# Purification of Memory

# Purification of Memory

## A Study of Modern Orthodox
## Theologians from a Catholic Perspective

Ambrose Mong

James Clarke & Co

**James Clarke & Co**
P.O. Box 60
Cambridge
CB1 2NT
United Kingdom

www.jamesclarke.co
publishing@jamesclarke.co


ISBN: 978 0 227 17513 2


*British Library Cataloguing in Publication Data*
A record is available from the British Library


First published by James Clarke & Co, 2015

*To the Brothers of the Dominican Province
of Our Lady of the Rosary*

[T]he Church must breathe with her two lungs! . . . And now, after a long period of division and mutual misunderstanding, the Lord is enabling us to discover ourselves as 'Sister Churches' once more, in spite of the obstacles which were once raised between us. If today, on the threshold of the third millennium, we are seeking the re-establishment of full communion, it is for the accomplishment of this reality that we must work and it is to this reality that we must refer.

Ioannes Paulus PP. II
*Ut Unum Sint: On Commitment to Ecumenism*
25 May 1995

# Contents

# Foreword

Writing the foreword to this work on modern Orthodox theologians affords me a special pleasure as it brings back memories of my first doctoral dissertation, written some four decades ago, which deals with the theology of the icon in the work of the Russian Orthodox theologian Paul Evdokimov. But more than a nostalgic trip down memory lane, it is for me a genuine excitement to see how Ambrose Mong, a rising star among Asian theologians, has taken a serious scholarly interest in Orthodox theology.

Currently the Orthodox Church does not have a large presence in Asia, compared with the Roman Catholic Church, the Protestant Churches, and the Evangelicals/Pentecostals. But it is important to note its ancient roots in this continent, as early as the apostolic age with, according to multiple traditions, the coming of Saint Thomas to India in AD 52, and in the seventh century with the coming of the Christians of the (Syrian) Church of the East (misnamed 'Nestorians') in China.

It is highly appropriate that Ambrose Mong titles his work *Purification of Memory*. This felicitous phrase comes from Pope (Saint) John Paul II's encyclical on Christian unity *Ut Unum Sint* (1995). That there is an urgent need to purify the memory of Roman Catholics and Orthodox in their mutual relationships is beyond doubt for anyone with an even hazy knowledge of the tragic event of ecclesiastical politics in 1054, the horrors of the Crusades, and the subsequent sack of Constantinople by the Muslim Turks in 1453.

But it is not only in the West that the Roman Catholic–Orthodox memory stands in sore need of purification and healing. Such a need is urgent also in Asia, especially in India. Again, this is clear to anyone who knows something about the arrogant and imperialistic efforts of the Roman Catholic Church to 'Latinize' the 'Nestorian' Christians of Malabar, India, especially under the Archbishop of Goa Alexis de Menezes and at the Synod of Diamper (1599), which provoked the oath at Koonen Cross taken by the leaders of the Saint Thomas Christians never to accept the authority of any bishop imposed on them by the Church of Rome (1653).

Fortunately, much has happened since then, especially at the Second Vatican Council (Vatican II), to heal the wounds between the two Christian communities in the West. In a historic gesture of reconciliation, in 1964 Pope Paul VI and the Ecumenical Patriarch Athenagoras I met in Jerusalem to rescind the excommunications of 1054 as a step to end the Great Schism and to restore union between the two sister churches. Much hope for full ecclesial communion was kindled under the pontificate of John Paul II, but so far it has not been achieved. Perhaps with Pope Francis, with his radical simple lifestyle and constant emphasis on mercy, the movement toward healing, reconciliation, and union among the churches will become a reality.

It is in this context that Ambrose Mong's book should be read and appreciated. He provides an insightful study of eight Orthodox theological movers and shakers and compares and contrasts them with their Roman Catholic counterparts. Interestingly, he finds that some Roman Catholic theologians are closer to the Orthodox theologians discussed than to their own confessional colleagues, and vice versa. Thus, for instance, Walter Kasper is shown to be closer to some Orthodox theologians in his ecclesiology of the local church than to his fellow German Joseph Ratzinger/Benedict XVI, and the Orthodox theologian John Zizioulas is shown to be closer to the Jesuit Henri de Lubac than to his fellow Orthodox Nicholas Afanasiev. It is these unusual but illuminating correspondences between these two theological communities that make Mong's work fascinating reading.

I am convinced that Ambrose Mong's theological research will make an important contribution not only to the dialogue between Roman Catholic and Orthodox theologians but also to the cause of ecumenical unity, especially in Asia, for which Christ has prayed.

*Peter C. Phan*
Ignacio Ellacuría Chair of Catholic Social Thought
Georgetown University

# Preface

In 2013, I taught an Introduction to Christianity course at the University of St Joseph in Macau. There are many ways to approach this subject. At first I began by using the geographical approach, which was helpful in many ways because it gave the students a sense of Christianity as a global religion. Besides using Todd M. Johnson's and Kenneth Ross' *Atlas of Global Christianity*, which is a wonderful teaching aid, I also found Douglas Jacobsen's *The World's Christians: Who they are, Where they are, and How they got there* an excellent textbook to help students acquire a perspective of Christianity as a growing global phenomenon. Jacobsen divides Christianity into four main traditions: the Orthodox tradition, the Roman Catholic tradition, Protestantism, and the Pentecostal/Charismatic movement. The last tradition, the Pentecostal/Charismatic movement, is the latest and fastest-growing phenomenon and it includes both Protestants and Roman Catholics. I find this inclusion of Protestants and Roman Catholics in one movement rather significant because boundaries are not easy to delineate when it comes to characterizing a particular Christian tradition such as this – the Spirit blows where it wills (John 3:8).

Another interesting feature of Jacobsen's text is that he starts first with the Orthodox tradition because, according to him, it has the longest history and it preserves most of the ancient customs and practices of Christianity. One would think that a religion with such a long history and tradition would be fairly well known. But this is not the case with Orthodox Christianity, especially in Asia. Many people still think of the Orthodox Church as antiquated, not much different from Roman Catholicism, except for its provincialism. In fact, my students did not have the foggiest idea about the Orthodox tradition. We are fortunate that nowadays we have the internet, YouTube, and other media to transmit information and pictorial representations. Through digital technology, the students were able to get a glimpse of the grandeur and beauty of the Orthodox Church, its worship and its iconography.

Besides these resources, I also needed a supplementary text that went beyond the introductory level. Given my interest in individual theologians, I decided to write a book that I hope will give a better understanding of Orthodox theology based on the writings of eight distinguished Orthodox thinkers. I hope that this book will also serve the needs of the ecumenical movement in their efforts to understand the 'other'. Writing this book has been a great learning experience for me as I have begun to appreciate the beauty and depth of Orthodox worship and also the hardships and sufferings that our separated brethren have undergone to keep their faith alive.

Special thanks to Peter C. Phan for writing the Foreword and to Lai Pan-chiu for his advice, guidance, and support. These two distinguished professors have inspired me by their commitment to academic rigour and discipline. I am also grateful to Anna Li for checking the manuscript. Many people have also assisted me in writing this book through proofreading, encouragement, and moral support. They are as follows: Ellen S. Ching, Anne Lim, Hilia Chan, David Liu, Patrick Tierney FSC, Columba Cleary OP, Mary Gillis CND, Jolene Chan, Josephine Chan, Henry Lo, Abraham Shek, Lydia and Roger Garcia, Tommy and Emily Lam, Javier González OP, Fernando Muñoz OP, Beinidict MacCionaoith OP, Bonifacio Solís OP, José Luis OP, Fauto Gómez OP, Philip Lee, and George Tan. Last but not least, I would like to thank Lisa Sinclair for her editorial assistance and dedication to this project, and Becky Chadwick and Adrian Brink of Lutterworth Press for their help in the publication of this work. It is a joy and pleasure to work with such an efficient and venerable press. Any errors that remain are, of course, my own.

*Ambrose Mong OP*
St Joseph House
Hong Kong, 2015
Feast of St Athanasius

# Introduction

The idea of purification of memory is that the church admits the wrongs and atrocities it has committed in the past and seeks forgiveness. It suggests that the church must be purified not only of the wrongs it has inflicted on others, but also of the memory of the violence and persecutions it has suffered in the past. This healing of memory is needed not only for the church's integrity of mission, but also as part of the ecumenical effort to encourage dialogue. Dialogue is important because through it we try not to allow our memories to dwell on the sins and wrongs we have committed or suffered, but to focus on and share what we have in common. This work attempts to demonstrate that, in spite of the mistrust and conflict between the Orthodox and Roman Catholic Churches, they actually share a common heritage that can serve as a basis for reunification.

Among the major Christian traditions, the Orthodox Church is the least known, and Orthodox theology is often shrouded in mysticism and misunderstanding. This is more serious in Asia, where the Orthodox Church is a minority faith and is perceived as an exotic branch of Christianity. Yet, in point of fact, the Eastern Church has been in China since the seventh century. The purpose of this work, therefore, is to acquaint the laity, theological students, and seminarians, with the teaching of Orthodoxy through a study of important modern Orthodox theologians. As the different ideologies are viewed from both Roman Catholic and ecumenical perspectives, it is my wish that readers will gain a deeper appreciation of church history in relation to the split between the Eastern and Western Churches.

As a Roman Catholic priest, I am very much inspired by the example of the late Pope John Paul II in his efforts to reach out to our Orthodox brothers and sisters. In an ecumenical gathering in Paris on 31 May 1980, John Paul II, now a saint, spoke of the 'healing and purification of memories'. This phrase was an important principle in his efforts to reach out to members of other Christian communities, especially to the Orthodox Church. In his encyclical *Ut Unum Sint*, a landmark document on Christian unity, he teaches that the 'commitment to ecumenism must be based upon the conversion of hearts and upon prayer, which will also lead to the *necessary purification of past memories*'.[1] More importantly for us here, in the context of this work, John Paul II, referring to the 1965 lifting of Orthodox-Roman Catholic excommunications, notes that such effort removed from our memory and from the church the painful events of the past through 'a solemn act which was at once a healing of historical memories, a mutual forgiveness, and a firm commitment to strive for communion'.[2] The concept of purification of memory therefore refers to historical memory.

Further, in 2001, in his address to Archbishop Christodoulos of Athens, the primate of the Orthodox Church in Greece, Pope John Paul II, said, 'certainly we are burdened by past and present controversies and by enduring misunderstandings. But in a spirit of mutual charity these can and must be overcome, for that is what the Lord asks of us. Clearly there is a need for a liberating process of purification of memory.'[3] He admitted that the Roman Catholic Church had sinned against their Orthodox brothers and sisters by their actions and omissions, and he asked the Lord for pardon.

Referring to the 'disastrous sack of the imperial city of Constantinople, which was for so long the bastion of Christianity in the East', John Paul II said, 'it is tragic that the assailants, who

---

1. Pope John Paul II, *Ut Unum Sint*, 25 May 1995, http://www. vatican.va/holy_father/john_paul_ii/encyclicals/documents/hf_jp-ii_ enc_25051995_ut-unum-sint_en.html, no. 2. The focus in this book is on the schism between Rome and the Chalcedonian Orthodox. For a good description of the other Eastern Churches (anti-Chalcedonian), the Church of Assyrian Christians, and the Churches of Oriental Orthodoxy, see Aidan Nichols OP (2010), *Rome and the Eastern Churches*. San Francisco: Ignatius Press, pp. 52–170.

2. *Ut Unim Sint*, 52. See also Adam A.J. DeVille, 'On the Healing of Memories: An Analysis of the Concept in Papal Documents', http://www.koed.hu/sw249/adam.pdf. 'Patient listening can uncover deep and wide agreement concealed by the polemics of the past,' Henry Chadwick (2003), *East and West: The Making of a Rift in the Church: From Apostolic Times until the Council of Florence*. Oxford: Oxford University Press, p. 275.

3. Pope John Paul II (n.d.), 'John Paul II, Pope (2001-05-04), "A liberating process of purification of memory"', *Origins* 31, no. 1, 3.

had set out to secure free access for Christians to the Holy Land, turned against their own brothers in the faith. The fact that they were Latin Christians fills Catholics with deep regret. . . . Together we must work for this healing if Europe now emerging is to be true to its identity, which is inseparable from the Christian humanism shared by East and West.'[1] He also acknowledged that from apostolic times to the present day, the Orthodox Church of Greece has influenced the Latin Church in its liturgy, spirituality, and jurisprudence. Hence the universal church acknowledges the debt it owes to Greek Christianity, especially for the teachings of the Fathers in the East.

The Roman Catholic Church continues to look towards the Eastern Church for theological enlightenment, as Pope John Paul II put it so clearly in his letter *Orientale Lumen*:

> Since, in fact, we believe that the venerable and ancient tradition of the Eastern Churches is an integral part of the heritage of Christ's Church, the first need for Catholics is to be familiar with that tradition, so as to be nourished by it and to encourage the process of unity in the best way possible for each. Our Eastern Catholic brothers and sisters are very conscious of being the living bearers of this tradition, together with our Orthodox brothers and sisters. The members of the Catholic Church of the Latin tradition must also be fully acquainted with this treasure and thus feel, with the Pope, a passionate longing that the full manifestation of the Church's catholicity be restored to the Church and to the world, expressed not by a single tradition, and still less by one community in opposition to the other; and that we too may be granted a full taste of the divinely revealed and undivided heritage of the universal Church which is preserved and grows in the life of the Churches of the East as in those of the West.[2]

Throughout his pontificate, John Paul II always insisted that true ecumenism could not take place without inner conversion and the purification of memory, without holiness and fidelity to the Gospel message, and without assiduous prayer that reflects the prayer of Jesus. Inner conversion implies that the church admits the wrongs

1. Ibid.
2. Pope John Paul II (1995), *Orientale Lumen* (Apostolic Letter), 2 May, http://www.vatican.va/holy_father/john_paul_ii/apost_letters/documents/hf_jp-ii_apl_02051995_orientale-lumen_en.html, no. 3.

and atrocities it has committed in the past and seeks forgiveness from God and also from the victims. Swiss Cardinal Georges Cottier says, 'The forgiveness of God is precisely the highest and most eminent form of the purification of memory. This is because the divine forgiveness really erases and destroys the sin, so that its weight does not burden the conscience anymore.'[1] Further, the churches, both Latin and Orthodox, must be purified of the memory not only of the wrong each has done to the other, but also of the cruelty and injustice each has suffered from the other.

A report by the Roman Catholic-Mennonite Dialogue states, 'although we are not in full unity with one another, the substantial amount of the Apostolic faith that we realize today that we share, allows us as members of the Catholic and Mennonite delegations to see one another as brothers and sisters in Christ.'[2] This statement can also be applied to members of other Christian churches. In this report, John Paul II also stressed the need for theological dialogue. This would assist in the healing of memories by helping the dialogue partners to discover to what extent they continue to share the Christian faith in spite of centuries of division. Explaining their traditions to one another would lead to a deeper mutual understanding and a deeper realization that they hold in common many aspects of their Christian heritage.[3] It is in light of the call for theological dialogue as a process of healing memory that I write the following chapters.

## Outline and Sequence of the Work

Chapter 1 will study the writings of John Meyendorff as he deals with issues that are fundamental to the understanding of the separation between the Orthodox and the Roman Catholic Churches. Besides his sincere search for unity, Meyendorff's work also handles the topics of catholicity, the history of the schism, the Petrine office, and others, with great insight and objectivity.

1. Georges Cottier (2004), 'The purification of memory'. *Nova Et Vetera* 2, no. 2 (September), 259.
2. 'Called Together to Be Peacemakers', Report of the International Dialogue between the Catholic Church and Mennonite World Conference (1998–2003), http://www.vatican.va/roman_curia/pontifical_councils/chrstuni/mennonite-conference-docs/rc_pc_chrstuni_doc_20110324_mennonite_en.html, no. 210.
3. Ibid., 207.

Chapter 2 will examine the eucharistic ecclesiology of Nicholas Afanasiev in comparison with the ecclesiology of Joseph Ratzinger. Both theologians share the belief that in spite of the difficulties encountered in the dialogue between the Orthodox and the Roman Catholic Churches, the love that is rooted in the Eucharist can help them overcome this impasse.

Chapter 3 will discuss the ecclesiology of John Zizioulas and his critique of Afanasiev, among other issues. This chapter also examines the debate between Walter Kasper and Joseph Ratzinger regarding the priority of the universal church over the local churches. Since John Zizioulas' writings were influenced by Georges Florovsky, Chapter 4 will discuss Florovsky's neo-patristic synthesis, which has had a great impact on Orthodoxy. Florovsky's support of Hellenistic Christianity reveals a striking similarity with Ratzinger's Eurocentric theology. This fascination with Greek thought brings us to the writings of Sergius Bulgakov. Chapter 5 explores Sergius Bulgakov's theory of Sophiology, which is key to the understanding of his works on ecclesiology, Christology, and Mariology. In many ways, his ecclesiology reflects the teachings of *Lumen Gentium*, a Vatican II document.

Chapter 6 will focus on Bulgakov's critic, Vladimir Lossky, who emphasized the apophatic character of Orthodox theology. Influenced by Pseudo-Dionysius and Gregory Palamas, Lossky's writings on the Trinity will be explored. As Lossky was deeply influenced by the negative theology of Orthodoxy, he was critical of social activism and worldly involvement, which he feared would hinder our spiritual growth. However, there is an Orthodox theologian who thought otherwise and who in many ways foreshadowed the liberation theology of Latin America. In view of this, Chapter 7 will study the contextual theology of Nicolas Berdyaev.

Finally, in Chapter 8 we will accompany Jaroslav Pelikan on his return to Orthodoxy after being a Lutheran scholar for most of his life. This chapter includes his writings on Christian doctrinal development, which present a critical yet sympathetic view of Roman Catholicism. However, it was his love of Hellenism that eventually led him to the bosom of the Orthodox Church.

In these eight chapters, we will explore interpretations of key theological issues that have kept the Orthodox and the Roman Catholic Churches apart as well as together. More often than not, it has been misunderstanding, suspicion, and mistrust due to ignorance and unfamiliarity that has kept the churches apart. Besides, as we shall see, divergent theological views can co-exist within the same church. For example, Walter Kasper's ecclesiology is more in accord with the Orthodox tradition than Joseph Ratzinger's emphasis on the priority of the universal church. At the same time, we find striking similarities between Ratzinger and Florovsky in their approach to Hellenization in the church. Within the Orthodox Church, John Zizioulas' ecclesiology is closer to Henri de Lubac's than to that of his fellow Orthodox theologian, Nicholas Afanasiev. Thus, such differences and divergent theological views need not be obstacles to reunification. Churches are like gardens, in which different kinds of flowers must be allowed to bloom.

Most of the recently published books on Orthodox theology are meant as general introductions. Only a few examine to a deeper extent topics such as trinitarian theology, deification, and Christology, and these are meant for specialists. I hope that this book on Orthodox theologians, seen from both Roman Catholic and ecumenical perspectives, will satisfy the needs of those seeking more than just a cursory introduction to Orthodox theology. This work explores the ideologies of Orthodox theologians from the nineteenth and twentieth centuries, so the theological issues they deal with are relevant to our present-day search for unity.

# Chapter 1
# John Meyendorff

John Meyendorff was born in Neuilly-sur-Seine, France, on 17 February 1926 to a prominent Russian family. He completed his theological studies at St Sergius Orthodox Theological Institute in Paris in 1949 and earned a doctorate from the Sorbonne in 1958 with his doctoral dissertation on the major works of St Gregory Palamas (1296–1359). After his ordination to the priesthood in 1958, Meyendorff left his teaching post at St Sergius for the United States to join the staff of St Vladimir's Seminary in New York. Jaroslav Pelikan said that Meyendorff was 'the last representative of the émigré Russian Orthodox community, with roots in and a strong hold on Russian culture. At the same time he was the most American of that generation.'[1] Meyendorff was a church historian who specialized in Byzantine theology and was highly regarded as one of the most articulate spokesmen for the Orthodox Church as well as for the ecumenical movement. Suffering from pancreatic cancer, he passed away on 22 July 1992.

Meyendorff was a great ecumenist and contributed much as a member of the Central Committee of the World Council of Churches (WCC). He also acted as a moderator of the WCC Faith and Order Commission from 1967 to 1975. His writings on Roman Catholicism are balanced, objective, and thoughtful. Robert Slesinski claims that Meyendorff was a great gift to his tradition and that '[his] fertile mind was committed to serious reflection [which] was coupled with a scrupulous intellectual honesty. It afforded his work a serene, irenic character not hesitant to

---

1. Jaroslav Pelikan (1996), 'In Memory of John Meyendorff' in Bradley Nassif (ed.), *New Perspectives on Historical Theology: Essays in Memory of John Meyendorff*. Grand Rapids, Michigan: William B. Eerdmans, p. 8. Some material in this chapter appeared as an article: Ambrose Ih-Ren Mong (2014), 'John Meyendorff on the Unity of the Church', *International Journal of Orthodox Theology* 5/2, 103–132.

tackle the great vexing ecumenical questions of our age, arising from some of the saddest pages of Christian ecclesiastical history.'[1] Although Meyendorff's ecumenical teaching was addressed to Protestants, the themes of some of his reflections concern the relationship between the Orthodox and Roman Catholic Churches. Therefore, such reflections have great relevance for Roman Catholics who wish to understand the position of Orthodoxy on ecclesiastical issues.

Meyendorff sought unity of the church by contending that the Orthodox Church is the true Church of Christ. This chapter elaborates on this theme by exploring Meyendorff's thoughts on the Great Schism of 1054 and his understanding of the nature of authority in the church and, in particular, the primacy of Peter.

## *Unity Through the Orthodox Church*

Meditating on John 17:21, 'that they may all be one. As you, Father, are in me and I am in you, may they also be in us so that the world may believe that you have sent me,' John Meyendorff believed that the search for unity constitutes a fundamental and positive aspect of church history. He urged Christians to demonstrate their unity in God so that non-Christians could be invited to share in this union. Unfortunately, our Christian history has been marked by discord and division. It seems that the Father has not heard the prayer of his Son and the salvation brought by Christ has not brought peace in the world. The Gospel message seems like one doctrine among others and, so far, only a fraction of humanity has been converted to the Christian faith. The Christian missionaries were the first to be aware of this 'scandal' and sought to be 'ecumenical', that is, to make Christians aware of this separation among those who professed their belief in Christ and of the presence of conflicts and mistrust among the different Christian churches.[2]

It is in the light of ecumenism that Meyendorff wrote on the history of the Orthodox Church. In seeking the Gospel and the church in its divine reality, we must also try to understand the historical problems that tore Christianity apart. This is an important issue, especially in Asia and Africa, where Christians are not natural inheritors of the conflict between the Greek and Latin Churches.

1. Robert Slesinski, 'John Meyendorff: A Churchman of Catholic Outreach'. *Diakonia*, 27, no. 1 (January), 8.
2. John Meyendorff (1996), *The Orthodox Church: Its Past and its Role in the World Today*. Crestwood, New York: St Vladimir's Press, p. vii.

Meyendorff posited that the Orthodox Church occupies a unique place in that it has kept a distance from the conflicts that continue to divide the Roman Catholic and Reformed Churches. In ecumenical debate, the Orthodox Church sees itself as the guardian of the faith that originated from the apostles and the Church Fathers.[1] Meyendorff further claimed that the Orthodox Church remains the church of continuity and tradition and that because of its fidelity to scripture and tradition, it maintains its orthodoxy as well as its catholicity. Therefore, as a condition for union, the Orthodox Church insists that all Christians must return to Orthodoxy, the faith of the first ecumenical councils. This reunion would involve a return to the sources of the faith, which means fidelity to revelation. It also involves distinguishing between the tradition of the church and human traditions, which tend to obscure revelation.

Meyendorff also believed that the merit of the Orthodox Church lies in its willingness to examine its conscience and its refusal to accept human institutions or even formulations of Christian dogma as infallible. The Orthodox Church contemplates scripture, the word of God spoken by human beings, not only in its literal sense, but also through the power of the Spirit who inspires us.[2]

## Catholicity and Apostolic Truth

Orthodox Christians claim to be 'catholic' but not 'Roman' or 'papal'. Meyendorff urged Orthodox Christians to recover the sense of catholicity demonstrated in St Ignatius of Antioch's letter to Smyrnaeans – 'Where Jesus Christ is, there is the Catholic Church' – whereby it signifies 'the fullness and the universality of salvation revealed in Christ within the Church'.[3] The original meaning of catholicity was the acceptance of the whole truth regarding divine presence in Jesus Christ. Catholicity was a sign of the presence of

1. Ibid., p. ix.
2. Ibid., p. x.
3. Meyendorff (1983), *Catholicity and the Church*. Crestwood, New York: St Vladimir's Press, p. 7. In a similar way, von Balthasar held that 'it is not (collegial) apostolicity but only the full petrine character that is rejected by the Orthodox Church, a situation which allows a still quite authentic even if imperfect unity of Catholica (with possible intercommunion) to be maintained.' Medard Kehl SJ and Werner Löser SJ (eds) (1982). *The von Balthasar Reader*, trans. Robert J. Daly SJ and Fred Lawrence. New York: Crossroad, p. 249.

Christ in the Word, the Eucharist, or the Christian assembly. It was not synonymous with universality or geographical expansion. Later, catholicity came to mean those who hold the right doctrines; the orthodox as opposed to the heretics and schismatics.

As it is Christ through the Spirit who makes the church 'catholic', we can say that no human being can create 'catholicity'. We can only co-operate with divine grace to show our concern for the salvation of souls. Meyendorff maintained that one can be a Christian only as a member of the Roman Catholic Church and through 'a continuous effort at manifesting the catholicity of the Church'.[1] This suggests that no church is fully catholic, even in apostolic times, because we are all journeying towards that fullness of catholicity that is yet to come. Protestants believe that all Christian churches are partial manifestations of catholicity. Hence, there are ecumenical meetings in which Christians come together to share what they have in common and also to discuss their differences. For Protestants, catholicity is shared to different degrees by all Christian denominations.

The Orthodox Church, however, believes itself to be the one holy, catholic, and apostolic church. These four characteristics come from Christ and the Holy Spirit. But the claim to be catholic and orthodox is valid only to the extent that the church remains faithful to the apostolic truth. Meyendorff admitted that there were times in the twentieth century when the Orthodox Church presented to the world 'an image of divisiveness, of theological unawareness, of missionary passivity, of dependence upon socio-political concerns'.[2] He classified this as the second order of betrayal; the first order of betrayal he described occurs when the whole church totally changes its apostolic structure. Perhaps he had the Roman Catholic Church in mind regarding the first order.

The catholicity of the Orthodox Church is manifest in its liturgy, canonical tradition, and theology. However, due to human inconsistencies, this catholicity can be obscured in practice. Nonetheless, Meyendorff proposed that at this present time the Orthodox Church is best placed to present to the world the true Christian message. The ecumenical movement presents a forum for the Orthodox Church and an opportunity to reach out lovingly to other Christian communities by expressing its catholicity.

Unfortunately, the impasse in ecumenism in its organizational form is due in part to the inability of the Orthodox Church 'to

1. Meyendorff, *op. cit.*, p. 9.
2. Ibid., p. 11.

express their message in an effective way, with sufficient love to make the hard truth accepted and understood by those who miss it'.[1] In other words, the Orthodox Church has failed to convert all other Christians to the one true Church of Christ. This is to be expected because divisions and conflicts are and were common, even in the early church. St Paul says, 'Indeed, there have to be factions among you, for only so will it become clear who among you are genuine' (1 Corinthians 11:19). Arguably, the most painful conflict in Christianity was the Great Schism of 1054, because since then the Eastern and Western Churches have been like two separate lungs.

## Schism

Rightly regarded as one of the most tragic events in church history, the separation between Byzantium and Rome shaped the destiny of the churches in the East and West, and this separation endures today. It was in 1054 'that all the elements of disunity which had come to light over the centuries were first concentrated into a single event', an event that was one of the greatest misfortunes in Christian history. This date marks the birth of a distinctly Western-Latin Church that has turned its back on the East. Despite this tragic division in 1054, Meyendorff rightly asserted that it would be a 'romantic fallacy' to think that there was an undivided church in the beginning.[2] Congar also claimed that the rupture between East and West was the product

---

1. Ibid.
2. Meyendorff, *The Orthodox Church*, p. 35. John McGuckin argues that 'increasingly from that time onwards, the Papacy regarded the Greeks as having become "schismatic" by having refused the rights of papal jurisdiction, and the Orthodox regarded the Western Church as having lapsed into heresy for elevating the Papacy to such extraordinary heights, while tampering with the ancient deposit of the faith in such matters as adding the *Filioque* to the Creed, and using unleavened bread in the Eucharist.' John A. McGuckin, *The Orthodox Church: An Introduction to its History, Doctrine, and Spiritual Culture* (2008). Oxford: Blackwell, p. 21. Aidan Nichols says, 'heresy and schism remain formally distinct. While heresy is unorthodox dissent, schism is orthodox dissent, expressing itself in the organisation of a distinct ecclesial life by people who in all other respects share the faith of the Church.' Further, he writes, 'to preconciliar eyes, the status of the Orthodox churches did not appear to be in an unconditional sense one of schism from the Catholic Church.' Nichols (2010), *Rome and the Eastern Churches* (San Francisco: Ignatius Press), pp. 28 and 41.

of cultural, political, and religious conflicts rather than the result of a single episode.[1] In fact, there were from the start a series of heresies and schisms over Christological issues, which affected Egypt, Ethiopia, Armenia, and Syria. In the ninth century, the Greco-Roman world was already divided along linguistic and political lines.

Linguistic, cultural, and political differences, in addition to deep theological conflicts, worked together to sharpen the divide. In spite of the division between the Greek and Latin Churches, they continued to manifest their catholicity and did not allow themselves to be transformed into national churches. Meyendorff admitted that although the Orthodox Church claims to be the only true church of Christ, it has witnessed the restriction of its cultural and geographical vision because of its identification with the Byzantine world. Meanwhile, the Orthodox Church believed that the Roman Church had lost its 'doctrinal and ecclesiastical balance', which eventually led to the Protestant Reformation. Among the various factors of division, Meyendorff suggested that the theological factors were the most difficult to overcome. These theological issues have continued to constitute a major obstacle to Christian unity.[2] First, we will consider the non-theological factors.

## *Start of the Conflict: Non-theological Factors*

According to Meyendorff, the conflict between the Greek and Latin Churches began with the founding of the Carolingian Empire in the West. When the marriage between Charles and the Byzantine empress was called off, the Frankish king decided to destroy Constantinople's claim to universal jurisdiction by accusing it of heresy. The heresy was that the Eastern emperor worshipped images (icons) and believed that the Holy Spirit proceeded 'from the Father by the Son' instead of 'from the Father and the Son' – the question of the *filioque*.[3]

---

1. Brett E. Whalen (2007), 'Rethinking the schism of 1054: authority, heresy and the Latin rite'. *Traditio* 62 (January), 2.
2. Meyendorff, *op. cit.*, p. 36.
3. Ibid., p. 37. The *filioque* ('and the son') clause was added to the Nicene Creed by the Latin Church: 'We believe in the Holy Spirit, the Lord, the giver of life, who proceeds from the Father *and the Son*.' The clause was introduced into the Creed in Spain in the sixth century to strengthen the anti-Arian position of the Spanish Church. Charlemagne used it against the Greeks, and Rome finally accepted it around 1014.

Furthermore, the new empire in the West was dominated by 'caesaropapism' – the exercise of supreme authority over ecclesiastical matters by the secular ruler. Meyendorff wrote: '[I]t seems that the Frankish court was influenced by the example of the iconoclastic emperors of Byzantium, whose theology was taken over by Charlemagne, at least in part – and it was intended to supplant both the traditional empire (in the East) and the papacy.'[1] Fortunately, the Roman Church was against Charlemagne's theological attack on Byzantium. Meyendorff acknowledged the efforts of Pope Hadrian I (772–795) and Pope Leo III (795–816) to preserve the unity of the church, if only for a short time, by defending the Council of Nicea and rejecting the *filioque*.

A consequence of the creation of Charlemagne's empire was the development of a new type of Christianity by northern Europeans who had little knowledge of Byzantium theology. Meyendorff also blamed the Byzantines for despising Carolingian learning and culture. In fact, Emperor Michael III regarded Latin as a 'barbarous and Scythian tongue'.[2] The East viewed the West as intellectually inferior and could not take its theological position seriously. Despite this, the Church of Rome was able to maintain the bridges between the East and West because it had preserved enough Greek tradition and was the only religious authority respected by the Franks. Some scholars believe that the solution to the schism is to recover the common tradition that was disintegrated.

The separation between the East and the West in the ninth and eleventh centuries took place 'when the political aims of the Frankish Empire became confused with the canonical pretensions of the popes and both found themselves united in a common opposition to the

---

Photius considered the *filioque* to be the 'crown of evils', 'an illegitimate interpolation', which destroys the authority of the Father and 'relativizes the reality of personal, or *hypostatic existence*, in the Trinity'. Maximus the Confessor taught that the Son is not the origin of the Spirit; the Father alone is the origin of the Son and of the Holy Spirit. At the Council of Florence, the Western Church attempted to accommodate Greek and Latin formulations; it 'adopted a basically Augustinian definition of the Trinity, while affirming that the Greek *formulations* were not in contradiction with it. This, however, was not a solution of the fundamental issue.' See Meyendorff (1983), *Byzantine Theology: Historical Trends and Doctrinal Themes*. New York: Fordham University Press, pp. 91–4.

1. Meyendorff, *The Orthodox Church*, p. 38.
2. Ibid., p. 39.

East'.[1] Meyendorff claimed that in the eighth, tenth, and eleventh centuries, the popes were merely puppets of the Western emperors, who were bent on adopting the ideals of caesaropapism. However, there were exceptions: great popes like Nicholas I in the ninth century, Leo IX (1049–1054), and Gregory VII (1073–1085) fought vigorously against secular domination of the church, which eventually led to the triumph of the papacy over the empire and brought a new awareness of Roman papacy. Rome saw itself as more than just a patriarchate of the West and more than just an apostolic see among others. In other words, it felt its primacy of authority must be transformed 'into a real power of jurisdiction, universal in scope and absolute in nature'.[2]

Meyendorff viewed the existence of these exceptional pontiffs not as a sign of church leaders succumbing to the temptation of domination, but as a sincere attempt to liberate the church from secular control. In addition, these popes fought against simony and raised the standard of clerical conduct, and the result of these efforts was the birth of a new Western Christian civilization. Unfortunately, these capable pontiffs, mostly from Northern Europe, had little knowledge of the Greek Fathers, and were not well disposed towards the East. Latin and Western in their outlook, they got along well with the Western emperors to the detriment of the East. In Meyendorff's opinion, 'the controversy between *Sacerdotium* and the *Imperium* appeared to be more of a political than a religious quarrel.'[3] In other words, the conflict between the church and the state was more political than theological. The popes were shrewd enough to turn the emperor's own weapons against him by adopting his strategy and plan to reduce the status of the old Roman Empire as well as that of Constantinople.

Orthodox historians do not doubt the sincerity of the popes, but they do question the theological basis of such political manoeuvres, which go against the spirit of the Gospel and traditional ecclesiology. Hence, the Orthodox Church rejects the medieval model of papacy, which is authoritarian and absolute. This rejection of the absolute nature of the papacy appeared in the form of secularism and anti-clericalism in the West. Further, the failure of the popes to extend their control of the Eastern Church only served to strengthen the uniformity and monolithic nature of Western Christendom.[4]

---

1. Ibid.
2. Ibid., p. 40.
3. Ibid.
4. Ibid., p. 41.

Meyendorff regarded Nicholas I (858–876) as one of the greatest popes in the Middle Ages; Nicholas I tried in good faith to reform the Eastern Church, for he believed that he had the right to do so, based on the absolute power and universality of the Roman see during that time. It was on this point that he clashed with the Eastern Church.[1] He was determined to strengthen Roman centralization by diminishing the powerful Byzantine patriarchate. The opportunity came when the supporters of Ignatius of Constantinople wanted the ex-patriarch to revoke his abdication in 857 to the great scholar Photius. They appealed to Rome for help. In Meyendorff's opinion, this move was an 'unprecedented act of difference' by the Byzantine Church towards the Roman see.[2]

Photius reacted against this interference by Nicholas I by accusing the pope of heresy, and broke off communion with him. Not long afterwards, Photius was deposed due to a revolution in Byzantium. With the help of Rome, Ignatius returned to head the patriarchate in Constantinople. Thus, Photius was condemned and Rome asserted its supremacy once more. But later Ignatius turned against Rome; he died in 877 before Pope Hadrian II could excommunicate him. Having reconciled with Ignatius, Photius returned to the patriarchate in the year Ignatius died.

Fortunately, peace and harmony were restored when the successor of Nicholas I and Hadrian II, Pope John VIII, did not pursue the policies of his predecessors. He respected the Greek liturgy and the exclusion of the *filioque* from the Creed.[3] The legates of Pope John VIII at the Council of Constantinople (879–880) also supported the restoration of Photius and condemned the inclusion of the *filioque* in the Creed. Photius was grateful to Pope John VIII for restoring unity to the church and considered him a good example to those who doubted Rome's sincerity. The Council of Constantinople became the model of unity for Orthodox and Roman Catholics – a 'unity in faith to which the Roman primacy may indeed bear witness, but of which it cannot itself be the source'.[4] Such was Meyendorff's view on the primacy of Rome.

---

1. Ibid., p. 42.
2. Ibid., p. 43. See also Henry Chadwick (2003), *East and West: The Making of a Rift in the Church: From Apostolic Times until the Council of Florence*. Oxford: Oxford University Press, pp. 124–92.
3. Meyendorff, *op. cit.*, p. 45. On the Photian schism and the *filioque*, see Nichols, *Rome and the Eastern Churches*, pp. 227–69.
4. Meyendorff, *op.cit.*, p. 46. John McGuckin, however, believes that 'the work of Photios marked the first time . . . that the Eastern and

From the tenth to the eleventh century there was peace between the Eastern and Western Churches. But, Meyendorff noted, during this period the papacy was deteriorating while the Byzantine Church was flourishing, with missionary expansion and cultural progress. The Byzantines could now ignore the pope as he was not in a position to enforce his authority. To widen the gap further, an incident occurred that led to more conflicts between the two churches. The *filioque* was sung in the Credo of the mass during the coronation ceremony of the German emperor Henry II by Pope Benedict VIII. Thus, from the beginning of the eleventh century, 'there was no longer any communio in sacris between Byzantium and Rome.'[1]

Meyendorff believed that the controversy over the *filioque*, as well as other problematic issues, could have been settled as easily as before. But the tragedy is that East and West had ignored each other for such a long time that there was no longer any determination to seek reunion. They had lost the common ground that in the past had kept them together. Furthermore, the lack of a common language led to differing understandings of the nature of the church. Rome believed it was the sole custodian of the Truth, while the Eastern Church believed that the Spirit of Truth resided in the whole church and expressed himself through ecumenical councils.[2]

There was an attempt at reunion when Patriarch Michael Cerularius, on behalf of the emperor, sent a letter to Pope Leo IX seeking communion with Rome. But when the Roman legates arrived in Constantinople, though welcomed warmly by the emperor, they were refused an audience with the patriarch. Cerularius questioned the authenticity of the legates' papal letters because Leo IX was in prison in Italy and was in no position to sign those documents. The legates reacted by excommunicating the patriarch and his priests for, among other things, omitting the *filioque* from the Creed and not enforcing the rule of celibacy for the clergy. It was a dramatic affair: the legates entered into Hagia Sophia during the celebration of the liturgy and placed the

Western churches officially and instinctively drew apart on profoundly significant theological issues, especially those related to the manner in which papal authority was felt by the Easterners to have changed the ancient pattern of the Christian ecumene.' Photius argued against papal supremacy and the *filioque* theology. McGuckin, *The Orthodox Church*, p. 20.

1. Meyendorff, *op. cit.*, p. 47.
2. Ibid.

decree of excommunication on the high altar. In return, Cerularius excommunicated the Roman legates.[1]

Despite its dramatic outcome, Meyendorff claimed that this event of 1054 did not end all contact between the Eastern and Western Churches. In fact, the other Eastern patriarchs still maintained communion with Rome for a while. Conflicts between the two churches began mainly with political issues, as described, but soon theological issues came into play, and the final break came with the Crusades.

## The Crusades

In Meyendorff's opinion, the Fourth Crusade was responsible for destroying the last traces of church unity. The Venetian fleet supposedly bringing the Crusaders to the Holy Land went instead to Constantinople to loot the city of its treasures. Considered one of the most disgraceful events in history, the sacking of Constantinople enriched the Western world, which also installed its own Venetian patriarch, Thomas Morosini, who occupied the throne of Photius with the approval of Rome. In addition to the theological differences between the Greeks and Latins, national hatred now made reunion in the future seem impossible.[2]

---

1. Ibid, p. 49. According to Erickson, 'for most Byzantine churchmen of the 11th and 12th centuries the principal point of disagreement with the Latins was not papal primacy or *filioque* but rather the use of unleavened bread in the Eucharist.' John H. Erickson (1970), 'Leavened and unleavened: some theological implications of the schism of 1054'. *St Vladimir's Theological Quarterly* 14, no. 3 (January), 157.

2. Meyendorff, *op. cit.*, p. 50. Steven Runciman claims that 'it was perhaps inevitable that the Church of Rome and the great eastern Churches should drift apart; but the whole Crusading movement had embittered their relations, and henceforward, whatever few princes might try to achieve, in the hearts of the east Christians the schism was complete, irremediable and final.' Thus it was the Fourth Crusade that destroyed all hope of reconciliation and reunion between the two churches. Chrysostomos puts it this way: 'The Fourth Crusade provoked a direct confrontation between the disparate social psychology of the Byzantines and that of the Latin West, the profound implications of which would foil all attempts – some of the rather major proportions in the subsequent years, before the fall of Constantinople to the Turks – at Church reunion. However, the sack of the city, as well as the events which followed it, was more the catalyst for a series of distressing conflicts in perception

During this time, the popes insisted on unity in ecclesiastical matters. Although the Byzantium Church was against political union, it was not against union with the Latin Church, based on ancient canons and ecclesiastical custom. The East insisted on holding ecumenical councils, which it believed would lead to the victory of Orthodoxy. In fact, the meeting of the council at Ferrara and then at Florence (1438–1439) symbolized a moral triumph for the East. Unfortunately, discussion broke down on many issues, not least the *filioque*. Further, when pressurized by the impending Turkish threat, the Greek delegates submitted themselves to Rome. Upon returning home, confronted by the wrath of the people, the Greek delegates repudiated their submission to Rome. Eventually, the Byzantine Empire collapsed when the Ottoman ruler, Mohammed II, entered Constantinople as a conqueror. Gennadios Scholarios, the new patriarch, officially repudiated the Union of Florence.[1]

From the eleventh century onwards, the emperors were in favour of reunion with Rome because of the political advantage it would bring. However, for non-political reasons, the patriarchs were equally consistent in opposing reunion with Rome because they believed that they were the custodians of the true faith.[2] Meyendorff doubted that reunion would have been possible at this point even if theological issues had been settled. He believed that agreement should be based on common tradition. Bishop Kallistos Ware called this the 'disintegration of a common tradition' and said that 'the problem is to find the original kinship in the common past.'[3]

---

and cognition that were destined to doom every attempt at union, than it was their single cause.' See Chrysostomos (2001), 'Evaluating the fourth crusade'. *Orthodox Tradition* 18, no. 2 (January), 30 and 35.

1. Meyendorff, *op. cit.*, pp. 51–2. For further details on the Council of Florence, see Nichols, *Rome and the Eastern Churches* pp. 303–21. According to Henry Chadwick, 'the Council of Florence came near to success: so near and yet so far. The decisions gave nothing to the Greeks for on every point of contention they were required to accept Latin positions. It was easy for them to come away feeling that the council had only reinforced the schism which it was designed to heal.' Thus modern Orthodox historians tend to think of decisions made at Florence or the sack of Constantinople in 1204 as the real break between East and West. Chadwick, *East and West*, p. 275.

2. Meyendorff, *op. cit.*, p. 53.

3. Bishop Kallistos T. Ware (1973), 'Scholasticism and Orthodoxy: theological method as a factor in the schism'. *Eastern Churches Review* 5, no. 1 (March), 16.

Most of the discussions concerning reunion in the thirteenth century were focused on political considerations and not on religious ones. Thus the Byzantium Church was marginalized. Meyendorff believed that doctrinal issues concerning the Holy Spirit and the nature of the church are the fundamental reasons for the schism between the East and the West. Efforts at reunion have failed because the basic issues of doctrinal differences have never beem dealt with in depth. The West mistakenly thought that once the Emperor John V was converted to Roman Catholicism, the rest would follow suit. But it did not work that way; the West was wrong about the existence of Byzantine caesaropapism.

## Scholasticism

Theological concerns, such as the approval of the *filioque* in 1274, doctrinal formulations, and definitions of Roman Catholicism based on scholasticism, made union between the Greek and Latin Churches seemingly impossible. Yves Congar posited that it was no accident that the rise of scholasticism in the twelfth century led to the worsening of the schism between East and West, referring to the change from a patristic to a scholastic worldview. Congar saw this as a change from a predominantly 'essentialist' view of the world to a 'naturalistic' view, a change from a universe of 'exemplarist causality' to a universe of 'efficient causality'. The first view means that things receive their reality from 'a transcendent model in which they participate' and the second view means that we search for truth in existing things themselves, in empirical studies. It was also a change from 'synthetic perception' to 'an attitude of inquiry and analysis'.[1]

There was also a movement from learning in the monastery to learning in the university: from the cloister to the lecture hall for study, from mystical and contemplative theology to the scientific study of theology. In the monastery, theological study was integrated with liturgy and prayer, but scholastic theology in the university depended very much on personal research rather than acceptance of tradition.[2]

To put it simply, the twelfth-century Western theologian appealed to reason and logical proof in his studies of divinity while the Eastern theologians relied more on tradition as embodied by the Fathers. In the West, theology became a science, which was unthinkable in

1. Ibid., 19.
2. Ibid.

the East. Eastern scholars emphasized the personal experience of the saints. St Gregory Palamas, for example, in his *Triads*, invoked the living experience of holy men, whom he regarded as the real theologians. Echoing this idea, for Evagrius of Pontus, theology was a matter of prayer and not philosophical training.[1]

Thus, to the Orthodox, the experience of the saints is what theology is all about. Western theology appeared to the Greeks 'too self-confident' and 'insufficiently sensitive to the necessary limitations of all human language and conceptual thinking'.[2] Orthodox theologians believe that in scholastic theology, the mystical and apophatic aspects are neglected. Whether or not these charges against the scholastics by the Orthodox are justifiable, it remains true that the rise of scholasticism and the changes it brought in regard to theology contributed greatly to the alienation between the East and West. Ware considers scholasticism a significant factor in the rupture of our common tradition.

Meyendorff also pointed out that not all of scholasticism was disruptive, as there were political factors that were supportive of union. In fact, from the thirteenth to the fifteenth centuries, the Byzantine emperors made several attempts to re-establish ecclesiastical communion with Rome so as to gain Western support against the Turks. As mentioned earlier, Meyendorff believed that it was theological issues that kept the two churches apart. The conflict was centred on the question of ecclesiology – the understanding of what it means to be a church. He argued that if the Eastern and Western Churches possessed a common ecclesiastical criterion, other issues could easily be solved.

### Ecclesiology – Unity in Faith

As we have seen, Meyendorff was of the opinion that a lack of a common ecclesiology is responsible for the schism. The Orthodox appeals to the authority of tradition and the West appeals to the authority of the pope.[3] Both sides fail to understand each other's

---

1. Ibid., 20.
2. Ibid., 22.
3. Meyendorff believed that 'There is no Orthodoxy without Holy Tradition, which implies communion in Spirit and in truth with the witness of the apostles and the fathers, based upon the belief that, by the power of God and in spite of all historical human weaknesses, there was and there is an uninterrupted, consistent and continuous Holy Tradition

position. While accepting the apostle Peter as head of the church, the East questions the nature of this succession. It refuses to accept Rome's claim of exclusive right to this succession because there is no evidence of such right in the New Testament regarding the ministry of Peter. The Orthodox Church recognizes the universal primacy of the Roman Church, but this primacy is not due to Peter's death in Rome. Roman primacy is not an exclusive and divine privilege coming from the Lord himself. This privilege comes from the church – 'a *de facto* authority which the Church had formally recognized by the voice of its councils'.[1] This means that the pope is not infallible and the council is above the pope. The presence of the pope and representatives of other episcopates is necessary for the council to be ecumenical.

Christ addressed Peter with the words '[Y]ou are Peter and on this rock I will build my church, and the gates of Hades will not prevail against it' (Matthew 16:18) and 'Feed my sheep' (John 21). These commands of Jesus, Meyendorff argued, do not refer exclusively to the bishop of Rome. They are Jesus' acknowledgement that Peter confessed his divinity when they were on their way to Caesarea Philippi. Peter is the rock of the church only to the extent that he is faithful to what he professes. This means that anyone who has made this profession of faith will be the rock of the church. This is the teaching of Origen and the Church Fathers. All bishops are to proclaim the true faith and hence they are all '*ex officio* the successors of Peter'.[2] This Orthodox conception of the Petrine office is clearly spelled out in the teaching of St Cyprian of Carthage from the third century. Thus, the controversy between East and West is due primarily to different understandings of the nature of the church and its authority.

The Orthodox Church views the church as a communion in which God is present 'sacramentally'. The church is thus a sacrament in which 'the death and resurrection of the Lord are "commemorated" and by which his Second Coming is proclaimed and anticipated'. The fullness of this reality is present in every local church where the

---

of faith held by the Church throughout the centuries. This belief in Tradition is not identical with simple conservatism. Holy Tradition is a living tradition. It is a witness to the unchanging Truth in a changing world.' Meyendorff (1990) in J. Breck, J. Meyendorff, and E. Silk (eds) (1990), *The Legacy of St Vladimir: Byzantium, Russia, America.* Crestwood, New York: St Vladimir's Seminary Press, p. 15.

1. Meyendorff, *The Orthodox Church*, p. 191.
2. Ibid., p. 192.

Eucharist is celebrated. The bishop in the Orthodox Church is not a successor of any particular apostle and therefore it matters little if the church was founded by Peter, Paul, or John. The function of the bishop is to teach according to the apostolic tradition in which Peter is the spokesman. This episcopal function is the same whether it is in Rome, Moscow, or Constantinople. God does not grant all special privileges to one particular see, but gives the fullness of his power to all. Hence, the local churches are not isolated but are united by the 'identity of their faith and their witness to the truth'.[1]

From the third century onwards, synods of bishops were organized to solve common problems and gradually a certain order of precedence emerged, with Rome occupying the first place among equals, followed by Constantinople. But this universal primacy is not of an ontological nature; it can be modified according to circumstances. This primacy of the universal church also does not reduce the importance of local churches. The difference between the Greek and Latin Churches, according to Meyendorff, is that the Roman Catholic Church, based on the First Vatican Council definition (1870), teaches that the pope possesses doctrinal infallibility and immediate jurisdiction of all the faithful. The bishop of Rome is the 'visible criterion of Truth and the unique head of the universal Church, without however possessing any sacramental powers different from those of other bishops'.[2]

The Orthodox Church, however, believes that no power can exist by divine right outside the local churches in a diocese. The relationship between bishops is governed by ecclesiastical norms that can be changed. In other words, the norms are man-made and not God-given. The consensus of the church or the ecumenical council is fundamental to Orthodoxy regarding the criterion of truth. As such, the Orthodox Church cannot accept the doctrine of papal infallibility so dear to the Roman Catholic Church.

Meyendorff taught that the unity of the church is, above all, unity in faith, and not uniformity in organization. This unity is not dependent on external or visible manifestations. He wrote: '[T]he reunion with the Church of the churches, separated from it presupposes, necessarily and absolutely, their agreement with it in the faith.' Therefore, in his opinion, future dialogue between Roman Catholic and Orthodox Churches should 'necessarily hinge on the role still left in Roman ecclesiology for the local church and the

1. Ibid., p. 193.
2. Ibid., p. 194.

episcopate'.[1] This implies that Rome must give greater freedom and autonomy to the local churches and individual dioceses. In other words, the local bishops must be given more power and authority to make decisions. The bishops of the Orthodox Church, on the other hand, must look for different and creative ways to express the common witness.

Meyendorff was hopeful that dialogue would remain possible between the Orthodox and Roman Catholic Churches on the basis that the two churches are united by a long and common biblical and patristic tradition. One of the hopeful signs is that the Roman Catholic Church has rediscovered the importance of understanding itself as 'communion', a concept that is central to Orthodox ecclesiology.

### The Church as Communion

The Congregation for the Doctrine of the Faith (CDF) teaches: 'The concept of *communion* (*koinonia*), which appears with a certain prominence in the texts of the Second Vatican Council, is very suitable for expressing the core of the Mystery of the Church, and can certainly be a key for the renewal of Roman Catholic ecclesiology.'[2] The idea of the church as communion finds its basis in the scripture where the concept of *koinonia* (κοινωνία) can be translated as 'participation', 'association', or 'contribution'. Christians are called into *koinonia* with Christ and with one another through faith and baptism. The Eucharist is described as a *koinonia* in the body

---

1. Ibid., p. 195.
2. 'Some Aspects of the Church understood as Communion', http://www.vatican.va/roman_curia/ congregations/cfaith/documents/rc_con_cfaith_doc_28051992_communionis-notio_en.html, no. 1. The Kenyan Catholic priest Vitalis Mshanga proposes a 'primacy in communion' according to which the pope, together with all the believers, acts as custodian of the faith. The model allows the pope particular primacy like any other local bishop and also universal primacy on the basis of the principle of apostolicity. This primacy in communion is a combination of service in love and juridical power to govern the church. Such an arrangement ensures unity of the church as well as freedom for the local churches. The church becomes a consultative or democratic body, it seems. See Vitalis Mshanga (2010), 'You are Peter: a critical analysis of the Orthodox view of papal primacy in view of an alternative way of exercising papal primacy'. *Journal of Ecumenical Studies* 45, no. 1 (December), 131–3.

and blood of Christ and the ministers of the Gospel are united in
*koinonia*. In the sharing of goods and financial resources, Christians
are engaged in *koinonia*. Thus, the idea of *koinonia* can be applied to
many aspects of Christian life.[1] Further, the faithful belong to the
church only when they are in communion with their bishop, and
the bishops recognize other bishops as being in communion with
themselves and with the universal church. Only a serious offence like
a schism can break the communion between churches.

Avery Dulles claimed that 'The Church of Rome, by reason of its
historical links with Peter and Paul, who had been martyred there,
and perhaps also by reason of the political prestige of the city, its
wealth, and its strategic importance as a center of communications,
gradually came to be recognized as having a universal primacy, the
exact nature of which was as yet somewhat undefined.'[2] This was also
Meyendorff's understanding of the nature of Rome's primacy, that it
was a matter of political and economic considerations and certainly
not of divine sanction. Meyendorff elaborated Roman primacy as
a matter of order and organizational efficiency. However, in times
of controversy, Dulles argued, venerable Fathers such as Ambrose,
Jerome, and Augustine chose to consult Rome. Perhaps this was due
to the fact that Rome seldom makes mistakes regarding dogmatic
formulations.

Because of the prestige of its location, the concept of church
as communion was gradually undermined when Rome became
stronger. By the end of the first millennium, all the churches in
the West were under the jurisdiction of Rome. However, in the
East, Constantinople was the dominant church as the churches in
Alexandria and Antioch lost their status due to heresy or schism. The
revival of Roman law in the West served to strengthen papal power,
and reciprocity among equals was not taken seriously. As Dulles
wrote, 'The vertical lines of authority from Rome to the bishops
replaced the horizontal lines of communion among bishops and
among churches.'[3] Eventually the pope was viewed as the supreme
and universal bishop of the church.

Scholastic theology also undermined the importance of
communion because the understanding of communion became
spiritualized. The significance of communion was narrowed to the

1. Avery Dulles SJ, 'The Church as Communion' in Nassif (ed.), *New
   Perspectives on Historical Theology*, p. 128.
2. Ibid., p. 129.
3. Ibid., p. 130.

reception of the sacrament: it 'was a mysterious grace-relationship of the individual with God'. This means that receiving the eucharistic bread and baptism were not seen as bringing one into communion with the local church and its bishop, but 'rather into a universal, undifferentiated communion of grace'.[1] In this regard, communion was considered interior and not an external manifestation. Interestingly, with this spiritual understanding of communion, the Protestants began to develop the idea of the invisible church against Roman domination.

Rome reacted against the Reformers by emphasizing the juridical aspect of the church – the church as the centralized body in which all the members, bishops, priests, and laity are subject to the authority of the pope. The local churches became administrative branches under the pope, who is absolute in power. The ecumenical councils are also restricted in their power to control the pope. It is now the pope who controls the council.[2] As we have seen, this goes against Orthodox ecclesiology.

While Rome developed its understanding of the papacy along juridical lines, Orthodox theology held fast to the idea of the church as a divine institution whose internal existence could not be defined in juridical terms. Meyendorff wrote: 'For them the Church was, first of all, a sacramental communion with God in Christ and the Spirit, whose membership – the entire Body of Christ – is not limited to the earthly *oikoumene* ("inhabited earth") where law governs society, but includes the host of angels and saints, as well as the divine head.'[3]

There were Roman Catholic theologians before Vatican II who sought to revitalize the church by going back to its patristic source. They had a vision of the church as 'an interpersonal communion, patterned on the mutual relations of the divine persons in the Trinity'. This idea is close to Orthodoxy. Here the local church celebrating the Eucharist presided over by the bishop is viewed as

---

1. Ibid.
2. Ibid.
3. Further, Meyendorff also asserted that the Byzantines were not juridically incompetent and were aware that certain canons reflect the divine nature of the church. Further, Roman traditions were always present in Byzantium and there were Latin canon lawyers who advised the emperors on decrees concerning the church. But these lawyers understood their role as subordinate to the divine nature of the church. They recognized that there 'was no canonical legislation in heaven'. Meyendorff, *Byzantine Theology*, pp. 79–80.

the 'paradigmatic realization of the Church'.[1] The bishops as heads of the local churches receive their power directly from Christ himself through the sacrament of ordination. Constituting a college, all of the bishops are responsible for the direction of the whole universal church. In other words, there is co-responsibility because authority is shared among the bishops.

The idea of church as communion is taken up in the teaching of Vatican II; the church is likened to a sacrament and within this communion, each local church is called to share its gift with others. Together with the pope, all bishops are linked to one another in communion. The pontiff is regarded not as an absolute ruler but as a moderator who presides over the church in charity. He helps to maintain legitimate diversity and is a symbol of unity. Communion theology is thus used to correct the extreme positions of centralism and clericalism in the church that have developed in recent years.[2] Vatican II has encouraged the local and regional churches to develop their distinct characteristics within the universal church. Most of the ideas about communion are spelled out in *Lumen Gentium*, the Dogmatic Constitution on the Church. One of the most significant changes that occurred during the Second Vatican Council was the introduction of the vernacular into the liturgy.

Recognizing the importance of ecumenism, Vatican II is determined to build on the incomplete communion that now exists among Christian communities, in the hope of achieving full communion. The Roman Catholic Church's emphasis on scripture, tradition, baptism, and works of charity, which are the gifts of the Holy Spirit, can act as a bond of communion with other Christian communities that lack apostolic heritage and the universal church. Dulles rightly claimed that this vision is particularly relevant to Western Christian communities' relationship with the Eastern Churches. The Decree on Ecumenism, *Unitatis Redintegratio*, states: 'These Churches, although separated from us, possess true sacraments, above all by apostolic succession, the priesthood and the Eucharist, whereby they are linked with us in closest intimacy.'[3] The Decree also acknowledges that some churches may have better appreciation of the divine mystery and express it better than others:

1. Dulles, *op. cit.*, p. 131.
2. Ibid., p. 132.
3. *Unitatis Redintegratio*, the Decree on Ecumenism (1964), http://www. vatican.va/archive/hist_councils/ii_vatican_council/documents/vat-ii_ decree_19641121_unitatis-redintegratio_en.html, no. 15.

It is hardly surprising, then, if from time to time one tradition has come nearer to a full appreciation of some aspects of a mystery of revelation than the other, or has expressed it to better advantage. In such cases, these various theological expressions are to be considered often as mutually complementary rather than conflicting. Where the authentic theological traditions of the Eastern Church are concerned, we must recognize the admirable way in which they have their roots in Holy Scripture, and how they are nurtured and given expression in the life of the liturgy. They derive their strength too from the living tradition of the apostles and from the works of the Fathers and spiritual writers of the Eastern Churches. Thus they promote the right ordering of Christian life and, indeed, pave the way to a full vision of Christian truth.[1]

Both Congar and Meyendorff saw clearly that communion derived from the triune God is fruitful and helps in maintaining diversities and the distinct characteristics of each party. In the universal church, we must have both universal and local bonds. The church is like a chorus of many voices that requires a universal bond to maintain harmony and some autonomy to prevent monotony. The 'diverse but concordant liturgies, spiritualities . . . law and doctrine' reflect the profound mystery of God,[2] and all should be invited to share and participate in this divine life without losing our cultural and spiritual identities. Related to this idea of communion is the touchy issue of the primacy of Peter, which we briefly discussed earlier.

## The Primacy of Peter

At the root of the debate on the division between East and West is the following question: 'Is the institution guaranteeing the truth, or Truth itself?'[3] Meyendorff acknowledged that the Second Vatican Council have recognized this problem. The Roman Catholic Church have attempted to solve the issue by re-emphasizing conciliarity, reaffirming the ecclesial context of Peter primacy, and redefining it by taking into consideration the view of Orthodoxy and others as well. In spite of this goodwill, the issue remains because Vatican II teaches that:

1. Ibid., 17.
2. Dulles, *op. cit.*, p. 139.
3. Meyendorff (ed.) (1996), *Primacy of Peter*. Crestwood, New York: St Vladimir's Press, p. 7.

[T]he college or body of bishops has no authority unless it is understood together with the Roman Pontiff, the successor of Peter as its head. The pope's power of primacy over all, both pastors and faithful, remains whole and intact. In virtue of his office, that is as Vicar of Christ and pastor of the whole Church, the Roman Pontiff has full, supreme and universal power over the Church.[1]

With this, the Roman Catholic Church has only reaffirmed its stand on the primacy of Peter. Nonetheless, Meyendorff gave credit to the Roman Catholic Church for elaborating on the meaning of the local church, its eucharistic structure, and the role of the people of God. The Roman Catholic Church also stresses that the normal exercise of papal powers must be done in collaboration with other bishops. In meeting with the Orthodox ecumenical patriarchs, Pope Paul VI emphasized 'equality and primacy of honor' and referred to the churches as 'sister-churches'.[2] In spite of this fraternal feeling, according to Meyendorff, this gesture did not resolve all other issues, such as the anathemas of 1439, and he condemned the Orthodox Church for not accepting the decrees of the Council of Florence.

The Eastern Churches had always acknowledged the particular authority of Rome in ecclesiastical affairs, but they did not see this as an affirmation of the right to absolute power. The Byzantines never understood the great authority of Rome as supreme and absolute; the prestige of Rome is due only to the Petrine character of the church. Although the East recognizes the pope as the successor of Peter and Peter is recognized as the head of the church, this is not considered 'decisive'.[3] This means that other apostolic sees, such as Jerusalem, Constantinople, or Antioch, also have the right to claim the title of successor of Peter.

The establishment of Petrine and Pauline apostolicity and Rome's position as the capital city gave the Bishop of Rome first place among equals, but only with the consensus of all the other churches, according to Meyendorff. Therefore, in the East, the '*personal ministry of Peter* and the problem of his *succession*' were two distinct questions.[4] This leadership position is not based on divine rights

---

1. Dogmatic Constitution on the Church – *Lumen Gentium* (1964), http://www.vatican.va/archive/hist_councils/ii_vatican_council/documents/vat-ii_const_19641121_lumen-gentium_en.html, no. 22
2. Meyendorff, *op. cit.*, p. 8.
3. Meyendorff, 'St Peter in Byzantine Theology', ibid., p. 68.
4. Ibid., p. 69.

but on human consensus, which can be changed. The Orthodox claim that their understanding of the Petrine ministry comes from scripture and the early Church Fathers.

## Origen and the Fathers

Based on Matthew 16:18, Origen interpreted Jesus' command as a consequence of Peter's profession of Christ's divinity on the way to Caesarea Philippi; Simon became the rock on which the church is established as the result of this profession. Thus, Origen taught that those saved by faith in Christ also receive the keys of the Kingdom. This means that the successors of Peter include all believers because Christ did not give the keys of the Kingdom to Peter alone. St John Chrysostom and St Augustine also affirmed the faith of Simon and believed that 'in a certain sense all those who share the same faith are his successors.'[1]

Regarding episcopal ministry in the patristic tradition, St Cyprian of Carthage taught, as part of the Roman Catholic tradition, that the 'See of Peter' is present, not only in Rome, but in every local church. In other words, it is the essence of early church teaching that the local bishop is the teacher of his flock and thus fulfils 'sacramentally, through the apostolic succession, the office of the first true believer, Peter'.[2] Hence, it is understandable that even after the Great Schism of 1054, Orthodox theologians still regarded Peter as the 'coryphaeus' (κορυφαῖος) or the chief, acknowledging his important function in the foundation of the church. But they did not equate this recognition with endorsing papal claims of infallibility.

Photius, the great patriarch of the ninth century, recognized Peter as the 'coryphaeus of the Apostles'. Even though he betrayed Christ, Peter was not deprived of his leadership in the apostolic college. Thus, Photius aligned the foundation of the church with Peter's confession. The Lord gave the keys to Peter as a reward for his confession, which laid the foundation of the church.[3] St Gregory Palamas, in the fourteenth century, regarded Peter as the 'first of the Apostles', comparing Peter to Adam. Palamas claimed that by giving Simon the name 'Peter' and by building on him his church, Christ made him 'father of the race of the true worshippers of God'. Like Adam, Peter was tempted, but he repented and was forgiven

1. Ibid., p. 70.
2. Ibid., p. 71.
3. Ibid., p. 72.

by Christ and thus became the supreme pastor of the whole church. Although Peter belongs to the 'choirs of the apostles', he is distinct from others because he 'bears a higher title'.[1]

Peter is indeed the apostles' coryphaeus and the foundation of the church. Nonetheless, Meyendorff reiterated that textual evidence in favour of Peter's primacy in no way supports Roman ecclesiology. Although Peter was the leader of the apostolic college, this authority depended on his faith. In other words, it could be taken away, which it was, but was restored after his repentance.[2]

According to the teaching of Cyprian on the Petrine office, there is no plurality of episcopal sees, but only one chair of Peter, and all the bishops have a share in it. This is the essence of Orthodox understanding of the succession of Peter in the church. On the level of '*analogy* existing between the apostolic college and the episcopal college', there exists another succession because of the need to organize the church as an institution or 'ecclesiastical order', as Meyendorff put it.[3] The power of this second succession is determined by the Councils, and therefore the authority of Peter is not God-given, but comes from the Councils. It appears to the Orthodox Church that Roman ecclesiology emphasizes rather disproportionately this analogical aspect of Peter and has neglected the idea that the succession of Peter is in the person of the bishop in every local church.[4]

While acknowledging that establishing the earthly church with juridical terms was necessary, Meyendorff insisted that these legal concepts could not exhaust the profound reality of the Church of God. The organization of the church could also be determined by the Councils at times. Meyendorff was hopeful that the Latin Church would restore this balance between Peter as the universal primate and also as the head of the local church. The Orthodox Church can contribute to this restoration by further research into its own ecclesiological tradition, which originates in primitive Christianity.

---

1. Ibid., p. 74. John Erickson claims that 'Papal primacy (or rather pre-eminence) is never directly attacked. Even Michael Cerularius refers to the Pope with the greatest respect and prefers to cast the blame for the whole affair on his old enemy Argyrus, the Byzantine military governor in southern Italy, or else on the "Franks".' Erickson, 'Leavened and unleavened', 156.
2. Meyendorff, *op. cit.*
3. Ibid., 89.
4. Ibid., 90.

In sum, the ideas of Meyendorff on the primacy of St Peter have great relevance and significance for Roman Catholics. Meyendorff was appreciative of the strength of the Roman Catholic position on the papacy, while also wishing to emphasize Orthodox theological convictions and objections to Roman Catholic understanding. Recognizing that Peter did occupy a special place in the church according to scripture and tradition, Meyendorff, however, disagreed with this primacy and the extent to which the Petrine power is interpreted and practised by Roman Catholics. In his view, episcopal sees rose in prominence more for political reasons than divine providence. For the good running of the church, primacies were needed as they were a political expediency. Therefore, every bishop is a successor of St Peter and participates in the Petrine office. Such is the Orthodox view generally.

The Petrine office should be juridical and collegial at the service of the people of God. The ecclesial rights and dignity of the local churches need to be protected, as demanded by the Orthodox Church, but not at the expense of juridical rights that are needed to keep the church together. It remains to be seen how the Petrine office can in the future accommodate the demands of the Orthodox churches in order for the church to be one. Meyendorff welcomed the idea of 'sister churches', an expression that means that the East and the West share a common ecclesiastical heritage based on a valid episcopate and Eucharist. Rome, of course, cannot accept the idea that the Petrine office can be shared by other bishops vis-à-vis the pope. Nonetheless, the notion of sister churches, used by the Patriarch of Constantinople, Athenagoras I, and favoured also by Pope Paul VI and Pope John Paul II, can be explored for further critical reflection. In the next chapter, we will discuss Nicholas Afanasiev and cover the issue of sister churches raised by Joseph Ratzinger.

# Chapter 2
## Nicholas Afanasiev

The eucharistic ecclesiology of Orthodox theologian Nicholas Afanasiev, with its emphasis on the unity of faith, on communion, and on the relationship between the local and universal churches, exerted great influence on Roman Catholic theology prior to Vatican II. Afanasiev attended the Council as an official observer and was also present when the anathemas from the eleventh century were lifted by Pope Paul VI and Ecumenical Patriarch Athenagoras I. In his essay 'Una sancta', written 'to the memory of John XXIII, the Pope of Love', Afanasiev expressed great hope for the reunification of the Christian churches when Vatican II was convoked. Concerned about the sinful division of Christianity, Afanasiev saw the Eucharist as the source of unity. He applied his understanding of the eucharistic assembly to exploring the nature of division and the possibilities of reunion between the Orthodox and Roman Catholic Churches.

While Cardinal Joseph Ratzinger was still prefect of the Congregation for the Doctrine of the Faith, his preference in ecumenical endeavours was for a slow, realistic, and theologically attentive approach. As a result, he was very critical of shortcuts to unity. Critical of the various approaches to ecumenism that relied on sociological or political models, Ratzinger believed it was unlikely that full Christian unity would happen in the near future. However, as Pope Benedict XVI, he confirmed his commitment to Christian unity as a priority in his pontificate. Not only did Ratzinger seek to correct a wrong interpretation of the Council's ecclesiological vision, he also wanted to stress Vatican II's conception of the local churches. In his ecclesiology, Ratzinger moved from an emphasis on the church as the mystical body of Christ to the church as the sacrament of salvation. This led to his understanding of the importance of the Eucharist as the foundation of the church.

This chapter seeks to examine the eucharistic ecclesiology of Nicholas Afanasiev and Joseph Ratzinger. It attempts to demonstrate that in spite of their differences, they share a belief that the impasse in the dialogue between Orthodox and Roman Catholic Churches can be overcome by 'a purification of memory' in 'a spirit of love' that is also rooted in the Eucharist. It is this purification of memory through the effort of love that will enable the process of healing to take place in their ecumenical efforts to achieve unity. Afanasiev categorized his understanding of the church into two fundamental types: universal and eucharistic.

## Universal Ecclesiology

Universal ecclesiology based on the principles laid down by Cyprian of Carthage gradually replaced eucharistic ecclesiology. Universal ecclesiology teaches that only the universal church possesses fullness, which means that the local churches do not possess fullness. The principle of unity of the universal church consists of 'a multiplicity united in peace' of the bishops. For Cyprian, 'the principle of the unity of the episcopate is the principle of the unity of the universal church. The unity of the Church demands the unity of the bishops, and the unity of the bishops protects the unity of the Church.'[1] Furthermore, 'The bishop is in the Church and the Church in the bishop, and if anyone is not with the bishop, he is not in the Church.'[2]

To Cyprian and the early Church Fathers, the church is one because Christ is one. Cyprian, with his Roman background, was precise in juridical formulae and thus, for him, the essential unity of the church is found in the one Christ. At the same time, the actual unity of the many local churches 'is preserved in the one episcopate which all bishops share, the one throne of Peter which all bishops occupy'.[3]

---

1. Nicholas Afanasiev, 'Una sancta', in Michael Plekon (ed.) (2003), *Tradition Alive: On the Church and the Christian Life in Our Time/ Readings from the Eastern Church*. Lanham: Rowman & Littlefield. For a detailed biography of Afanasiev, see Aidan Nichols OP (1989), *Theology in the Russian Diaspora*. Cambridge: Cambridge University Press. Some material in this chapter appeared as an article: Ambrose Ih-Mong (2012), 'Purification of memory in the spirit of love: An examination of the ecclesiology of Nicolas Afanasiev and Joseph Ratzinger'. *International Journal of Orthodox Theology*, 3 March, 129–57.
2. Afanasiev, 'Una sancta', p. 13.
3. M. Edmund Hussey (1975), 'Nicholas Afanasiev's Eucharistic ecclesiology: a Roman Catholic viewpoint', *Journal of Ecumenical Studies* 12, no. 2 (March), 236.

Universal ecclesiology implies that outside the episcopate there is no church. As such, Afanasiev believed that the schism existing between the Orthodox and Roman Catholic Churches has been perpetuated by uncritical acceptance of Cyprian's formula. He wrote: '[T]his doctrine [universal ecclesiology], and above all the doctrine on the unity of the Church and on the principle of this unity, has greatly supported the division.'[1] Thus there can be no hope of reunion between the Orthodox and Roman Catholic Churches from the perspective of universal ecclesiology, which teaches that local churches are rooted in the universal church, for this means that no local churches separated from the universal church can remain as part of the church. Regarding the status of the Orthodox and Roman Catholic Churches, universal ecclesiology would convince each of them that there can only be one true church, not two. Hence, an ecumenical dialogue based on universal ecclesiology is doomed to fail.

In sum, universal ecclesiology based on the principles formulated by Cyprian of Carthage is not the primitive structure of the church, but a development caused by external factors in the Christian community during the time of Constantine. A universal ecclesiology implies the idea of primacy, but Afanasiev's preference was for priority given to the local church. He believed that a return to the eucharistic ecclesiology of the early church would have the potential to heal the rift between the Orthodox and Roman Catholic Churches and to recover the unity that was there from the very beginning.

### Eucharistic Ecclesiology

According to Afanasiev, 'in the apostolic age, and throughout the second and third centuries, every local church was autonomous and independent – autonomous, for it contained in itself everything necessary to its life; and independent, because it did not depend on any other local church or any bishop whatever outside itself.'[2]
Furthermore:

[T]he local church is autonomous and independent, because the Church of God in Christ indwells it in perfect fullness. It is independent, because any power, of any kind, exercised over it would be exercised over Christ and His Body. It is

1. Afanasiev, *op. cit.*, p. 11.
2. Afanasiev, 'The Church which Presides in Love' (1992) in John Meyendorff (ed.), *The Primacy of Peter: Essays in Ecclesiology and the Early Church*. New York: St Vladimir's Seminary Press, p. 107.

autonomous, because fullness of being belongs to the Church of God in Christ, and outside it nothing is, for nothing can have being outside Christ.[1]

Christ is fully present in the Eucharist and each local church together with its bishop during eucharistic celebrations manifests the full body of Christ. Afanasiev taught that 'Where the Eucharist is, there is the Church of God, and where the Church of God is, there is the Eucharist. It follows that the eucharistic assembly is the distinctive empirical sign of the Church.'[2] As such, the limit of the church is determined by the limit of the eucharistic assembly.

The bishop is not excluded because he is 'the distinctive empirical sign of the local church'. In fact the bishop is 'included in the very concept of the Eucharist'.[3]

However, Afanasiev was critical of universal ecclesiology that maintains the principle of unity in the episcopate which lies above eucharistic assembly. For him, the role of the bishop is important for the church, but it is not the full manifestation of the church. Although nothing can stand above the local eucharistic assembly, Afanasiev also argued that the *una sancta* (the church) is not subordinate to the local church and thus maintained a proper balance between the universal and local aspects of the church. He wrote:

> Each local church would unite in herself just the local churches, for she possessed all the fullness of the Church of God and all the local churches together were united because the same Church of God dwelt in them all. . . . It is the union of the Church of God with herself, through diverse representations. Within eucharistic ecclesiology the principle of the union of the local churches is that of the unity of the Church of God, which is found in the local church herself.[4]

Therefore what was celebrated in one church was also celebrated in others as they all possess the fullness of the church of God. The local churches are not provincial in nature, but possess a universal nature.[5] Hence separated churches are also in some ways in communion with the church.

1. Ibid., p. 109.
2. Afanasiev, 'Una sancta', p. 14.
3. Ibid.
4. Ibid., p. 15.
5. Quoted in Radu Bordeianu (2009), 'Orthodox–Catholic dialogue: retrieving Eucharistic ecclesiology,' *Journal of Ecumenical Studies* 44, no. 2 (March), 242–3.

According to Afanasiev, both the Orthodox Church and the Roman Catholic Church celebrate the same Eucharist, and as a result, he contended, the two communities are united in spite of dogmatic differences. Cyprian, however, argued that separated churches are not in communion with the church (*una sancta*) and as such their sacraments are not valid. Unfortunately, both the Orthodox and the Roman Catholic Church adopted Cyprian's position. Each considered itself the true church and thereby dismissed the other as having a 'diminished existence of the Church'.[1] But Afanasiev considered such a position to be untenable because 'the nature of the Church presupposes that either she exists in her fullness or she does not exist at all, but there can be no partial existence nor can there be vestiges existing here and there. The Church is one in all the fullness of her nature and she is the only true Church, and it is not possible to have the Church where there is error.'[2]

According to the Nicene Creed, the church is 'one, holy, catholic and apostolic,' and thus Afanasiev insisted that the church would always be one in spite of differences. He wrote: '[I]f one recognized the quality of church in the other part of the divided church, one would be minimizing the importance of dogmatic differences, leaving them integral as they are. If one or the other parts are both the church, then this means the sacraments are celebrated and salvation is possible in both, for this is the purpose of the church.'[3] In his ecclesiology, Afanasiev stressed fewer doctrinal differences, but emphasized that:

> For eucharistic ecclesiology, the orthodox church and the catholic church are both Churches, or to be more exact, each local church of both groups remains a Church – as it was before so it is after the 'separation.' I put 'separation' in quotation marks for it did not take place and there is no separation. The Church of God is forever and remains one and unique. The break in communion was not able to produce the division of the Church which, by her very nature, cannot be divided into parts.[4]

---

1. Ibid., 243.
2. Afanasiev, 'Una sancta', p. 8. Bordeianu argues that ironically Afanasiev did not accept different degrees of belonging to the church and thus he implicitly followed Cyprian's position that there is no church outside the universal Church. Bordeianu, *op. cit.*, 243.
3. Afanasiev, *op. cit.*, pp. 5–6.
4. Ibid., p. 22.

Afanasiev believed that the East–West schism did not affect union at the deeper level. Thus the Orthodox and Roman Catholic Churches are still united in essence, even though they still lack eucharistic communion, because the separation is based on canonical principles:

> [O]ur separation, even if provoked by dogmatic differences, nevertheless has a canonical character. The separation always remains but on the surface of ecclesial life and never extends to its depths. Our canonical division (provoked by dogmatic differences), a division that in turn has given rise to even more profound dogmatic differences, has despite all of this never entirely broken our eucharistic unity. Although this unity does not find concrete expression for reasons of canonical order, we are not able to transform in reality our ecclesiological *koinonia*, our fellowship.[1]

Eucharistic unity remains intact in spite of doctrinal differences. While acknowledging that exclusion from the Eucharist happens when there is a schism, Afanasiev argued that:

> The nature of the break in communion indicated that the local church deprived of communion with the other churches ceased to exist for the latter, for there were no longer links by which this communion could be realized. But such a church did not cease to remain in itself the Church of God despite its isolated situation. If we think that such a local church is no longer the Church, we reject the only distinctive sign by which we can judge the existence of a Church: where there is the eucharistic assembly, there is Christ, and there is the Church of God in Christ.[2]

Thus in the ecclesiology of Afanasiev, the churches scattered throughout the world remain one with the rest as manifested in the eucharistic celebration. In other words, the unity of the churches depends primarily on the same Eucharist being celebrated in different local churches. They are not dependent on local communities, doctrinal uniformity, episcopal union or even the bond of love. Afanasiev lamented that both the Orthodox and the Roman Catholic Church have forgotten these eucharistic principles and instead have focused on their doctrinal differences. He called for a return to the eucharistic ecclesiology of the early church, believing this would

---

1. Ibid., p. 49.
2. Ibid., p. 18.

eventually lead to unity when believers from the two churches received the Eucharist. This means that as long as there is a valid Eucharist in the Orthodox and Roman Catholic Churches, the unity has never completely been broken – the link is the Eucharist.[1]

Afanasiev's eucharistic ecclesiology has been criticized for its one-sidedness manifested in congregationism, and he has also been accused of favouring the local church over the universal church.[2] Nonetheless, his understanding of eucharistic ecclesiology has an ecumenical significance in explaining the idea that the problems of a divided church cannot be separated from the issue of the Eucharist. Influential in the Roman Catholic Church, Afanasiev was the only Orthodox theologian whose work was mentioned in the documents of Vatican II. In *Lumen Gentium*, we see that the Eucharist is important in the life of the church because it signifies and effects unity in the church:

> Really partaking of the body of the Lord in the breaking of the Eucharistic bread, we are taken up into communion with Him and with one another. 'Because the bread is one, we though many, are one body, all of us who partake of the one bread.' In this way all of us are made members of His Body, 'but severally members one of another.'[3]

The fundamental idea in eucharistic ecclesiology is that the local church contains the fullness of the church. *Lumen Gentium* also expresses this perspective:

> In any community of the altar, under the sacred ministry of the bishop, there is exhibited a symbol of that charity and 'unity of the mystical Body, without which there can be no salvation.' In these communities, though frequently small and poor, or living in the Diaspora, Christ is present, and in virtue of His presence there is brought together one, holy, catholic and apostolic Church. For 'the partaking of the body and blood of Christ does nothing other than make us be transformed into that which we consume.'[4]

1. Bordeianu, *op. cit.*, 245.
2. Anastacia Wooden (2010), 'Eucharistic ecclesiology of Nicolas Afanasiev and its ecumenical significance: a new perspective'. *Journal of Ecumenical Studies* 45, no. 4 (September), 544.
3. Dogmatic Constitution on the Church – *Lumen Gentium*, http://www.vatican.va/archive/hist_councils/ii_vatican_council/documents/vat-ii_const_19641121_lumen-gentium_en.html, no. 7.
4. Ibid., no. 26.

As we can see, Vatican II affirms that the one church is fully present in the local church. However, it also emphasizes the principle that local churches are part of the universal church – they are not autonomous and independent, as taught by Afanasiev. *Lumen Gentium* affirms that:

> The Roman Pontiff, as the successor of Peter, is the perpetual and visible principle and foundation of unity of both the bishops and of the faithful. The individual bishops, however, are the visible principle and foundation of unity in their particular churches, fashioned after the model of the universal Church, in and from which churches come into being the one and only Catholic Church.[1]

The above statement means that the local church is just a portion of the universal church. Afanasiev saw the Eucharist as the source of unity. In contrast, Vatican II sees the pope as the 'principle and foundation of unity', and the Eucharist as a sign and means of fostering that unity.

## Spirit of Love

Putting aside all dogmatic differences, Afanasiev urged both churches to work towards strengthening their common bond in the Eucharist in a spirit of love:

> By an effort of Love, the orthodox church *could* reestablish communion with the catholic church, the dogmatic divergences notwithstanding and without demanding that the catholic church renounce the doctrines that distinguish her from the orthodox church. . . . Certainly, to attain this the effort in Love is necessary, a great sacrifice, an element of self-renunciation. To restrict the doctrine of the power of the pope within the limits of the catholic church would be, for the church of Rome, the result of a great sacrificial spirit toward the goal of reestablishing the union-of-the-churches-joined-in-Love.[2]

In view of the above, Afanasiev called for the Orthodox and Roman Catholic Churches to act in the spirit of love to renew their communion in spite of disagreements over many aspects of church

---

1. Ibid., no. 23.
2. Afanasiev, 'Una sancta', pp. 25–6.

life and teaching. Not minimizing the importance of dogmatic formulations nor advocating doctrinal relativism or indifferentism, Afanasiev believed that differences could be resolved through the power of charity. He claimed that Christians 'have forgotten that "our knowledge is imperfect and our prophesying is imperfect" (1 Corinthians 13:9). When Love is raised higher than knowledge, then knowledge itself will be perfected. Knowledge is not opposed to Love and Love does not exclude knowledge.'[1] Thus Orthodox and Roman Catholics need to strengthen the bond of love in order to re-establish eucharistic communion.

When Afanasiev wrote about 'the agreement in Love of the local churches', he was not referring to love as an emotion or general friendliness.[2] Love for him was a commitment, an effective binding force:

> If the power founded upon love is insufficient in actual life, which has lost the principle of love, it is on the contrary completely sufficient in the Church, where love is the first and the last principle. Juridical power is a substitute for love in actual social life, a substitute as perfect as possible in a very imperfect life. In the Church, perfect love dwells, there is no need for such a substitute.[3]

In sum, Afanasiev contended that the main difference between universal ecclesiology and eucharistic ecclesiology is in the principle of unity of the local churches. Universal ecclesiology stresses the fullness and unity of the church in the multitude of local churches and is guaranteed by the episcopacy. Eucharistic ecclesiology, however, stresses the fullness of the one church manifested in each local church. Afanasiev was convinced that eucharistic ecclesiology existed in the early church and he saw it as a primordial way of being church. Universal ecclesiology borrowed ideas and structures from the civil society and gradually replaced eucharistic ecclesiology. This 'slippage of the Eucharist from the central, defining action of the Church to merely one of many services performed' caused the meaning of the Eucharist to be obscured.[4] Afanasiev understood that one of the most serious problems in the life of the church was due to 'the separation of the structures and organization of the Church

---

1. Ibid., p. 28.
2. Ibid., p. 17.
3. Quoted in Wooden, *op. cit.*, 554.
4. Ibid., 555.

from the Holy Spirit and the Eucharist'.[1] In the same way, Ratzinger
has claimed that the separation of the doctrine of the Eucharist from
ecclesiology represents a distortion in theology.

## The Ecclesiology of Joseph Ratzinger

Pope Emeritus Joseph Ratzinger believes that:

> the separation of the doctrine of the Eucharist and ecclesiology,
> which can be noted from the eleventh and twelfth centuries
> onwards, represents one of the most unfortunate pages of
> medieval theology . . . because both thereby lost their centre. A
> doctrine of the Eucharist that is not related to the community
> of the Church misses its essence as does an ecclesiology that is
> not conceived with the Eucharist as its centre.[2]

The institution of the Eucharist is the making of a covenant and
thus it is the concrete foundation of the new people. This means
that the people come into being through the covenant relationship
with God. Jesus brings his disciples into his communion with God
and also into his mission to draw all people at all times and places to
himself. These disciples become a 'people' through communion in
the Eucharist.[3]

The Old Testament theme of covenant is appropriated by Jesus
and receives a new centre: communion with Christ's body. Thus the
church, the people of the new covenant, takes its origin from the
Eucharist; the church is regarded as the people of God only through
its communion with Christ. It is only this relationship with Christ
that allows men and women to gain access to God. In *Called to
Communion: Understanding the Church Today* (1996), Ratzinger
writes:

> [T]he Eucharist, seen as the permanent origin and centre of the
> Church, joins all the 'many,' who are now made a people, to the
> one Lord and to his one and only Body. The fact already implies
> that the Church and her unity are but one. It is true that the many
> celebrations in which the one Eucharist will be realized also

---

1. Ibid.
2. Joseph Ratzinger (1965), 'The pastoral implications of episcopal
   collegiality'. *Concilium* 1, 28.
3. Ratzinger (1996), *Called to Communion: Understanding the Church
   Today*. San Francisco: Ignatius Press, p. 28.

point ahead to the multiformity of the one Body. Nevertheless, it is clear that these many celebrations cannot stand side by side as autonomous, mutually independent entities but are always simply the presence of one and the same mystery.[1]

Influenced by Henri de Lubac, Ratzinger asserts that the church as the mystical body of Christ refers to the Eucharist. St Paul and the Early Fathers also connected the idea of the church with the Eucharist. Eucharistic ecclesiology implies that Jesus' Last Supper was the event that founded the church:

> [T]he Eucharist joins human beings together, not only with one another, but also with Christ, and . . . in this way it makes people into the Church. At the same time this already determines the fundamental constitution of the Church: Church lives in eucharistic communities. Her worship service is her constitution, for by her very nature she is service of God and therefore service of men, the service that transforms the world.[2]

The mass is the church's form, through which it develops the new relationship of multiplicity and unity. This means that the ecclesiology of local churches has its origin in the formulation of the eucharistic ecclesiology.[3] Thus we also see Ratzinger's ecclesiology seeking to clarify the role of the local churches through an understanding of the church as a sacrament of salvation and the Eucharist as the foundation of the church. In *Rome and the Eastern Churches* (2010), Aidan Nichols sums up the significance of eucharistic ecclesiology when he writes:

> The value of a eucharistic ecclesiology is that it derives the ministerial, and therefore governmental, structure of the Church from the pattern of her eucharistic life and in so doing

---

1. Ibid., p. 29.
2. Ratzinger (2008), *Church, Ecumenism and Politics*. San Francisco: Ignatius Press, pp. 17–18. Claude Geffré is more radical when he writes: 'the visible belonging to the church guaranteed by the confession of the same creed and the communion in the eucharistic body of Christ can be a sacrament of an invisible belonging to Christ, who transcends the borders of the visible church and who may coincide with belonging to the other great non-Christian traditions.' Claude Geffré (2002), 'Double Belonging and the Originality of Christianity as a Religion', in Catherine Cornille (ed.), *Many Mansions?* Maryknoll, New York: Orbis, p. 104.
3. Ratzinger, *op. cit.*, p. 18.

suggests how we should understand the relation of the local church, which celebrates the Eucharist in a particular place, to the universal Church, the *Catholica*. The Eucharist is always celebrated by a particular group, yet that which is so celebrated is, in fact, the Eucharist of the whole Church. The local church, therefore, manifests the plenitude of the Church – yet only in the measure of its communion with all the other churches.[1]

Ratzinger emphasizes that the church is not a human construction. We can only receive the church from where it is really present: 'from the sacramental communion of his Body as it makes its way through history.'[2] This leads to his preference for an ecclesiology of *communio*.

## *Ecclesiology of Communion*

Joseph Ratzinger teaches that the concept of communion lies '"*at the heart of the Church's self-understanding*" insofar as it is the mystery of the personal union of each human being with the divine Trinity and with the rest of mankind, initiated with the faith, and, having begun as a reality in the Church on earth, is directed towards its eschatological fulfilment in the heavenly Church'.[3] This concept of communion must be understood in the biblical sense, and in the biblical context, communion has theological, Christological, soteriological, and ecclesiological characteristics.[4]

There is also a sacramental dimension as acknowledged by St Paul: 'The cup of blessing which we bless, is it not a communion in the blood of Christ? The bread which we break, is it not a communion in the body of Christ? Because there is one bread, we who are many are one body' (1 Corinthians 10:16–17). Thus the ecclesiology of communion forms the basis for Eucharistic ecclesiology. Ratzinger writes:

---

1. Aidan Nichols OP (2010), *Rome and the Eastern Churches*. San Francisco: Ignatius Press, pp. 359–60.
2. Ratzinger, *op. cit.*, p. 20.
3. Ratzinger, Congregation for the Doctrine of the Faith (1992), 'Letter to the Bishops of the Catholic Church on some aspects of the Church understood as Communion', http://www.vatican.va/roman _curia/congregations/cfaith/documents/rc_con_cfaith_doc_28051992_ communionis-notio_en.html.
4. Ratzinger, 'The Ecclesiology of Vatican II', Conference of Cardinal Ratzinger at the opening of the Pastoral Congress of the Diocese of Aversa (Italy), http://www.ewtn. com/library/curia/cdfeccv2.htm.

In the Eucharist, Christ, present in the bread and wine and giving Himself anew, builds the Church as His Body and through His Risen Body He unites us to the one and triune God and to each other. The Eucharist celebrated in different places is universal at the same time, because there is only one Christ and only a single body of Christ. The Eucharist comprehends the priestly service of 'repraesentatio Christi' as well as that network of service, the synthesis of unity and multiplicity which is expressed in the term 'communio'.[1]

Communion has two dimensions: the vertical that is communion with God and the horizontal that is communion with one another. Christians must understand that communion is a gift from God given to us through the paschal mystery. Ecclesial communion is both invisible and visible. The invisible reality refers to our communion with the Father through Christ in the Holy Spirit. The visible reality is our communion with one another as sharers in the divine nature, in the passion of Christ, and in the same faith. In the church on earth, there is this close relationship between the invisible and visible aspects of communion. The link between these two dimensions of communion, invisible and visible, constitutes the church as the sacrament of salvation. From this sacramentality, Ratzinger argues, the church is open to missionary and ecumenical work. It is sent out to the world to spread the mystery of communion which is essential to its nature: 'to gather together all people and all things into Christ; so as to be for all an *"inseparable sacrament of unity"'*.[2]

Another important point that Ratzinger makes is the idea that the church is a communion of saints. This communion brings spiritual solidarity among the members of the church when they are members of one body. The invisible element means that communion exists not only among those still living, but also between those who have died in Christ in the hope of rising again. Ratzinger writes:

> [T]here is a *mutual relationship* between the pilgrim Church on earth and the heavenly Church in the historical-redemptive mission. Hence the ecclesiological importance not only of Christ's intercession on behalf of his members, but also of that of the saints and, in an eminent fashion, of the Blessed

---

1. Ibid.
2. Ratzinger, 'Letter to the Bishops of the Catholic Church', no. 4.

Virgin Mary's. *Devotion to the saints*, which is such a strong feature of the piety of the Christian people, can thus be seen to correspond in its very essence to the profound reality of the Church as a mystery of communion.[1]

Ratzinger's understanding of communion became the official ecclesiology while he was prefect of the Congregation for the Doctrine of the Faith. Meanwhile, the word 'communion' was interpreted differently by different people. But Ratzinger regards these different interpretations as 'handy slogans'. He says that, like the expression 'People of God', the word 'communion' becomes a slogan, its meaning distorted and devalued, when people emphasize the horizontal aspect only and abandon the vertical dimension. In this case the ecclesiology of communion was reduced to a concern with relations between the local churches and the universal church. The egalitarian emphasis on equality in communion was gaining popularity. In 'Eucharist, Communion and Solidarity', Ratzinger expresses his concern clearly:

> It was unavoidable that this great fundamental word of the New Testament, isolated and employed as a slogan, would also suffer diminishment, indeed, might even be trivialized. Those who speak today of an 'ecclesiology of communion' generally tend to mean two things: (1) they support a 'pluralist' ecclesiology, almost a 'federative' sense of union, opposing what they see as a centralist conception of the Church; (2) they want to stress, in the exchanges of giving and receiving among local Churches, their culturally pluralistic forms of worship in the liturgy, in discipline and in doctrine.[2]

In this erroneous understanding, according to Ratzinger, communion is seen as 'emerging from a network of multiple communities'. He is opposed to the horizontal idea of communion with its emphasis on the idea of 'self-determination within a vast community of churches' that dominates the thinking of the church.[3] Ratzinger admits the need to correct the imbalance and excessiveness of Roman centralization. But he reminds us that questions of this

1. Ibid., no. 6.
2. Ratzinger (2002), 'Eucharist, Communion and Solidarity', lecture at the Bishops' Conference of the Region of Campania in Benevento (Italy), http://www.vatican.va/roman_curia/congregations/cfaith/documents/rc_con_cfaith_doc_20020602_ratzinger-eucharistic-congress_en.html.
3. Ibid.

sort should not distract us from the main task of proclaiming Christ to the world. He rightly asserts that the church should be proclaiming not itself but God.[1]

At the same time, Ratzinger insists that communion is related to the universal church, understanding the importance of ecclesial hierarchy and papal primacy. Thus there are criteria to be met for Christian communities to be qualified as a 'valid church'. These criteria centre on the requirements of valid ministerial orders and the celebration of a valid Eucharist. Above all, for Ratzinger, communion with Rome is an important prerequisite.[2]

Ratzinger has been criticized for his assertion concerning the priority of the universal church: 'The universal Church in her essential mystery is a reality that ontologically and temporally is prior to every particular Church.' He responded to the criticism by saying, '[T]he ontological priority of the universal Church – the unique Church, the unique Body, the unique Bride – vis-à-vis the empirical, concrete manifestations of various, particular Churches is so obvious to me that I find it difficult to understand the objections raised against it.'[3] Those objections are possible only if we look at the church with its shortcomings and not as something willed by God. For Ratzinger, these oppositions are 'theological ravings' by people who see the church only as a human institution. Thus 'in this case one has abandoned not only the ecclesiology of the fathers, but the ecclesiology of the New Testament and the understanding of Israel in the Old Testament as well. It is not just the later deutero-Pauline letters and the Apocalypse that affirm the ontological priority of the universal Church to the particular Churches.'[4]

## Priority of the Universal Church

When the ecclesiological concept of communion is applied analogously to the relationship between the universal church and particular churches, Ratzinger vociferously asserts the priority of the universal church. He dismisses the idea that the particular church is a subject complete in itself. According to Ratzinger:

1. Ratzinger, 'The Ecclesiology of Vatican II'.
2. Lieven Boeve and Gerard Mannion (eds) (2010), *The Ratzinger Reader*. London: T & T Clark, p. 83.
3. Ratzinger, *op. cit.*
4. Ibid.

In order to grasp the true meaning of the analogical application of the term *communion* to the particular Churches taken as a whole, one must bear in mind above all that the particular Churches, insofar as they are '*part of the one Church of Christ*', have a special relationship of '*mutual interiority*' with the whole, that is, with the universal Church, because in every particular Church '*the one, holy, catholic and apostolic Church of Christ is truly present and active.*'[1]

Consequently, Ratzinger insists, the universal church is not merely the sum of all the particular churches or a federation of churches. It is also not the result of the communion of all the churches, but 'it is a reality *ontologically and temporally* prior to every *individual* particular Church.'[2] The universal church is the mother and not the offspring of the particular churches.

In its original and first manifestation, the church is universal. The local churches that have arisen in different places are particular expressions of the one unique Church of Jesus Christ. 'Arising *within* and *out of* the universal Church, they have their ecclesiality in it and from it.'[3] Ratzinger argues that the relationship between the universal church and the particular churches is a mystery, and cannot be compared to any human organization. We become members of the one, holy, catholic, and apostolic church through faith and baptism. However we do not belong to the universal church in a *mediate* way, through belonging to a particular church. Instead we belong to the universal church in an *immediate* way, although we enter it through a particular church. Ratzinger says, 'from the point of view of the Church understood as communion, this means therefore that the universal *communion of the faithful* and the *communion of the Churches* are not consequences of one another, but constitute the same reality seen from different viewpoints.'[4] This means that when one becomes a Roman Catholic through a particular church, one automatically belongs to the one, holy, catholic, and apostolic church.

Ratzinger's ecclesiology is different from and even contrary to the ecclesial vision of Afanasiev, who favoured the local churches over the universal church. As an Orthodox theologian, Afanasiev was naturally wary of the principle of primacy in ecclesiology. Ratzinger, on the other hand, stresses the ontological priority of the universal

1.  Ratzinger, 'Letter to the Bishops of the Catholic Church', no. 9.
2.  Ibid.
3.  Ibid.
4.  Ibid., no. 10.

church and the necessity of communion with Rome. Be that as it may, below is discussion of a letter written by Ratzinger that reveals his true feelings regarding the relationship between the Orthodox and Roman Catholic Churches. Here we see Ratzinger concurring with Afanasiev on many points regarding efforts to forge greater unity between the two churches.

## Purification of Memory

In his letter to the Metropolitan Damaskinos of Switzerland on 20 February 2001, Joseph Ratzinger expressed his cognisance that the Orthodox Church and the Roman Catholic Church belong to one another. Therefore none of their doctrinal disputes are insurmountable. Ratzinger thinks that the obstacle that stands between the two churches is not so much a question of doctrine as the memory of old hurts that alienates the two communities: '[T]he power of the confused tangles of history seems to be stronger than the light of faith that ought to be transforming them into forgiveness.'[1] This means that both churches need a purification of memory to begin the process of healing that will eventually lead to unity.

Many people believe that the main obstacle to the full restoration of unity between the Roman Catholic Church and the Orthodox Church lies in the pope's primacy of jurisdiction. Ratzinger thinks that this is a problem of language. The pope's jurisdiction over the whole church is based on honour, not in the worldly sense, but in the sense of service and obedience to Christ. The pope presides over the church in charity. This *agape*, expressed fully in the Eucharist, is connected to the theology of the cross, which is the deepest expression of God's love for us in Jesus Christ.[2]

Joseph Ratzinger also claims that without the primacy of the pope's jurisdiction over the whole church, the Roman Catholic Church would long ago have split into various national churches or various different rites. This would make it impossible to have a general view of the ecumenical situation. The primacy of the pope makes possible the steps of reconciliation towards unity. Ratzinger believes that the problem of autocephalous churches ('self-headed' Eastern Orthodox churches whose primates do not report to higher

---

1. Ratzinger (2005), *Pilgrim Fellowship of Faith*. San Francisco: Ignatius Press, p. 232.
2. Ibid., p. 233.

authorities) shows 'the necessity for an instrument of unity' that must also be 'correctly balanced with the independent responsibility of the local Churches'.[1]

Orthodox believers were offended when Ratzinger asserted that it is not appropriate to refer to the Orthodox Church and the Roman Catholic Church as two 'sister churches'. He explained that the term 'sister churches' refers to particular churches only. It is a matter of setting the plural 'churches' and the singular 'the church' in the right relationship to one another.[2] In the Credo we confess that there is only one church of Christ, which of course exists concretely in many particular churches. At the same time, these particular churches form part of the one church. Therefore, according to Ratzinger, to speak of the Orthodox Church and the Roman Catholic Church as sister churches would be 'setting up a plural above and beyond which no singular is apparent. A dualism would remain at the ultimate level of the concept of "Church", and the one Church would thus become a phantom, a utopia, whereas bodily existence is the very thing that is essential to her.'[3]

Ratzinger laments that the term 'universal church' is very often misinterpreted when he insists on the ontological and temporal precedence of the universal church over the particular churches. To interpret this understanding as favouring Roman centralism is 'complete nonsense', according to Ratzinger. He argues that the local Church of Rome is a local church that is entrusted with a special responsibility for the whole church, 'but she is not herself the universal church'.[4]

---

1. Ibid., p. 235.
2. Ibid., p. 236.
3. Ibid., p. 237.
4. Ibid., p. 239. Ratzinger is following the teaching of Vatican II, which attempted to depict the one Church of Christ as united in *koinonia*. Before the Council, the Catholic Church identified itself with the one true church, implying that other Christians are living outside the church. The Council fathers applying the theology of *koinonia* used the term 'subsist in' rather than 'is' to depict the relationship of the Church of Christ to the Catholic Church. This means that instead of saying the Church of Christ *is* the Catholic Church, Vatican II teaches that the Church of Christ *subsists in* the Catholic Church. The aim of this new understanding of the church is to avoid sociological identification of the church with the present structure of the Roman Catholic institutions. It also avoids implying that the Eastern Churches that are not in communion with Rome are not real churches. The Decree on Ecumenism also states that other Christian communities contain elements of the true Church. Thus members of these ecclesial

Maintaining the ontological and temporal priority of the universal church over the particular churches is 'not a declaration that the local Church of Rome should seek to acquire as many privileges as possible', Ratzinger insists.[1] It is not a question of the distribution of power, but is about the mystery of the church. In *Pilgrim Fellowship of Faith* (2005), he writes:

> [T]his is strictly a matter of theology, not of juridical questions or of Church politics: the fact that God's idea of the Son's one bride, eschatologically oriented toward the eternal wedding feast, is the first and the one essential idea of God that is at stake in matters to do with the Church, while the concrete realization of the Church in local Churches constitutes a second plane that is subsequent to the first and always remains subordinated to it.[2]

For the Orthodox Church to be in communion with Rome, Ratzinger suggests, the only condition is that they accept the teachings of the primacy of the pope during the first millennium:

> Rome must not require more from the East with respect to the doctrine of primacy than had been formulated and was lived in the first millennium. . . . Rome need not ask for more. Reunion could take place in this context if, on the one hand, the East would cease to oppose as heretical the developments that took place in the West in the second millennium and would accept the Catholic Church as legitimate and orthodox in the form she had acquired in the course of that development, while, on the other hand, the West would recognize the Church of the East as orthodox and legitimate in the form she has always had.[3]

communities are saved 'through the mediation of their communities, and not in spite of them'. This change in language from *est* to *subsistit* allows the possibility of expressing the reality of the church as transcendent and not merely a sociological structure. Other Christian communities are also recognized as having elements of the church, its spiritual and mystical reality. See *Unitatis Redintegratio*, the Decree on Ecumenism, http://www.vatican.va/archive/hist_councils/ii_vatican_council/documents/vat-ii_decree_19641121_unitatis-redintegratio_en.html; and Jeffrey Gros FSC, Eamon McManus and Ann Riggs (1998), *Introduction to Ecumenism*. New York: Paulist Press, pp. 68–9.

1. Ratzinger, *op. cit.*
2. Ibid.
3. Ratzinger (1987), *Principles of Catholic Theology*. San Francisco: Ignatius Press, p. 199.

Ratzinger also stresses the importance of apostolic succession in preserving the unity of the church. Both the Roman Catholic Church and the Orthodox Church have accepted that the church came into existence from the scripture. The bishops by virtue of their sacramental consecration and ecclesial tradition personify this unity of the church. This church unity, Ratzinger claims, is based on the concept of *successio apostolica,* intrinsically part of the structure of the church, as expressed since the second century.[1] He writes:

> The Apostolic succession is not a purely formal power; it is part of the mission for the gospel. That is why the concepts of succession and tradition were not separated in the early Church and why Vatican Council II is justified in linking the two closely together. The *successio*-structure is the expression both of the link with tradition and of the concept of tradition in the Catholic Church. On this question, there is, so far as I can see, no essential difference between the Catholic Churches of East and West.[2]

The structural unity between the two churches has not been destroyed. Afanasiev would be delighted to hear this. Perhaps this is the reason Ratzinger says that Rome should not demand from the East that it accepts any doctrine of papal jurisdiction other than the one formulated during the first millennium.

Ratzinger understands the Orthodox Church's aversion to papal primacy, but he thinks that they developed an incorrect interpretation of the Petrine office. According to the Orthodox point of view, the development of *monarchia papae* (papal monarchy) destroyed the ecclesial structure and, as a result, the primitive church was replaced by something different. This means that the Western Church is no longer under the bishops in their collegial unity. Instead the church has become a 'centrally organized monolith' and the idea of a perfect society has replaced the idea of succession. According to Ratzinger, the Orthodox Church has developed the mistaken idea that, in the Roman Catholic Church, the faith that is handed down no longer serves as a normative rule. It is no longer a rule that can be interpreted with the consensus of all the local churches. The Eastern Church has thus held that in the Roman Catholic Church, the will of the supreme pontiff creates a new authority.[3]

---

1. Ibid., p. 194.
2. Ibid., p. 245.
3. Ibid., p. 194.

This understanding by the Orthodox Church was reinforced in 1870 by the Roman Catholic teaching on the primacy of jurisdiction exercised by the bishop of Rome. On the one hand, only tradition serves as a valid source of the law.[1] On the other hand, the source of the law appears to be the will of the sovereign, who creates new laws that are binding for all. The Orthodox Church thus believes that the sacramental structure of the church has been replaced by a new concept of law; the papacy, which is not a sacrament but only a juridical institution, has set itself above the sacramental order.[2] Thus the Eastern Church must reject papal authority.

The Orthodox Church also contends that the Roman Catholic understanding of papal primacy, with its insistence on the universal jurisdiction of the papacy, goes against the eucharistic foundations of the church.[3] Since the eucharistic communities are wholly the body of Christ under their bishops, they are 'fundamentally equal and may not be subordinated to one another'. The Orthodox Church admits that historically Rome played a prominent role among the five ancient patriarchates: Rome, Constantinople, Alexandria, Antioch, and Jerusalem. However, it challenges traditional Roman Catholic understanding of the role of the patriarch in Rome.[4]

The Orthodox Church is opposed to the Roman Catholic tradition of papal primacy, with its strong emphasis on the universal jurisdiction of the pontiff. It believes that the authority of the patriarch was 'an expression of synodality' and bound to the communion of the churches.[5] It has rejected the notion of Roman primacy that assumes a 'supra-episcopal authority', as well as 'any primacy understood as a power *over* other local bishops and their Churches'. Instead, for the Orthodox Church, the essential form of primacy lies in the synod of bishops.[6] Simply put, primacy lies in the episcopacy it belongs to.

---

1. Ibid.
2. Ibid., p. 195.
3. Ibid., p. 292.
4. Richard Gaillardetz (1997), *Teaching with Authority: A Theology of the Magisterium in the Church*. Collegeville, Minnesota: Liturgical Press, p. 47. Russian Orthodox theologians stress the notion of *sobornost*, the organic unity of the whole Church. This unity applies particularly to the relationship between bishops and the whole Church. The bishop is the presider over the local eucharistic community in relation to the Church he serves. This authority is always 'exercised *within* rather than *above* the Church'. Ibid., p. 33.
5. Ibid., p. 47.
6. Ibid., p. 48.

According to Joseph Ratzinger, the removal of the anathema of 1054 reflects a holy and historic responsibility that goes beyond mere courtesy.[1] It is an important historical action involving the dialogue of love and the theological dialogue. Quoting the Metropolitan Meliton's words in his *Principles of Catholic Theology* (1987), Ratzinger states that the act of reconciliation brings 'no modification whatever in the status of dogma, in the existing canonical order, in the liturgy or in the life of the Church. . . . It does not mean a restoration of the sacramental community.'[2] The fundamental aim of the event was the restoration of ecclesial love – a community of love between bishopric and bishopric, between church and church. Ratzinger claims that this ecclesial love 'is not yet a sacramental community but possesses in itself the necessary dynamism to become such. It is to be regarded as an actual ecclesial union that binds churches as churches.'[3]

This restoration of love means that, as St Paul says in Philippians 3:13, we must forget the past. Memory has the dangerous power of causing the poison of yesterday to become the poison of today. Thus Ratzinger believes that reparation of the past can take place through a 'purification of memory'. This would mean amending our past mistakes through forgetting, resulting in a purification of memory that will serve to heal the wounds. In practical terms, both churches would erase from memory the excommunication that took place in the past. Forgetting is forgiving.[4]

This purification of memory taught by Joseph Ratzinger is what Nicholas Afanasiev was urging those who work for the reconciliation between the Roman Catholic and Orthodox Churches to consider. For Afanasiev, dogmatic divergence was of secondary importance, because reconciliation is about forging the bond of love that is already there in those who are baptized in Christ.

In the next chapter, we will discuss the ecclesiology of John Zizioulas, including his critique of Afanasiev's eucharistic ecclesiology. In relation to this subject, the chapter will also present Walter Kasper's response to Ratzinger's understanding of the

---

1. This refers to the mutual lifting of excommunications in a joint Catholic–Orthodox declaration, approved by Pope Paul VI and Ecumenical Patriarch Athenagoras I of Constantinople, and read simultaneously on 7 December 1965 at a public meeting of the Ecumenical Council in Rome and at a special ceremony in Istanbul.
2. Ratzinger, *Principles of Catholic Theology*, p. 209.
3. Ibid., p. 210.
4. Ibid., p. 211.

priority of the universal church over the local churches. As we shall see, divergent theological views exist in both the Orthodox Church and the Roman Catholic Church and thus, there is always room for debate and mutual learning. Dialogue between churches is, after all, a process of discovering the 'other' in all its complexities and changes.

# Chapter 3
## John Zizioulas

Regarded by Yves Congar as 'one of the most original and most profound theologians of our age', John D. Zizioulas was born in 1931 and studied in Thessaloniki and Athens. His doctoral dissertation was on the bishop in the early church and was published in English as *Eucharist, Bishop, Church: The Unity of the Church in the Divine Eucharist and the Bishop During the First Three Centuries*. He also studied in Chicago before becoming the Professor of Systematic Theology at the University of Glasgow. Later he was Visiting Professor at Geneva; King's College, London; and the Gregorian University, Rome. He was a layman, but in 1986 he was called upon to become the Metropolitan of Pergamon. Very much involved in the ecumenical movement, he became a member of the committees for dialogue with the Roman Catholic Church and with the Anglican Church, and was the Secretary of Faith and Order in the World Council of Churches in Geneva. He is now the Chairman of the Academy of Athens.

Zizioulas has expressed concern that the Eastern Church has been influenced by the West, first by scholasticism after the fall of Byzantium in 1453, and later by secularism. He follows in the footsteps of his teacher, Georges Florovsky, who sought to liberate Orthodox theology by returning to the early Church Fathers through a patristic synthesis.[1] Ironically, it was the

---

1. Zizioulas agrees with Florovsky that the main problem in Orthodox scholasticism was the separation of theology from its liturgical roots: 'the *lex orandi* and the *lex credendi* no longer coincided.' See Paul McPartlan (1993), *The Eucharist Makes the Church: Henri de Lubac and Zizioulas in Dialogue*. Edinburgh: T & T Clark, pp. 127–9. Some material in this chapter appeared as an article: Ambrose Ih-Ren Mong (2014), 'The one and many: an examination of John Zizioulas' ecclesiology'. *Canadian Journal of Orthodox Christianity*, IX, 3 (Fall), 44–59.

Western theologians who first called for a return to the ancient patristic source as a way to revive and reform the church. Zizioulas acknowledges his debt to these theologians, especially Henri de Lubac, in his effort to revive Orthodoxy. This chapter examines the influence of Henri de Lubac on Zizioulas' thought regarding the relation between the Eucharist and the church, which is connected to his insights on the relation between Christology and pneumatology. It also seeks to understand Zizioulas' position on the relation between the universal and the local churches, which is also a key issue in the Roman Catholic Church, as demonstrated in the debate between Joseph Ratzinger and Walter Kasper. Before we examine these topics, a brief discussion of Zizioulas' fundamental theological principles will give us a better grasp of his ecclesiology.

## *Theological Presuppositions*

Unlike the Roman Catholic Church, which has the magisterium as its teaching authority, the Orthodox Church claims that the only authoritative sources it has are the Bible and the Fathers, which are common to all Christians. But it is how the Orthodox Church interprets these common sources that distinguishes it from the other Christian communities. According to Zizioulas, its interpretation is based on some basic theological presuppositions:

   i.  *Ecclesiology must be situated within the context of Trinitarian theology.* We must begin with a clear distinction of Persons in the Trinity.
   ii. *Christology must be conditioned by pneumatology in a constitutive way.* [The Holy Spirit] is above all the one who makes Christ *be* what he is, i.e. *Christos* – Christ.
   iii. *The Church does not draw her identity from what she is but from what she will be.* Eschatology is absolutely crucial to ecclesiology. . . . [W]e must think of the *eschata* as the *beginning* of the Church's life, the *arche*, that which brings forth the Church, gives her the identity, sustains and inspires her in her existence.
   iv. *Finally, there is the cosmic dimension of ecclesiology.* The Church is not a community of human beings unrelated to the non-personal cosmos. Salvation is for the entire

creation which is subject to the yoke of death, and until death is eliminated from the entire cosmos there can be no salvation for the human being.[1]

In view of the above, according to Zizioulas, the church is both human and divine at the same time. Further, we can only understand Christology in the context of ecclesiology – Christ in the church. He insists that Christ is a 'corporate personality' – 'the firstborn among many brethren' – which means the 'last Adam in whom the many become one and the one becomes many'.[2] Ontology is thus an important consideration for Zizioulas' theology.

## Ontology

This metaphysical principle, 'the one and many', sums up Zizioulas' approach in his studies of ecclesiology. First he points out that during the Last Supper, Jesus identified the bread and wine with his body and blood. The Lord said to his disciples, 'This is my blood of the covenant, which is poured out for many' (Mark 14:24). According to him, these words of the Lord are linked to the 'Servant of God', a figure who takes upon himself the sins of the 'multitude' (Isaiah 40:55), which means that he identifies himself with the 'many'. This idea of Zizioulas that the 'one' represents the 'many' has its origin in the eucharistic tradition in Pauline writings: 'The cup of blessing that we bless, is it not a sharing in the blood of Christ? The bread that we break, is it not a sharing in the body of Christ? Because there is one bread, we who are many are one body, for we all partake of the one bread' (1 Corinthians 10:16–17). In St John's Gospel, the 'Son of Man' incorporates the 'many': 'Those who eat my flesh and drink my blood abide in me, and I in them' (John 6:56).[3]

In view of the above scriptural evidence, Zizioulas highlights that the synoptics, St Paul and St John, shared the same fundamental belief that in the Eucharist the 'many' become 'one' and the 'one' incorporates the 'many'. Furthermore, it is wrong to interpret Johannine theology, as some scholars do, as a tendency towards individualism in the eucharistic community. St John actually spoke

---

1. Metr. John D. Zizioulas (1988), 'The mystery of the church in Orthodox tradition'. *One In Christ* 24, no. 4 (January), 295–6.
2. Ibid., 301.
3. See Zizioulas (2011), *The Eucharistic Communion and the World*, ed. Luke Ben Tallon. London: T & T Clark, pp. 12–13.

of the communicant as an individual within the community. There is also a 'curious philological phenomenon' here when Jesus says, 'Very truly, I tell you, we speak of what we know and testify to what we have seen; yet you do not receive our testimony. If I have told you about earthly things and you do not believe, how can you believe if I tell you about heavenly things? No one has ascended into heaven except the one who descended from heaven, the Son of Man' (John 3:11–13). In this quotation, Zizioulas points out the mixing of the first person singular with the first person plural: the 'I' and the 'we', the 'one' and the 'many'.[1]

In *Catholicism*, Henri de Lubac mentions St Peter Damian, a strong supporter of the papacy who claimed that 'the whole Church forms, in some sort, but one single person. As she is the same in all, so in each one is she whole and entire; and just as man is called a microcosm, so each one of the faithful is, so to say, the Church in miniature.'[2] Using this metaphysical principle, 'the one and many', Zizioulas attempts in his works to understand and explain the nature of the church in terms of its universality and particularity.

### Ecclesial Being

For Zizioulas, the church is 'a way of being' and 'a mode of existence'. The mystery of the church is closely tied to the being of man in the world and to the being of God himself. The church is here to serve the existential needs of humankind. As a member of the church, the human being is also 'an image of God', which means that he or she exists as God himself exists, taking on God's 'way of being'. As such, the human being is able to relate to the world, to other people, and to God in communion. This ability is not an achievement on the part of the individual person but a gift from God, an 'ecclesial fact'. The church, for its part, must strive to be an image of God by making sure that its structures and ministries conform to this way of existence. In other words, the church must possess the right faith and vision in accordance with God's being. This is not a luxury for the Orthodox Church, according to Zizioulas, but 'an existential necessity'.[3]

1. Ibid., p. 14.
2. Quoted in Henri de Lubac (1988), *Catholicism: Christ and the Common Destiny of Man*, trans. Lancelot C. Sheppard and Sr Elizabeth Englund OCD. San Francisco: Ignatius Press, p. 315.
3. Zizioulas (1993), *Being as Communion*. New York: St Vladimir's Seminary Press, p. 15.

This theory of the 'one and many' goes back to the Greeks, whose philosophy was monistic in outlook. They believed that the being of the world and the being of God are one, forming an unbreakable unity. But the Church Fathers, such as Ignatius of Antioch, Irenaeus, and Athanasius, helped to break this ontological monism of Hellenistic philosophy. The Fathers 'approached the being of God through the experience of the ecclesial community, of *ecclesial being*'. They found that God's being can only be known through personal relationships and love: 'Being means life, and life means *communion*.'[1] This breakthrough of the Fathers originated from the eucharistic experience of the church that understands God as communion. Thus Zizioulas claims that there is no true being without communion; the person exists only through communion.

Furthermore, the human person in the church becomes the 'image of God' due to the '*economy* of the Holy Trinity', which means the activities of Christ and the Holy Spirit in 'history'. This economy is the foundation of ecclesiology: 'The Church is built by the historical work of the divine economy but leads finally to the vision of God "as He is", to the vision of the Triune God in his eternal existence.'[2] This eschatological aspect of the church is part of the Orthodox tradition that emphasizes liturgical worship, especially in the celebration of the Eucharist.

Zizioulas believes that there is a need to bring the ecclesial being and the being of God closer by rediscovering the importance of the Eucharist in the primitive church. In the olden days, the Eucharist was not just one sacrament among others, merely a means of grace, as taught by the scholastics, administered by the church in the gathering of the people; it was above all an 'eschatological act' – a foretaste of the very life of the Trinity. In *Being as Communion* (1993), Zizioulas writes: '[T]he Eucharist was not the act of a pre-existing Church; it was an event *constitutive* of the being of the Church, enabling the Church to *be*. The Eucharist *constituted* the Church's being.' As such, the Eucharist serves to unite the work of Christ and the work of the Holy Spirit. In the Eucharist, the 'dialectical relationship' between God and the world is preserved. The Eucharist is not just a memorial of Christ's death and resurrection; it looks to the future, to the *eschata*, where we get a foretaste of life with God in heaven.[3]

---

1. Ibid., p. 16.
2. Ibid., p. 19.
3. Ibid., p. 21.

## Ecclesial Identity

As the Eucharist is given such a prominent place in Zizioulas' theology, it is not surprising when he claims that the Orthodox Church has its roots in the divine Eucharist. The Roman Catholic and the Protestant Churches, in his opinion, focus primarily on mission, namely preaching and proselytizing. But when an Orthodox goes to church, he or she goes there not primarily to listen to the preaching of the Gospel but to participate in the liturgy, which includes the eucharistic celebration. In other words, the Orthodox Christian goes to church to worship God.

Be that as it may, Zizioulas thinks that the emphasis on mission, preaching, and individual piety in the Western Churches is beginning to affect the Orthodox Church, especially its liturgy. He fears that Orthodox liturgy has deteriorated due to pugnacious Western influence. For Zizioulas, the Orthodox Church's main objective is not missionary enterprise; it does not seek to convert others as such because its liturgy does not attempt to explain the faith. At the centre of the Orthodox tradition is worship: the eucharistic celebration and the recitation of the Creed. Such understanding of the church goes back to its early history when there was only divine worship and the celebration of the Eucharist. It is the liturgy that defines the Orthodox tradition.[1]

## The Eucharist Makes the Church

According to Zizioulas, in the primitive church, the Eucharist was closely tied to the mystery of the church. In fact, the words *ekklesia* and Eucharist mean the same thing. A study of 1 Corinthians 11 shows that the 'Lord's Supper' or 'coming together in the same place' and 'church' signify the same reality. St Paul considered the church to be the concrete community that celebrates the Eucharist: 'The local community becomes the very "Church of God" when it gathers to celebrate the Eucharist.' This close identification of church and Eucharist was developed further by St Ignatius of Antioch, who taught that the Eucharist makes the church catholic, meaning 'the

---

1. Zizioulas (2008), *Lectures in Christian Dogmatics*, ed. Douglas Knight. London: T & T Clark, p. 122. The other aspect of Orthodox tradition is monasticism, which Zizioulas seems to downplay. Perhaps he fears that individualism found in ascetic practices might affect the communitarian aspect of the church.

full and integral body of Christ'.[1] For Ignatius, the church derives its catholicity from the celebration of the Eucharist, thus every local church is 'catholic'. When the local community gathers together with the bishop, priests, deacons, and laity to worship, the 'catholic Church' is present because the fullness of Christ is found in the Eucharist.[2]

Borrowing from Aristotelian language, the term 'catholic' originally referred to the concrete local churches. The catholicity of the church was also linked to the *parousia*, the eschatological reality, and at the same time, 'its nature [was] revealed and realistically apprehended *here and now* in the eucharist.' The Eucharist was understood as 'an *act* and a *synaxis* of the local Church, *a "catholic" act of a "catholic" Church*'.[3]

Things changed when St Augustine of Hippo (354–430), the great Western doctor, came on to the scene. Augustine emphasized the universality of the church against the particularism of the Donatists. Due to Augustine, 'catholic', for the first time, referred to the universal church. This new meaning of catholicity implies qualitative as well as geographical expansion.[4] As Augustine was a towering figure with tremendous influence, the Latin Church evolved into a single monolithic organization with the bishop of Rome as its head.

Nonetheless, up to the thirteenth century, the Eucharist continued to be the sacrament of the church that expressed its unity; the body of Christ and the body of the church were identical. Henri de Lubac spoke of the Eucharist as the sacrament 'which contains the whole mystery of our salvation' and also as the 'sacrament of unity'.[5]

After the thirteenth century, scholastic theologians began to distinguish between the terms 'body of Christ', 'body of the church', and 'body of the eucharist'.[6] In the Latin Church, sacramental theology became independent from Christology and ecclesiology. There is now a separation between the Eucharist and ecclesiology: the Eucharist is seen as just one of the many sacraments; it is no longer identified with the church. As a result, in Western practice, we now have a private celebration of the Eucharist, something that was unheard of in the ancient church. Now the priest alone can

1. Zizioulas, *The Eucharist Communion and the World*, p. 100.
2. Ibid., p. 101.
3. Zizioulas, *Being as Communion*, p. 145.
4. Zizioulas, *The Eucharistic Communion and the World*, p. 101.
5. de Lubac, *Catholicism*, p. 89.
6. Zizioulas, *op. cit.*, p. 102.

celebrate a valid Eucharist without the bishops, deacons, and the people in the Roman Catholic Church. De Lubac spoke against such individualism creeping into the church:

> True Eucharistic piety, therefore, is no devout individualism. It is 'unmindful of nothing that concerns the good of the Church.' With one sweeping, all-embracing gesture, in one fervent intention it gathers together the whole world. It recalls the commentary that, according to St. John, Jesus himself gave . . . the prayer of unity and the approach of the 'supreme token of love.' It is on these things that true Eucharistic piety bases thoughts and resolutions; it cannot conceive of the action of the breaking of bread without fraternal communion. . . . [I]t will be noticed that in the ancient liturgies, and still nowadays in the East, the prayers for union form the culminating point of the Epiclesis.[1]

The celebration of the Eucharist occupies a central position in the Orthodox Church. However, according to Zizioulas, '[I]n spite of the continuous centrality of the Eucharist in Orthodox Church *life*, an ecclesiology developed in the academic level which regarded the Eucharist as *one* sacrament among many (usually seven), and which actually distinguishes very clearly between Church and Eucharist in its methodology.'[2] Perhaps this was due to the way universities and seminaries organized their curriculum.

What Zizioulas is emphasizing here is that there is a gap or dichotomy between academic ecclesiology and the liturgical practice in the Orthodox Church. Fortunately, in our own time, Zizioulas argues, the situation has changed for the better due to the revival of biblical, patristic, and liturgical studies by Western scholars since the beginning of the twentieth century. One of the good things to come out of this revival is the restoration of the ancient link between the Eucharist and the church that was forgotten in the Middle Ages. Zizioulas acknowledges that it is through the influence of these Western theologians and liturgists that Orthodox thinkers themselves began to appreciate 'the patristic concept of the Eucharist as *leitourgia*, i.e. *a work of the people* and as gathering *epi to auto* to realize the ecclesial event *par excellence*'.[3]

---

1. de Lubac, *op. cit.*, pp. 109–10.
2. Zizioulas, *op. cit.*, p. 103.
3. Ibid. Regarding the work of Western scholars in liturgical revival, Zizioulas was referring to the writings of G. Dix (1945), *The Shape of*

One of those who sought to revive this close connection between the Eucharist and the church was Nicholas Afanasiev. The main principle of Afanasiev's eucharistic ecclesiology was 'wherever there is the Eucharist there is the Church'. Zizioulas, however, is critical of such one-sided theory, and thus has accused Afanasiev of promoting '*eucharistic* presupposition of ecclesiology and not so much of the ecclesiological presuppositions of the Eucharist'.[1]

The first problem in Afanasiev's eucharistic ecclesiology, according to Zizioulas, is that the local church in the present time does not comprise only one parish, as in the primitive church. In other words, in the past, all the members of the local church assembled in one place in the presence of all the presbyters and with the bishop at its head, thus overcoming social and cultural divisions and fulfilling all the conditions of catholicity. Nowadays, however, the eucharistic community does not meet all of these conditions. In Zizioulas' opinion, since there is more than one parish in the local church these days, we cannot have all the faithful gathered together in one place when the Eucharist is celebrated. Therefore, the parish is not a 'complete' and 'catholic' church.[2]

The idea that the parish by itself is not 'catholic' contradicts Orthodox teaching. It seems that Zizioulas' understanding of catholicity is limited to geographical and spatial dimensions in the Augustinian sense. According to Orthodox understanding, the catholicity of the church is not an empirical or a geographical reality but refers to its ontological nature. The church is 'catholic' or *sobornost* because of its wholeness and integrity.[3] Catholicity in the Orthodox tradition has nothing to do with physical expansion. At the same time, Zizioulas admits that where the Eucharist is celebrated, there is the church.

The other problem has to do with the relationship between the local and the universal churches. Zizioulas thinks that Afanasiev's eucharistic ecclesiology suggests that each local church is independent

*the Liturgy*; O. Casel (1999), *The Mystery of Christian Worship*; W. Elert (2003), *Eucharist and Church Fellowship in the First Four Centuries*.

1. Zizioulas, *op. cit.*, p. 104.
2. Zizioulas, *Being as Communion*, p. 24. For further studies on this issue see Eamon McManus (2000), 'Aspects of primacy according to two Orthodox theologians'. *One In Christ* 36, no. 3 (January), 234–50.
3. Fr Milan Savich (1986), 'Catholicity of the Church: "Sobornost"', http://www.orthodoxresearchinstitute.org/articles/dogmatics/savich_catholicity.htm.

of each other. Further, in giving priority to the local churches over the universal church, Afanasiev runs the risk of localism. Zizioulas is looking for a solution that will maintain the right balance between localization and universalization of the Church. It is a solution that transcends both localism and universalism.[1]

In *The Eucharistic Communion and the World* (2011), Zizioulas puts the issue in this way: '[D]oes the Eucharist make the Church or is the reverse true, namely that the Church constitutes the Eucharist[?]'[2] Scholastic theologians say it is the church that makes the Eucharist; Afanasiev and other Orthodox theologians say it is the Eucharist that makes the church. Zizioulas argues that the question is related to the relation between Christology and pneumatology. Thus when we say that the church precedes the Eucharist, we imply that Christology precedes pneumatology. This means that it is the institutional church that makes the celebration of the Eucharist possible. Zizioulas writes: 'This position forms part of an ecclesiology which views the Church as the Body of Christ which is *first* instituted in itself as an historical entity and *then* produces the "means of grace" called sacraments, among them primarily the Eucharist.'[3] The order suggested by traditional dogmatic manual in the Latin Church is as follows: first comes Christ; second, the Holy Spirit; then the church; and, last, the sacraments, including the Eucharist. This line of thinking, of course, is unacceptable to the Orthodox Church. Zizioulas is merely stating the traditional teaching of the Roman Catholic Church.

As far as Zizioulas is concerned, there is no question of priority between the church and the Eucharist. His position is that 'the Church constitutes the Eucharist while being constituted by it.'[4] In other words, church and Eucharist coincide; they are identical, as it were. As stated earlier, Afanasiev taught that 'wherever there is the Eucharist there is the Church.' He gave priority to the Eucharist over the church and supported '*eucharistic* presupposition of ecclesiology'.[5] Zizioulas, however, avoids the pitfall of giving priority either to the church or to the Eucharist. He believes that they are inter-dependent.

1. Zizioulas, *op. cit.*, p. 25.
2. Zizioulas, *The Eucharistic Communion and the World*, p. 104.
3. Ibid., p. 105.
4. Ibid.
5. Ibid., p. 104.

Henri de Lubac argued, 'the Eucharist makes the Church. It makes of it an inner reality. By its hidden power, the members of the body come to unite themselves by becoming more fully members of Christ, and their unity with one another is part and parcel of their unity with the one single Head.'[1]

At the same time, de Lubac also admitted that the Eucharist cannot explain everything in the church, for example its structure, which is needed for the church to spread itself physically. Thus for practical purposes, especially for missionary endeavours, to facilitate the administration of the sacraments, it is the church that makes the Eucharist. Hence, in *The Splendour of the Church*, de Lubac writes, 'The Church makes the Eucharist. It was principally to that end that her priesthood was instituted. "Do this in memory of me."'[2] Further, he argues that 'the ministry of the twelve' was instituted for the purpose of celebrating the Eucharist. In this sense, it is the church that makes the Eucharist.

Monsignor Paul McPartlan, Professor of Systematic Theology and Ecumenism at the Catholic University of America, sums up the two principles in this way: 'We see that, for de Lubac, the transition between the principles that the Church makes the Eucharist and the Eucharist makes the Church takes place via the presence of Christ in the eucharistic elements.'[3] As we can see, de Lubac's thought has it both ways – the Eucharist makes the church and the church makes the Eucharist. This is quite similar to Zizioulas' understanding that 'the Church constitutes the Eucharist while being constituted by it.' The influence of de Lubac is clearly evident in Zizioulas' understanding of the Eucharist in the church. As mentioned earlier, this understanding is connected to his view on the relation between Christ and the Spirit.

---

1. Henri de Lubac, *Corpus Mysticum: The Eucharist and the Church in the Middle Ages* (2006), trans. Gemma Simmonds, CJ with Richard Price and Christopher Stephens, ed. Laurence Paul Hemming and Susan Frank Parsons. London: SCM, p. 88. Von Balthasar says: 'The Church's sacrifice is, therefore, at once distinct from that of Christ and identical with his, since it consists in a (feminine) consenting to the sacrifice of Christ (and to all the consequences that flow from the Church).' Hans Urs von Balthasar (1990), *Mysterium Paschale*, trans. and with an introduction by Aidan Nichols OP. Edinburgh: T & T Clark, p. 99.
2. Quoted in Paul McPartlan (1993), *The Eucharist Makes the Church: Henri de Lubac and Zizioulas in Dialogue*. Edinburgh: T & T Clark, p. 100.
3. Ibid., p. 104.

## Christology and Pneumatology

Following his understanding of the Eucharist in the church, Zizioulas claims that Christ and the Spirit appear at the same time – one cannot do without the other and neither has priority over the other. First of all, the biblical accounts show that Christ was constituted by the Holy Spirit. Therefore, Zizioulas argues, the person of Christ is always related to the Holy Spirit; they form a community: '[T]he Church is part of the definition of Christ. The body of Christ is not first the body of an individual Christ and *then* a community of "many", but simultaneously both together.' Further, Zizioulas points out, 'the Eucharist is the only occasion in history when these two coincide.'[1]

Just as we cannot separate the Eucharist from the church, we also cannot separate Christ from the Holy Spirit. Zizioulas therefore insists that Christology and pneumatology exist simultaneously and not as separate phases of God's activity in the world. This simultaneity is seen during 'creation in which Christ and the Spirit acted as "two hands of God"'.[2] Church Fathers such as Irenaeus, Athanasius, Cyril of Alexandria, and Basil the Great taught that the Son and the Holy Spirit belong together, but this synthesis has not been well assimilated, especially in relation to ecclesiology. In *The One and the Many* (1993), following the view of the Fathers of both East and West, Zizioulas argues: '[T]hat the operation God *ad extra* should be regarded as one, leaves no room for a division of the Economy between Christology and Pneumatology. No matter how specific the role of the Spirit is . . . it is extremely dangerous for the unity of the Economy to speak of a special "Economy of the Spirit".'[3]

To avoid this danger, Zizioulas attempts a synthesis of Christology and pneumatology that will assist our understanding of the nature of the church. Beginning with the New Testament, there are two views concerning the priority of Christ in relation to the Holy Spirit: first, that the Spirit is given by Christ; and second, that there is no Christ until the Spirit acts as a forerunner announcing his coming.[4] Both these contrasting views could co-exist like other

1. Zizioulas, *op. cit.*, pp. 105–6.
2. Zizioulas (1993), *The One and the Many: Studies on God, Man, the Church and the World Today*. New York: St Vladimir's Seminary Press, p. 76.
3. Ibid., p. 77.
4. Zizioulas, *Being as Communion*, p. 127.

diverse accounts in the Gospels. This diversity allows the churches to take up different positions depending on how they interpret the scripture and tradition of the Fathers.

The Western Church gives priority to Christology over pneumatology while the Eastern Church gives priority to pneumatology over Christology. In *Being as Communion*, Zizioulas posits:

> For various reasons which have to do with the idiosyncrasy of the West . . . a certain priority will always be given by it to Christology over Pneumatology. . . . Equally, for the East Pneumatology will always occupy an important place given the fact that a liturgical meta-historical approach to Christian existence seems to mark the Eastern ethos.[1]

Attempting to synthesize these two different approaches to Christology and pneumatology, Zizioulas says that we must bear in mind that the activity of God *ad extra* is indivisible: where the Son is there is also the Father and the Holy Spirit and where the Spirit is there is also the Father and the Son. Their contributions, however, are distinct.[2] For example, only the Son is 'incarnate'; the Father and the Spirit enter into history, but the 'Son *becomes* history' and therefore there is only the '*Christ event*'. Even Pentecost, a pneumatological event, is attached to the Christ event so as 'to qualify as part of the *history* of salvation'. The 'Son *becomes* history' and it is the Holy Spirit who liberates the Son from this bondage of history by raising him from the dead. The Spirit is 'beyond' history and is associated with the *eschaton*, the last days. By raising Jesus from the dead, the Spirit makes Christ an 'eschatological being, the "last Adam"'.[3] The involvement of the Holy Spirit in the economy of salvation enables Christ to be a 'corporate personality', which means the one Christ becomes many through the Holy Spirit. This is possible because the Spirit is associated with the notion of communion: 'Pneumatology contributes to Christology this dimension of communion.'[4]

Following the tradition of the Orthodox Church, Zizioulas tends to emphasize pneumatology rather than Christology in the economy of salvation. The Spirit is described in the scriptures in terms of 'power', 'sanctification', 'Spirit of Truth', 'Spirit of Freedom', 'life-

---

1. Ibid., p. 129.
2. Ibid.
3. Ibid., p. 130.
4. Ibid., p. 131.

giver', and 'communion'. Zizioulas sees the Spirit as 'life-giver' and 'communion' as relating directly to the church. Both qualities are in fact synonymous: 'The life of God that the Spirit gives is a life of communion of persons, and it is as such that He creates power and dynamic existence as well as sanctification, miracles, and prophecies, and leads to Truth; He provides the preposition *in*, in which all of this takes place.' Zizioulas also maintains that 'in being conceivable only in the Spirit, Christ appears to be a relational being to an absolute degree. . . . He is not an individual but a Person in the true sense of the word.'[1] In other words, as mentioned earlier, he is a 'corporate personality', the Son of Man, Servant of God, who alone gives his life for the many. Thus the church is a mystery of the unity of the 'one' and the 'many'.

Regarding the relation between Christology, pneumatology, and ecclesiology, de Lubac explained this more simply when he wrote:

> The Spirit lives in the Church and animates her as her soul is the Spirit of the Son, the Spirit of Jesus, the Spirit of Jesus Christ, the Spirit of Christ. If Jesus himself depends on the Spirit in whom he exults, the Spirit is for us henceforth he whom Jesus sends and confers. The Spirit bears witness to Jesus and enables us to say 'Jesus is Lord.'[2]

It appears that de Lubac's commentary on the relation between the Spirit and Jesus is in accord with Zizioulas' understanding of communion. On the same topic, Yves Congar, in his detailed study of the Holy Spirit, comments:

> Because of the originality of his [Zizioulas'] approach, I have tried to present it as it stands. I reached my own position, however, before reading his article, which in fact owes a great deal to studies made before my own. I hope to have conveyed an idea of the enrichment, possibly the corrections, that an Orthodox insight can bring to our Western thought, however valuable and convincing this may be.[3]

---

1. Zizioulas, *The One and the Many*, p. 78.
2. Henri de Lubac (1986), *Christian Faith: The Structure of the Apostles' Creed*, trans. Illtyd Trethowan and John Saward. London: Geoffrey Chapman, p. 131.
3. Zizioulas' article refers to a French essay on the theology of apostolicity, 'La continuité avec les origines apostoliques dans la conscience théologique des Eglises orthodoxes'. Yves M.J. Congar, *I Believe in the Holy Spirit*, Vol. II, trans. David Smith. New York: Seabury Press, p. 51.

Zizioulas' emphasis on communion makes him critical of the individualism found in the monastic practice of self-purification. He fears that the individual piety of the monks and ascetics might affect the central role of the liturgy, especially the celebration of the divine Eucharist. How does this come about?

## Orthodox Monasticism

Influenced by Origen, Clement, and other Alexandrian theologians of the time, Orthodox monasticism took on platonic ideas. For Plato, everything that exists has an ideal form. What we see, however, is the material embodiment of this 'original idea', which is incomplete and corruptible. The things we see are just a reflection of this 'unchanging archetype'. Using this platonic idea, the Alexandrian theologians looked upon the heavenly church of Jerusalem as timeless and perfect: 'The Church is true to its identity when its members are brought together by participation in this original universal Logos.' However, worldly distractions can prevent the soul from being united with the Logos. The practice of self-purification in monastic life is one way in which the soul can be freed from distractions and passions that prevent it from being united with God. The monastery is seen as 'a kind of rehabilitation centre'.[1]

Origen and Clement of Alexandria taught that the liturgy is of secondary importance because 'the original perfection of the Church is demonstrated by the "logos" of the world as a whole. The *logoi* of all separate beings will unite again within the one Logos of God that existed before the creation of the world. In this teaching the eucharistic gathering and unity of the Church makes no constitutive contribution to bringing all things together in the one eternal Logos.'[2] This means that the salvation of the world involves the purification of the soul so that we can be reunited with the Logos who existed before time. This ecclesiology is essentially an individualistic one as it downplays the church as an 'ordered community imaging the future kingdom'.[3]

Zizioulas questions the validity of self-purification as the main objective of the church. He emphasizes the fact that 'in the Church we are being brought together as the recapitulation of the world, body and spirit, in the *incarnate*, materially embodied Logos.' This

1. Zizioulas, *Lectures in Christian Dogmatics*, p. 122.
2. Ibid., p. 129.
3. Ibid., p. 130.

means that the material body is not to be despised. Origen believed in the immortality of the soul and his ideas continue to influence Christian thinking. Zizioulas, however, emphasizes the Eucharist where we encounter Christ, the Word made flesh: 'Christ has taken all material nature into his human nature, and this makes the event of the Eucharist, and is the source of the Church and of all who are made holy within it.'[1]

Following the example of St Maximus the Confessor (580–662), who taught that the Eucharist best expresses the identity of the church, Zizioulas argues that 'the Church is the place in which this purification takes place, but rather than producing incorporated angels, it brings about salvation of this material world by giving it eternal communion with God.' Purification is a means of getting rid of all negative elements that hinder our relationship with God, but it is not the main purpose of the church. It must be understood as part of the 'eucharistic transformation of the world'.[2] The material world is not to be rejected or devalued. Entering the monastic life is often seen as a rejection of the material world – fleeing from the world to live a life of perfection. Such perception of monastic life is rejected by Zizioulas, who understands the significance of the Incarnation.

It is not surprising that tension exists in the conflict between self-purification spirituality, which is associated with the monastic life, and eucharistic theology, which is associated with the bishop who presides over the Eucharist. Eventually the monasteries were brought under the control of the bishop in the ninth century. Critical of 'spiritual elitism and individualism' associated with monastic practice, with minimum reference to the church at large, Zizioulas emphasizes the importance of participating in the liturgy of the church. For him, liturgy simply means 'the realisation of our relationship to God, the whole communion of his saints and the entire world'.[3] This has nothing to do with having the right thought, action, or emotion

---

1. Ibid., p. 123. Gregory Palamas reaffirmed 'the Biblical doctrine of man and of the incarnation. Man is a single, united whole: not only man's mind but the *whole* man was created in the image of God. Man's body is not an enemy, but partner and collaborator with his soul. Christ, by taking a human body at the Incarnation, has "made the *flesh* an inexhaustible source of sanctification."' Timothy Ware (1972), *The Orthodox Church*. Harmondsworth: Penguin, p. 77.
2. Zizioulas, *op. cit.*, p. 124.
3. Ibid., p. 125.

when approaching the divine. Liturgy is about having a relationship with God in the community of other worshippers. Zizioulas' critical view of monasticism stems from his strong belief in the idea of the church as people of God without any distinction or sense of spiritual superiority.

For Zizioulas, the church is the people of God, which includes everyone in the world united in Christ in the Holy Spirit. This is true not only for the church but also for the world in the future. He stresses the eschatological dimension of the church: 'The Church lives in history, but its true identity is to be found in the future.'[1] This idea is expressed in the liturgy, which anticipates the coming of the Kingdom of God. Thus the church transcends all secular institutions.

Orthodoxy places less emphasis on social and charitable works than the Roman Catholic and Protestant Churches. Zizioulas explains: 'Love cannot be turned into an institution.' This does not mean that the Orthodox Church does not care about the welfare of the people. It means that 'the more eschatological identity you carry with you, the more you will love and come to the aid of whoever needs your help, whatever it costs you.'[2]

Believing that if the eschatological identity is in place, the church will automatically reach out to those in need, Zizioulas insists that the church does not have to be absorbed in social activities – this is not its vocation. Organized social work rightly belongs to the state. Zizioulas is against social and political activism and argues that mission work does not constitute the identity of the Orthodox Church. Its focus must be in the future: 'The Church is primarily a foretaste of the eschatological assembly of the Lord, made present in the world. The resurrection of Christ and Pentecost makes the Church and its worship the presence of the future.'[3] The implication of this theological outlook means that Orthodox Christians attend church services to worship God in the liturgy. Orthodox Christians go to church primarily to get a glimpse of that intangible future that cannot be found in secular institutions, but when the liturgy is performed in the divine eucharistic celebration, the future makes itself felt.

Zizioulas is not only critical of monasticism, which involves a retreat from the world; he is also critical of social activism, which involves being completely absorbed by the world. He wants a

1. Ibid., p. 127.
2. Ibid.
3. Ibid.

spirituality that is down to earth and yet looks forward to the future; it is a spirituality that is neither contemplative nor active, but eschatological in outlook, with its foundation in the liturgy of the church. Throughout church history, monastic ecclesiology and eucharistic ecclesiology have existed side by side; sometimes they have moved towards integration and at other times, they have come into conflict with one another. Obviously, Zizioulas favours a kind of eucharistic ecclesiology that emphasizes the church as a communion. The kind of ecclesiology he adopts has to do with the relationship between the universal and particular churches.

### Universal and Local Churches

Western theology gives priority to *being*, making the particular less important than the universal. This means that the universal church has priority over the particular churches. Thus the one church stands over the rest of the local churches, and the pope over the rest of the bishops. This was expressed by the First Vatican Council's teaching on the infallibility of the pope. Critical of this position, Zizioulas argues that this is not merely 'a judicial matter, but a consequence of placing essence before existence, the one before the many'.[1] He claims that Vatican II did not overrule Vatican I but in fact asserted that the new ecclesiology was in continuity with that of the previous council. Zizioulas, however, views the decisions of these two councils as contradictory, which the Roman Catholic Church needs to clarify. In his ecclesiology, Zizioulas avoids giving priority to either the universal or the particular church.

Zizioulas teaches that local churches are related to one another, and that what binds them together is the seven Ecumenical Councils, which express the teaching of the entire church. But he acknowledges that the balance between the Councils and churches is not easy to maintain. 'Conciliarism' is the term used in the West to express the supreme authority of the council. In the Orthodox Church, only the first seven general councils are accepted as genuinely ecumenical and thus binding on them. As a consequence, in the East no ordinary church council is allowed to interfere with

---

1. Ibid., p. 141. Although Vatican II has taught that each local church is the whole church in each place, it has not officially repudiated the teaching of Vatican I, and thus there seems to be a dilemma in Roman Catholic ecclesiology. This is revealed by two different viewpoints regarding the primacy of the universal church.

the affairs of the local churches. This principle was articulated in the third century by St Cyprian: '[E]very bishop is to lead his own diocese, ordain whomever he wishes, and be responsible directly to God.'[1]

In Orthodox ecclesiology, there are patriarchates and auto-cephalous churches, which are seen as expressing the conciliarity of the church. Tradition accords the Bishop of Constantinople as first in honour among all the Eastern Orthodox bishops. It is not him personally but the Patriarchate of Constantinople that holds honour or primacy, and this is only the honour of being seated as the first among equals. It carries no administrative privileges or jurisdictional powers. The church is considered 'healthy' if there is consultation between him and the other churches, and vice versa. In other words, the Patriarch of Constantinople does not hold absolute power over the other churches. In his *Lectures in Christian Dogmatics*, Zizioulas points out that this is very different from Roman Catholicism, in which the pope has the authority to intervene in any local church without consulting the local authority: the pope makes the final decisions alone. But there is no such 'papal element' in the ecclesiology of the Orthodox Church.[2]

While Henri de Lubac acknowledged that the Orthodox belief in eucharistic communion would provide a good platform for dialogue between Orthodox and Roman Catholics, he felt it would be a mistake to 'deduce "a real priority of the local church over the universal"'.[3] In agreement with Yves Congar, de Lubac believed that there is 'mutual interiority' between the local and the universal churches. This mutual interiority means that a bishop is consecrated for the service of the local church as well as the universal church. It follows that the local church cannot claim priority over the universal church. Although de Lubac appreciated the Orthodox position, he was not convinced by it. Neither was he convinced of the priority of the universal church over the local churches. It is an issue that de Lubac admitted he could not resolve.[4] This topic was the subject of a widely publicized debate between Joseph Ratzinger and Walter Kasper. As we shall see, Walter Kasper's position is more in accord with Zizioulas' approach regarding the priority of the local churches over the universal church.

---

1. Ibid., p. 142.
2. Ibid., p. 145.
3. McPartlan, *The Eucharist Makes the Church*, p. 106.
4. Ibid., p. 110.

## The Ratzinger-Kasper Debate

The strong assertion by Joseph Ratzinger (Pope Emeritus Benedict XVI) of the priority of the universal church led to a prolonged debate between him and Cardinal Walter Kasper in 2001, before Ratzinger was elected pontiff. In a series of exchanges, Kasper accused Ratzinger of reversing the traditional order of priority, because 'the local church is neither a province nor a department of the universal church; it is the church at a given place.'[1] Kasper said he had reached this position regarding the relationship between the universal church and particular local churches through his pastoral experience. He analyzed the question in terms of praxis, not doctrine. Kasper accused Ratzinger of approaching the problem from a purely abstract and theoretical point of view, without taking actual pastoral situations into consideration.

Kasper is against Ratzinger's assertion that 'in its essential mystery, the universal church is a reality ontologically and temporally prior to every individual church,'[2] and contends that the Congregation for the Doctrine of the Faith identifies the one, holy, catholic, and apostolic church with the universal church in a way that excludes the particular churches. Another serious problem with Ratzinger's assertion of the ontological and temporal priority of the universal church is the unspoken assumption that 'the Roman church is *de facto* identified with the pope and the curia'.[3]

Unlike Ratzinger, Kasper believes that the problem of the relationship between the universal church and the local churches cannot be approached by theoretical deduction because the church is a concrete reality. Like Ratzinger, he starts off with scripture, but arrives at a different conclusion. Kasper also asserts that in the Gospel of Luke, the word *ecclesia* refers to a domestic and local community. The early church was developed from local communities, presided over by a bishop: '[T]he one church was present in each and all, they were all in communion.' Kasper acknowledges that the See of Rome, 'presiding in charity', was the guiding and leading authority

---

1. Walter Kasper (2001), 'On the Church'. *America*, 23 April, 9. See also Kilian McDonnell (2002), 'The Ratzinger/Kasper debate: the universal church and local churches'. *Theological Studies*, 63, 2 (June), 227–50; and Maximilian Heinrich Heim (2007), *Joseph Ratzinger: Life in the Church and Living Theology*. San Francisco: Ignatius Press, pp. 357–82.
2. Kasper, *op. cit.*, 10.
3. McDonnell, *op. cit.*, 231.

in determining orthodoxy. For the Eastern Church, this authority of Rome did not include jurisdictional power.[1] Thus, in his article 'On the Church', Kasper concludes that the ecclesiology of the first millennium stressed the primacy of neither the universal church nor the local churches.

Besides Walter Kasper, the Dominican Jean-Marie Roger Tillard (1927-2000), a well-known ecclesiologist in the French-speaking world, offered a more open and accommodative ecclesiological model for ecumenism. He rejected the question of priority as a misleading notion, arguing that the universal church is a communion and not a confederation of local churches, 'a communion of communions'. Tillard agreed with the idea that each local church exists only in communion with the universal church and the universal church does not exist apart from the communion of local churches. He argued that the local and the universal churches are 'simultaneous',[2] implying that insistence on the priority of the universal church shows a misunderstanding of unity and diversity.

## The Episcopal Office

In his *Lectures in Christian Dogmatics*, Zizioulas reminds us that in the early church, bishops were identified with Christ. But by the third century, in the West, under the influence of Cyprian, the notion of bishops as representatives of Christ changed to one of them as representatives of the apostles. Thus we now regard bishops as successors to the apostles and their main duty is to teach. Zizioulas laments that this is a divergence from the original understanding of the church; now we have the priests celebrating the Eucharist while the bishop is regarded as an administrator of the church.[3]

Henri de Lubac, however, had no problem accepting the bishops as successors of the apostles – 'the bishop as the *High Priest* and, correspondingly, as the primary celebrant of the Eucharist'.[4] In fact, de Lubac anticipated Vatican II's teaching on episcopal collegiality when he said, '"the whole episcopal body" is the "successor of the

---

1. Kasper, *op. cit.*, 11.
2. Christopher Ruddy (2006), *The Local Church: Tillard and the Future of Catholic Ecclesiology*. New York: Crossroad, p. 100.
3. Zizioulas (2008), *Lectures in Christian Dogmatics*, ed. Douglas Knight. London: T&T Clark, p. 147.
4. McPartlan, *The Eucharist Makes the Church*, p. 100.

apostolic college".' Based on the teaching of Cyprian, de Lubac argued that 'the Eucharist is the reason for episcopal collegiality.'[1] McPartlan holds that:

> De Lubac located the hierarchy's power of jurisdiction and teaching *within* its priestly power of sanctifying. The latter is 'both the origin and final flowering of the other two', in the 'one single mission' [which] the Church has from Christ and he from the Father. Its 'supreme exercise' occurs in the hierarchy's celebration of the Eucharist, that is, de Lubac says characteristically, when the hierarchy is 'consecrating Christ's body and thus perpetuating the work of the Redemption'.[2]

De Lubac also affirmed that the bishop as teacher brings members of the church around the eucharistic table and, through his work, seeks to maintain the unifying power of the Eucharist over which he presides.[3]

## Synodality

To conclude, Zizioulas believes that the problem regarding the priority of churches lies in the extent to which we are prepared to give the local church a 'primary and constitutive role' in ecclesiology. If the local church has a primary constitutive role, diversity will be established. Zizioulas insists that diversity is necessary for the church because without it, the church ceases to exist. The church must be a local reality. Further, if we stress the importance of the Holy Spirit in ecclesiology, the one church will be understood as many 'Churches incarnating'.[4] He assures us that diversity will not destroy unity, and vice versa.

To safeguard both unity and diversity, Zizioulas recommends a historical solution – synodality – an institution that ensures the right balance between the 'one' and the 'many'. Synods serve as 'instruments of communion' for churches to safeguard unity and harmony. To do this, synods must not interfere with the internal affairs of the local church. Further, all matters relating to other local churches should be brought to the synod of the bishops concerned. In all synods, the head or primus must decide with the rest of the

1. Ibid., p. 101.
2. Ibid., p. 103
3. Ibid., p. 103.
4. Zizioulas, *The One and the Many*, p. 339.

bishops who also cannot act without consulting him. All these rules and regulations ensure that the local church remains in communion with the other local churches without any losing their independence. For Zizioulas, the universal church is not above the local churches but 'a communion of full and "catholic" Churches'.[1] For him, unity does not destroy diversity. This means that we should not have an authority that requires the 'many' to be 'one'. After all, unity is not to be confused with uniformity.

The idea of synodality is what Pope Francis has in mind in relation to his interest in fostering greater unity between the Roman Catholic and Orthodox Churches. Enzo Bianchi, a newly appointed adviser to the Pontifical Council of Promoting Christian Unity, said, 'the Pope could allow a council of bishops including Orthodox bishops to assist in governing the Church.' This move would include promoting the development of synodality by making the papacy less authoritarian and the church more decentralized. Bianchi said, 'I believe the Pope has one particular concern, that unity should not be achieved in the spirituality of unity but rather in a command by Christ that we must carry out.' Reform of the papacy would involve striking a new balance between collegiality and primacy.[2] According to Bianchi, it is possible to have an episcopal body that helps the pope in governing the church without emphasizing papal primacy. Thus during the pontificate of Francis, the potential for unity between the Orthodox and Roman Catholic Churches is very promising.

1. Ibid., pp. 340–1.
2. Hannah Roberts (2014), 'Francis "plotting a path to unity with the Orthodox Churches"'. *The Tablet* 268, no. 9060 (2 August), 30.

# Chapter 4
## Georges Florovsky

In the last chapter, we noted that John Zizioulas, influenced by his teacher Georges Florovsky, has attempted a neo-patristic synthesis in an effort to reinstate the importance of the divine Eucharist in the Orthodox Church. Georges Vasilievich Florovsky was born in Odessa in 1893. Because of the civil war, he left Russia, together with his family, in 1920 and went to Sofia, Bulgaria. Later he moved to Czechoslovakia and became a lecturer on the philosophy of law at the Russian Academic Collegium in Prague. In 1922, he married Xenia Simonova, the daughter of a Russian teacher in Finland. In 1925, he was appointed Professor of Patristics at St Sergius Orthodox Theological Institute in Paris. Florovsky's ecumenical work began in 1926 when he joined Protestants, Roman Catholics, and fellow Orthodox in an ecumenical dialogue started by Nicolas Berdyaev. After his ordination to the priesthood in 1932, he pursued research on many aspects of theology and church history, and wrote about many topics. In his massive work *Ways of Russian Theology*, he criticizes the Western influence of scholasticism, pietism, and idealism in Russian theology. While the work was received with great enthusiasm among Russian intellectuals, it was not immune to criticism. In 1949, he emigrated to the United States to take the post of Dean of St Vladimir's Seminary in New York. He also taught at Harvard Divinity School from 1956 to 1964 and later at Princeton from 1964 to 1972. Florovsky passed away in 1979.

Ecclesiology was the point of departure for Florovsky's theological vision, and hence his works have great significance for ecumenical studies. In his writings, he sought to achieve a genuine reintegration of the divided Christian churches. Whether or not one agrees with his approach to ecumenism, one has to appreciate the fact that he sincerely wanted to heal the wounds of a divided Christianity. Florovsky was convinced that to be more Greek is to be truly catholic and Orthodox. His writings reveal a striking similarity with those of Joseph Ratzinger. He was close to the Protestants and helped in the formation of the World Council of Churches. An intimate knowledge of the Church Fathers and the philosophical and theological tradition of the West provided him with a solid platform from which to address the other Christian communities.

This chapter examines Florovsky's thoughts on Hellenism, ecumenism, catholicity, tradition, and monasticism. It also attempts a critical review of Florovsky's call to return to the patristic source as the only way to revive Orthodox theology and to forge Christian unity. He believed that to be a true Christian, one must be Hellenic and, thus, he called for a re-Hellenization of Christianity.

## *Christian Hellenism*

As Shakespeare says, 'The course of true love never did run smooth,' and the marriage between Hellenism and Christianity was not a smooth affair. In 'Christianity and civilization', Florovsky asserts that initially Hellenism and Christianity were opposed to one another and that the tension and conflict between the two must not be underestimated. Since the church did not attempt to eradicate Hellenism, Christianity was very much influenced by it, resulting in the formation of a distinct Christian culture. At the same time, Christianity had also contributed much to the development of Hellenistic civilization: 'The ancient world was reborn and transfigured in a desperate struggle. . . . The process was slow and dramatic, and finally resolved in the birth of a new civilization, which we may describe as Byzantine.'[1]

For a long time, the one Christian civilization was the same for both the East and West. This civilization originated in the East and subsequently, a distinct Western civilization came into existence. Thus, until the eighth century, Rome was still Byzantine in its outlook. This Byzantine era started with Theodosius and reached its peak under Justinian when a complete systematic Christian culture, a synthesis of all creative traditions, was established. Florovksy called it a 'New Hellenism' because the old heathen world was baptized. In other words, it was a conversion of the Hellenistic mind and heart, and not just a fusion of pagan heritage and Christian belief. As he put it, 'Hellenism was mightily dissected with the sword of Christian Revelation, and was

---

1. Georges Florovsky (1952), 'Christianity and civilization'. *St Vladimir's Seminary Quarterly* 1, no. 1 (September), 14.

utterly polarized thereby.'[1] Greek culture and tradition were preserved but reinterpreted through the lens of Christianity, which became the essence of Byzantine culture. Christian Hellenism is defined as follows:

> Hellenism in the Church has been, so to speak, immortalized, having been incorporated into the very fabric of the reality of the Church as an eternal category of Christian existence. This does not mean, of course, ethnic Hellenism or the contemporary Hellas or Levant, nor the recent and wholly unjustified Greek 'phyletism.' What is meant is 'Christian antiquity,' the Hellenism of dogmatics, of the liturgy and the icon. The Hellenistic style of 'mysteriological piety' has been so eternally established in the liturgy of the Eastern rite that, in a certain sense, it is impossible to enter into the rhythm of the liturgical sacraments without some degree of mystical re-Hellenization.[2]

Convinced that Christian tradition can only be understood and creatively developed within the category of Hellenism, Florovsky said, 'let us be more Greek to be truly catholic, to be truly Orthodox.' He called for a spiritual renewal in Orthodox faith through a process of re-Hellenization:

> And still, all these traditional schemes and formularies are through and through hellenistic or Greek. This hellenism is really so-to-say canonised. It is a new, Christian Hellenism. It is a common atmosphere of the Church, created by a series of generations. Our Christian worship in its essential is hellenistic. . . . The same one has to say of our icons. The same is true of our doctrinal formularies too. In a sense the Church itself is hellenistic, is a hellenistic formation, – or in other words, Hellenism is a standing category of the Christian existence. . . . And thus any theologian must pass an experience of a spiritual hellenisation (or re-hellenisation).[3]

1. Ibid.
2. Ross Joseph Sauvé (2010), 'Florovsky's tradition'. *Greek Orthodox Theological Review* 55, no. 1–4 (March), 232–3.
3. Georges Florovsky's note on the offprint of his lecture, 'Patristics and Modern Theology: advance proof copy from the acts of the I Congress of Orthodox Theology', Athens, 1936 (Pyrsos, Athens, 1938), 6–7, quoted in Ivana Noble and Tim Noble (2012), 'A Latin appropriation of Christian hellenism: Florovsky's marginal note to Patristics and modern theology and its possible addressee,' *St Vladimir's Theological Quarterly* 56, no. 3 (January), 270–1.

As we can see, Florovsky's understanding of Hellenism in this context is not nationalistic, but sacred and Christian, which he claimed to be normative for the church. This means that the catholicity of the church and its theology can only be formulated in Greek terms – catholicity and Hellenism in theology are inextricably connected. Hellenism remained in Florovsky's thinking an eternal and timeless category and a permanent feature in Christianity. For him, it was the criterion for verifying the authenticity of any theological work and its fidelity to the tradition of the church.

Florovsky was not trying to promote the superiority of Hellenistic culture and language, but he was anxious to respond to the accusations levelled by the German theologian, Adolf von Harnack. In his classic work, *Das Wesen des Christentum* (1900), von Harnack called for a return to the original biblical and Semitic spirit of the Christian faith. He sought to overcome the deviation due to the Hellenization of Christianity, which he believed was the product of the platonizing Fathers of the Church and the systematization of dogma. Critical of such studies by Harnack, Florovsky desired to expunge German idealism and romanticism from Orthodox theology. Some of his colleagues at St Sergius, particularly Sergei Bulgakov, were influenced by such Western philosophy. Florovsky's wholehearted embrace of Hellenism as the norm for Christianity, although it did not exclude other Christian traditions from the church, did regard them as incomplete or deficient.[1] But for Florovsky, a return to patristic source meant more than just a critical or exotic study of the Fathers; it was a return to the spirit and living source of the primitive church.

The aim of re-Hellenization was to revive Christianity in his times by returning to its source through re-immersion in the ancient and venerable teachings of the early Church Fathers. Florovsky was convinced that the neglect of patristic teaching was harmful to Christianity. This unfortunate situation came about when church statements were isolated from their patristic source. He wanted a 'catholic transfiguration' that would lead to a permanent profession of Christian faith, overriding the particularity of a denomination or branch of Christianity. Critical of both the modern attempt at theological synthesis and the traditionalist attempt to conserve the past, Florovsky wrote: 'Patristic texts are kept and repeated. Patristic mind is too

---

1. Pantelēs Kalaitzidēs and Gregory Edwards (2010), 'Orthodoxy and Hellenism in contemporary Greece'. *St Vladimir's Theological Quarterly* 54, no. 3–4 (January), 385–6.

often completely lost or forgotten.'[1] The modernists selectively and discriminately insert patristic ideas into a modern secular framework, which distorts the patristic message. The traditionalists suffocate the patristic mind by their tight grip on tradition. In Florovsky's view, both approaches were equally futile. He sought a creative re-invention of patristic teaching: 'This call to "*go back*" to the Fathers can be easily misunderstood. It does not mean a return *to the letter* of the old patristic documents. . . . What is really meant and required is not a blind or servile imitation and repetitions but rather a further *development* of this patristic teaching, but homogeneous and congenial.'[2]

Florovsky thus called for a neo-patristic theology that highlighted the 'spirit of the Fathers' as a fundamental characteristic of Orthodox theology. This recovery of the 'spirit of the Fathers' he characterized as 'acquiring the mind of the Fathers'. As mentioned earlier, neo-patristic theology is essentially a reaction against a perceived Western domination of Orthodox theology influenced by scholasticism and German idealism. The neo-patristic movement, in contrast, emphasizes the primacy of the teaching of the Church Fathers, liturgical tradition, and monastic life. It is above all ecumenical in its thrust, and respected by both the Western and Eastern Churches.[3] This recovery of patristic thought was central to Florovsky's ecumenical vision and to theological renewal in the Western Churches.

## *Striking Similarity*

Florovsky's calls for a Christian Hellenism reveal a striking similarity to the thought of Joseph Ratzinger. In *Truth and Tolerance* (2004), Ratzinger deals with the question of Hellenization and takes to task Roman Catholic theologians who think that Greek philosophy is no longer relevant to the church in its various cultures. These theologians

1. Quoted in Noble and Noble, *op. cit.*, 278.
2. Ibid., 279.
3. See Paul Ladouceur (2012), 'Treasures new and old: landmarks of Orthodox neopatristic theology'. *St Vladimir's Theological Quarterly* 56, no. 2 (January), 194–5. In this article (198), Ladouceur asserts that the most significant achievement of neo-patristic theology is the stress on apophatic (negative) theology, the theology of divine energies, and the idea of deification (theosis) as the ultimate aim of human beings. These three theological ideas are the characteristic of Orthodox theology in relation to Latin theology. Originating with the Cappadocian Fathers, these theological notions were developed by St Gregory Palamas in the fourteenth century.

believe that the Greco-Latin culture of the church is just one cultural form among others. Ratzinger, however, highlights the fact that the first encounter between Greek thought and biblical faith took place, not in the early church, but in the Old Testament – the Greek translation of the Old Testament, the Septuagint, which represents an 'independent textual tradition'.[1] This intercultural encounter was continued and developed by the Church Fathers. According to Ratzinger, 'The distinguishing mark of Greek philosophy was that it did not rest content with traditional religions or with the images of the myths; rather . . . it put the question about truth.'[2]

Hence, in Ratzinger's view, the encounter between biblical faith and Greek thought was providential; in other words, it was willed by God himself. He teased out this idea in his address at Regensburg University in 2006:

> The encounter between the Biblical message and Greek thought did not happen by chance. The vision of Saint Paul, who saw the roads to Asia barred and in a dream saw a Macedonian man plead with him: 'Come over to Macedonia and help us!' (cf. Acts 16:6–10) – this vision can be interpreted as a 'distillation' of the intrinsic necessity of a rapprochement between Biblical faith and Greek inquiry.
>
> This inner rapprochement between Biblical faith and Greek philosophical inquiry was an event of decisive importance not only from the standpoint of the history of religions, but also from that of world history – it is an event which concerns us even today.[3]

It was not a coincidence that the early apostles went to the Greeks, who valued rational thinking. The early Christians wanted to learn from the genius of Hellenistic culture. Ratzinger believes that it was providential that Christianity was cast in Hellenistic categories and expressions. In other words, it was not an accident, but part of God's design for his people. The Church Fathers also developed this synthesis; they did not merely combine Christian thought with static

---

1. Joseph Ratzinger (2004), *Truth and Tolerance*. San Francisco: Ignatius Press, p. 92.
2. Ibid., p. 95.
3. Pope Benedict XVI (2006) 'Faith, Reason and the University', lecture at the University of Regensburg, 12 September, http://www.vatican. va/holy_father/benedict_xvi/speeches/2006/september/documents/hf_ ben-xvi_spe_20060912_university-regensburg_en.html.

Greek categories, but started a dialogue with Hellenistic philosophy and made it an instrument of the Gospel. Thus, it is important for both Florovsky and Ratzinger that we return to our spiritual ancestors to understand how Christianity came about.

## Return to the Fathers

Florovsky saw the teaching of the Fathers as more than just an intellectual exercise; it contains a certain 'existential character', which in concrete terms means a vision of faith that includes an encounter with the living Christ. This vision is fundamental to understanding Orthodox theology: 'Apart from the life in Christ theology carries no conviction, and, if separated from the life of faith, theology may easily degenerate into empty dialectics, a vain *polylogia*, without any spiritual consequence. Patristic theology was rooted in the decisive commitment of faith.'[1] In other words, patristic theology is not just a speculative study but a spiritual engagement and a commitment of faith. As such, it cannot be divorced from the concrete life experience of prayer and the practice of virtue. Florovsky desired that Christians adopt the disposition of the Church Fathers; this 'does not mean simply to quote their sentences. It means to acquire their mind, their *phronema*. The Orthodox Church claims to have preserved this *phronema* and to have theologized *ad mentem Patrum*.'[2] This recovery of the mind of the Fathers includes adopting their attitude of piety and holiness.

Florovsky regarded the influence of modern Western philosophy on Orthodox theology as a 'Babylonian captivity'. It was a deviation from traditional patristic thought: '[T]he style of theology has been changed. Yet, this did not imply any change in doctrine. It was, indeed, a sore and ambiguous *Pseudomorphosis* of Eastern theology, which is not yet overcome even in our own time. This *Pseudomorphosis* actually meant a certain split in the soul of the East.'[3] The only way to escape this captivity is to return to the tradition of the Fathers, which is preserved in the celebration of its sacred liturgy.

---

1. Florovsky (1960), 'The ethos of the Orthodox Church'. *Ecumenical Review* 12, no. 2 (January), 188.
2. Ibid., 189.
3. Ibid., 191. In a similar vein, Joseph Ratzinger thinks that the church is in a 'situation of Babylonian captivity' in the modern world, divided by various factions and contaminated by all kinds of new ideas. Lieven Boeve and Gerard Mannion (eds) (2010), *The Ratzinger Reader*. London: T & T Clark, p. 94.

This return to the wellspring of patristic teaching also has ecumenical significance. For centuries the Christian world was united
under the theology of the Greek Fathers. Florovsky regarded St
Augustine's theology as basically Greek thought vested in Latin attire.
In fact, the rest of the Latin Fathers, such as St Ambrose, St Jerome,
and St Hilary, were interpreters of Greek tradition. When Western
civilization fell into decay after Augustine, the Greek language was
forgotten. Therefore, in order to revive Christianity, we need to
return to the Greek Fathers, who are recognized as competent and
safe theological guides. Florovsky believed that this patristic revival
would guarantee a reintegration of Christian tradition, 'a recovery
of the true Catholic mind'.[1] This means that the legacy of Orthodox
theology, with its emphasis on patristic teaching, is relevant to all
Christian churches. The Orthodox Church is still the custodian of
patristic treasures and the other separated brethren are invited to
share this rich legacy as a way of coming together as one family.

Florovsky was pleased to acknowledge that there have been
valuable studies on patristic theology by Russian scholars. He stated
that the return of the philosophers to the church and their efforts
to interpret patristic tradition in new situations is most significant,
despite the dangers involved. These dangers include the adoption of
the German idealism of Hegel and Schelling. Although he was critical
of his fellow Russian thinkers, Vladimir Solovyov, Sergius Bulgakov,
and Nicolas Berdyaev, he acknowledged their great contributions to
Orthodox thought, which proved that Eastern theology is not as
exotic as the West like to believe. Further, the writings of Berdyaev
show that the modern person who remains steadfast in his faith and
loyal to the teaching of the church can still be free and responsive to
the needs of the world.[2]

Present-day Orthodox theologians must address an ecumenical
audience because Orthodox theology is essentially ecumenical and
universal. But Orthodox theologians must not be servile repeaters of
patristic and biblical texts. Such repetition of texts or ideas is contrary
to the spirit of the biblical and patristic writings. Both the scripture
writers and the Fathers were bold, courageous, and adventurous
in seeking divine truths. However, renewal is not possible without
returning to the source, Florovsky was eager to remind us – we must
return to the wellspring of living water and not retire to the library or

1. Florovsky (1949), 'Legacy and the task of Orthodox theology'. *Anglican
   Theological Review* 31, no. 2 (April), 66–7.
2. Ibid., 69.

museum. Patristic teaching is not so much 'a binding and restricting authority, as a life in the Spirit, a living experience, a communion with the Truth, with the living Lord, who is not only an authority, but the Truth, the Way and the Life'.[1]

Further, true theology, according to Florovsky, originates in profound liturgical experience: 'It must become once more, as it has been in the age of the Fathers, a witness of the Church, worshipping and preaching, and cease to be merely a school-exercise of curiosity and speculation.'[2] This liturgical approach to practising theology has always been a distinctive feature in the Orthodox Church. It is only through this approach, Florovsky argued, that Orthodox theology can quickly recover from what he called 'pseudomorphosis', which has been paralyzing its spirit for a long time. This does not mean that Orthodox theology must cut itself off from the Latin School, but it does mean that it should not be subservient to the Western tradition. It must approach other traditions critically and yet fraternally:

> All reaches of the Orthodox tradition can be disclosed and consummated only in a standing intercourse with the whole of the Christian world. The East must face and meet the challenge of the West, and the West perhaps has to pay more attention to the legacy of the East, which after all was always meant to be an ecumenical and catholic message.[3]

Neo-patristic synthesis, for Florovsky, is the beginning of a healing process in a divided Christendom – an ecumenical co-operation in practising theology by going back to its patristic source. It is time for the Orthodox to join in this concerted effort, to bring Christians back together by returning to the home of their spiritual ancestors. This brings us to Florovsky's approach to the question of the unity and disunity of the Christian churches, and his involvement in the World Council of Churches.

## The Unity and Disunity of the Christian Churches

Florovsky was honest, objective, and direct in his approach to Christian ecumenism. He did not believe in easy compromise, diplomatic gestures, or overlooking fundamental differences to achieve unity. Convinced that the Orthodox Church possesses the

1. Ibid., 70.
2. Ibid.
3. Ibid.

fullness of truth, he insisted that this did not betray his desire for unity. In fact, it cleared confusion and suspicion. On this, he wrote:

> As a member and Priest of the Orthodox Church, I believe that the Church in which I was baptized and brought up is in very truth the Church, i.e., the true Church and only true Church. I believe this for many reasons: by personal conviction and by the inner testimony of the Spirit which breathes in the sacraments of the Church and by all that I could learn from Scripture and from the universal tradition of the Church. I am therefore compelled to regard all other Christian churches as deficient, and in many cases I can identify these deficiencies accurately enough. Therefore, for me, Christian reunion is simply universal conversion to Orthodoxy. I have no confessional loyalty; my loyalty belongs solely to *Una Sancta*.[1]

Although his statement may sound arrogant, Florovsky argued that this conviction regarding the truth of the Orthodox Church places great responsibility on the believer to proclaim the Gospel.

1. Quoted in George C. Papademetriou (1996), 'Father Georges Florovsky: a contemporary Church Father'. *Greek Orthodox Theological Review* 41, no. 2–3 (June), 123. In another passage, Florovsky claimed: 'The Orthodox Church claims to be the Church. There is no pride and arrogance in the claim. It implies rather an awful responsibility. Nor does it mean perfection. The Church is still in pilgrimage, in via. The Orthodox Church is fully aware and conscious of her identity through the ages, in spite of all historical perplexities and tribulations. She has kept intact and immaculate the sacred heritage of the Early Church and of the Fathers. . . . And for that reason she recognises herself, in this distorted Christendom of ours, as being the only guardian of the primitive Faith and Order, in other words, as being the Church.' Florovsky (1950), 'The doctrine of the church and the ecumenical problem'. *Ecumenical Review* 2, no. 2 (December), 157. This is similar to Ratzinger's attitude towards his own church, which he regards as possessing the fullness of truth while others are deficient. In fact, he regards some Protestants not as church in the Catholic sense, but as Christian communities. Regarding other religions, the Vatican declaration, *Dominus Iesus*, signed by Ratzinger, states: 'If it is true that the followers of other religions can receive divine grace, it is also certain that *objectively speaking* they are in a gravely deficient situation in comparison with those who, in the Church, have the fullness of the means of salvation.' http://www.vatican.va/roman_curia/congregations/cfaith/documents/rc_con_cfaith_doc_20000806_dominus-iesus_en.html, no. 22.

Although Florovsky was aware that Christian disunity is a bleeding wound in the body of Christ, he also believed that the church is on a pilgrimage toward final unity, which cannot be achieved by human efforts alone because it is ultimately a gift from God. Thus, we must get rid of our prejudices and short-sightedness in order to understand the cause of our division. He was optimistic that one day the Christian churches will be united.

Though divided, Florovsky argued that Christianity is still one, at least in aspiration: 'The body of Christians has been utterly disrupted. The hope of unity alone has not been fully lost, and perhaps this is the only token of unity still left in divided Christendom.'[1] As such, he cautioned us not to be satisfied with this schismatic state of affairs because the spirit of schism is contrary to the true spirit of the church. On the split between the Greek and the Latin minds that started early in the church, Florovsky posited that although the division was not complete, it had great repercussions in history. At the heart of the break-up was the issue of language. Greek was the language of early Christianity, but the Gospel had to be translated into other tongues so that the message would be meaningful to other nations. He held that Greek is still important because as a language it carries within itself the categories that are used to explain the Christian faith: it is, as we discussed earlier, the original language in which the Gospel was transmitted and received.

Although the East and the West are very different, the feeling of universal fellowship is still strong as Christians from the East and the West feel at home when they visit each other. Unfortunately, the Greek language was neglected during the time of Augustine. The East did not take the rise of Latin Christianity seriously and very few of the works of Augustine were translated into Greek. Furthermore, there was minimal translation of the Greek Fathers into Latin, and this led to deeper division: 'Latin Christian civilization steadily decayed since Augustine, and fresh nations came on the historical

---

1. Florovsky, 'The doctrine of the church and the ecumenical problem', 152. 'The Church is One. And for that reason she is Universal, the same Church in the whole world. Her unity transcends all barriers and boundaries, whether of race or language, or of social rank and learning. Even in the early times, when Christians were but a scattered minority in an unconverted world, the Church was fully conscious of her intrinsic Universality'. Florovsky (1954), 'The Church Universal'. *St Vladimir's Seminary Quarterly* 2, no. 4 (June), 2.

scene, but when the recovery came very little of the Greek heritage was saved, and living continuity with the common past of the Church universal was broken, except what has been preserved in the treasury of worship.'[1]

In spite of the rupture, for Florovsky, the split between the Eastern and Western Churches was never complete because common ground still exists. But the most tragic thing is that Christians from the East and the West have forgotten that they share a common heritage. In fact, what is common is thought to be something distinctive or peculiar. For example, the West looks upon the Greek Fathers as 'exotic Orientals'. Florovsky objectively described this mutual ignorance and suspicion:

> The total outcome of this age-long estrangement was the inability, on both sides of the cultural schism, to ascertain even the existing agreements and the tendency to exaggerate all the distinctive marks. . . . [T]here was another motive for this mutual misunderstanding which is still relevant in our day. Both sides were on the defensive: everything Greek smelt 'schism' for the Roman taste, and everything Latin suggested 'Popery' to the Eastern.[2]

In spite of all these suspicions and misgivings on both sides, Florovsky was hopeful that disagreement alone could not be the cause of total division. He believed that in spite of their differences, there is still hope for reconciliation and reintegration of the various churches into one universal church. His emphasis was on synthesis and integration, and not mere tolerance of differences or particularities. This begins when we realize that we share a common legacy that existed long ago. For Florovsky, this is the most urgent task for the ecumenical movement. He believed that the Orthodox Church has something special to contribute to the work of bringing Christians together:

> The witness of the Eastern Church is precisely a witness to the common background of ecumenical Christianity because she stands not so much for a local tradition of her own but for the common heritage of the Church universal. Her voice is not merely a voice of the Christian East but a voice of Christian

1. Florovsky (1950), 'Eastern Orthodox Church and the ecumenical movement'. *Theology Today* 7, no. 1 (April), 70.
2. Ibid., 71.

antiquity. The Eastern witness points not only to the East but to an *Oikoumene,* in which East and West belong together in the peace of God and in the fellowship of the primitive tradition.[1]

This implies that the Orthodox Church has a duty to remind Christians, by her witnessing, of their common heritage and background. It is both a challenge and a duty that the Eastern Church must undertake: 'the witness of the undivided Church of Christ'.[2] The burden of responsibility falls on the Orthodox Church because she is the survivor of ancient Christianity and remains faithful to the early Ecumenical Councils and Fathers. She stands for patristic tradition, which is also the tradition of the Western Churches, and here lies its unifying force.

After so many centuries of conflicts and estrangement, Florovsky admitted that it can be tempting to take sides. Both the East and the West will tend to emphasize their uniqueness as representatives of their specific traditions. Such a tendency will not help in the process of reintegration of the various Christian churches. However, he believed that the major task for Christians working towards unity would be this reintegration of diverse Christian traditions sought in patristic synthesis. The first step is learning to read and study the Fathers not as historical documents, but as a source of life and truth. This is the 'greatest ecumenical promise of our age'.[3]

Many Christian communities emerged at a later date due to dissent or nonconformity with the universal church. Motivated by the desire to go back to the church of the apostolic age, these Christian groups felt that the visible church distorted the Gospel and thus ceased to remain as the true church. But Florovsky believed that from an Orthodox perspective, the Church of God can never lose her identity because the Orthodox Church is the Church of Christ. Regarding the status of non-Orthodox Christians, Florovsky seemed to follow the position taken by the Roman Catholic Church, which does not recognize other Christian communities as 'church', but at the same time regards these Christians as in some ways related to the one true Church of Christ. This implies that there are degrees of church membership and thus, unity is present in some ways. This brings us to Florovsky's involvement in the World Council of Churches.

---

1. Ibid., 72.
2. Ibid.
3. Ibid., 79.

## The World Council of Churches

Florovsky played a significant role in helping to found the World Council of Churches (WCC), a role that began with his participation in the Faith and Order Conference in 1937. He was a realistic man and not afraid to confront the difficulties encountered when various churches met for discussion because he believed that ecumenical dialogue is enhanced by an honest recognition of differences. Dialogue must involve painful clarification of fundamental and irreconcilable differences, rather than a superficial search for unity based on easy compromise. Convinced that the Orthodox Church possesses the fullness of truth, as we have seen, he held that there is only one church. But he was not a fundamentalist and his open personality enabled him to embrace those with whom he did not agree, especially in the area of Christian ecumenism.

At the Second World Conference on Faith and Order held in Edinburgh in 1937, Florovsky pointed out that we cannot overcome doctrinal differences that have separated churches for centuries by ignoring them. This leads to the 'confusion of churches' rather than unity.[1] Although he continued to make positive contributions, he did not refrain from making critical interventions on what he considered important ecclesiastical or theological principles. At the First Assembly of the WCC, he proposed dividing churches on the basis of apostolic succession. But later, influenced by Karl Barth and Michael Ramsay, the formulation chosen was the difference between Roman Catholics and Protestants.

There was a debate at the WCC in 1950 as to whether 'Membership [in the Council] does not imply that each church must regard the other member churches as churches in the true and full sense of the word'.[2] It was a sensitive and controversial issue. Some members of the WCC regarded some other churches as deficient or incomplete. Florovsky felt that it was undesirable to retain such members and advised them to leave the organization because 'this was no matter of editorial revision, but a matter of principle'.[3] From his strong conviction, it became clear to the WCC that it

---

1. Willem Adolph Visser't Hooft (1979), 'Fr Georges Florovsky's role in the formation of the WCC'. *St Vladimir's Theological Quarterly* 23, no. 3–4, 135.
2. Ibid., 136.
3. Ibid., 137.

needed a deeper dimension of ecumenism that could accommodate the tension and conflict between different ecclesiologies.

At the Second Assembly of the WCC in Evanston in 1954, Florovsky appeared to take a more open approach when he gave an important address entitled 'Our Oneness in Christ and our Disunity as Churches'. In this speech he said that the greatest achievement of the ecumenical movement is the courage to acknowledge our theological disagreements. The tragedy, however, lies in the fact that we hold on to our differences because of our loyalty to Christ and our zeal for the true faith. As a result, some members cannot accept others on equal footing as full churches or living parts of the universal church. Following their conscience, they abstain from any action that betrays their loyalty. But this does not mean that the ecumenical movement has reached a dead end. It is this very tension that provides true ecumenicity to the organization.[1] It would make things easier if some of the communions were to drop out, but that would not make the movement ecumenical.

## Catholicity of the Church

A discussion of true ecumenicity and its relation to the Orthodox Church cannot be had without a view of catholicity through Florovsky's eyes. First and foremost, Florovsky asserted that the catholicity of the church is not a geographical conception because the global extension is only an outward sign, not absolutely necessary. The church was already catholic even when small Christian communities existed in remote islands among non-Christians. The meaning of catholicity is to be understood as an inner wholeness and integrity of the church's life. It is not just a simple empirical communion, but an ontological reality:

> The Church is catholic, not only because it is an all-embracing entity, not only because it unites all its members, all local Churches, but because it is catholic all through, in its very smallest part, in every act and event of its life. The *nature* of the Church is catholic; the very web of the Church's body is catholic. The Church is catholic, because it is the one Body of Christ; it is union in Christ, oneness in the Holy Ghost – and this unity is the highest wholeness and fullness.[2]

---

1. Ibid., 138.
2. Florovsky (1972), *Bible, Church, Tradition: An Eastern Orthodox View*, Vol. I of the *Collected Works of Georges Florovsky*. Belmont, Massachusetts: Nordland, p. 41.

The catholicity of the church consists of two aspects: objectively, catholicity means the unity of Spirit, and subjectively, catholicity means the church is a communion. It is a love that binds all Christians together, a love that calls us to deny ourselves:

> We must 'reject ourselves' to be able to enter the catholicity of the Church. We must master our self-love in a catholic spirit before we can enter the Church. And in the fullness of the communion of the Church the *catholic transfiguration of personality is accomplished*. But the rejection and denial of our own self does not signify that personality must be extinguished, that it must be dissolved within the multitude. Catholicity is not corporality or collectivism.[1]

Self-denial in love does not mean that we have to deny our personality, and catholic consciousness does not separate us from those who are not catholic. This catholicity is achieved not by an elimination of our personality, but by a deeper awareness of our relationship to God and to one another. In fact, this is our calling as Christians – to be the person that God calls us to be – which means the call to attain catholic completeness.

## *Tradition*

The 'catholic unity' of the church also has two aspects: the objective aspect, which Florovsky referred to as the 'uninterrupted sacramental succession', and the subjective aspect, which is loyalty to the apostolic tradition.[2] He demanded that Orthodox Christians reject 'individualistic separatism' and embrace catholicity. In addition, he felt that church history is not just something that occurred in the past, but something that has been accomplished and exists in the 'catholic fullness of the one Body of Christ'; 'tradition reflects this victory over time.' In other words, to learn from tradition is to learn from the timeless wisdom of the church. Loyalty to this tradition is not just fidelity to an outward authority, but 'it is a living connexion with the fullness of Church experience.'[3] This loyalty not only allows us to appreciate the past; it also liberates us from the past. This is because tradition is not only a conservative principle; it is primarily a principle of growth

1. Ibid., p. 43.
2. Ibid., p. 45.
3. Ibid., p. 46.

and regeneration: 'Tradition is the constant abiding of the Spirit and not only the memory of words. Tradition is a *charismatic*, not a historical, principle.'[1] This means that tradition is not static, but living.

It is a living tradition because of the presence of the Holy Spirit in the church, and thus, there is a continuity of divine guidance and enlightenment. Since it is a living entity, tradition in the church has nothing to do with rites, rules, and regulations. For Florovsky, the church is not bound by letter, but it is moved by the Spirit, the Spirit of Truth, spoken through the prophets, which guided the apostles, and continues to guide the church today. In addition, 'true tradition is only the tradition of truth.'[2]

In the early church, tradition was a hermeneutical principle and method for interpreting scripture. It provided the living context in which the intention and design of God could be understood. Tradition was not just a channel for the transmission of doctrines, but a continuous life of truth. It was not a set of binding principles, but an insight into the meaning of God's revelation.[3] It is tradition that guides the Church Fathers in their interpretation of scripture and the formulation of doctrine. However, the ultimate criterion of truth is simply Christ, who is the truth.

This truth has two aspects – the person of Christ and the truth of revelation. Florovsky appealed to the faith of the church and the *kerygma* of the apostles in deciding how truth is to be arrived at. Scripture is to be understood within the context of the church. The appeal to the apostles' understanding of truth is seen as an appeal to the mind of the church; it is an appeal to the apostolic *kerygma* that was handed down in the church. Therefore, we confess what the entire church professes and without deviating from the teaching of the Fathers. The church is both apostolic and patristic. Florovsky understood the proclamation of faith in two stages: the proclamation of the church and the teaching of the Fathers. He wrote:

> Our simple faith had to acquire composition. There was an inner urge, an inner logic, an internal necessity, in this transition — from *kerygma* to *dogma*. Indeed, the teaching of

---

1. Ibid., p. 47.
2. Florovsky (1960), 'Saint Gregory Palamas and the tradition of the fathers'. *Greek Orthodox Theological Review* 5, no. 2 (December), 120.
3. Florovsky (1964), 'Function of tradition in the ancient church'. *Greek Orthodox Theological Review* 9, no. 2 (December), 187.

the Fathers, and the dogma of the Church, are still the same 'simple message' which has been once delivered and deposited, once for ever, by the Apostles. But now it is, as it were, properly and fully articulated.[1]

Yves Congar, the eminent Roman Catholic theologian, who had great influence on Vatican II, shared similar ideas about tradition: 'Tradition is an offering by which the Father's gift is communicated to a great number of people throughout the world, and down the successive generations, so that a multitude of people physically separated . . . are incorporated in the same, unique, identical reality, which is the Father's gift, and above all the saving truth, the divine Revelation made in Jesus Christ.'[2] Tradition is a sharing of a treasure, which is timeless, and this also represents a victory over time and space. It essentially means a living transmission of the Christian message.

Congar also believed that liturgy, formed by tradition, is the primary influence in shaping the Christian spirit. He spoke of the sum total of tradition, which includes the 'Catholic spirit or the mind of the Church'.[3] Objectively, it refers to the practice of the faith by the people through the ages, from the time of the apostles to the present day. Subjectively, it refers to the 'Catholic spirit', which includes a certain feeling or disposition that springs from a deep awareness of the church's identity.[4]

In the next section, we will discuss a tradition that is highly revered in both the Orthodox and the Roman Catholic Churches and, to some extent, in the Anglican Church as well: monasticism. In keeping with his call for a return to the teaching of the Early

---

1. Florovsky, 'Saint Gregory Palamas and the tradition of the fathers', 121.
2. Yves M.J. Congar (1965), *Tradition and the Life of the Church*. London: Burns & Oates, p. 17. On the influence of Orthodox theology on Congar, see Joseph Famerée (1995), 'Orthodox influence on the Roman Catholic theologian Yves Congar, OP: a sketch'. *St Vladimir's Theological Quarterly* 39, no. 4 (January), 409–16.
3. Congar, *op. cit.*, p. 35. The Catholic spirit is like the 'genius of a people, or a national spirit, *Volkgeist*; a living link between the past and the present, this spirit is embodied and realized objectively in laws and institutions, and supremely in the State. Such is Tradition: the community spirit whose profound inner force is the Pentecostal Spirit, and which lives, is transmitted within the ecclesiastical fellowship and is expressed in the monuments of the Church's faith', ibid., p. 77.
4. Ibid., p. 36.

Fathers as an antidote to the prevailing modern philosophy that poisons the church, Florovsky viewed monasticism as a reaction of the Christian spirit against the hedonism of our age. Besides, like the monks, many of the Church Fathers were also associated with the desert.

## *Monasticism*

Ironically, when the Empire was established, it became a great temptation for many Christians to settle into an easy and comfortable life, which distracted them from living according to the values of the Gospel. In fact, many Christians succumbed to this worldly allurement. Providentially, there were some in the East who decided to flee to the desert, not so much from worldly troubles as from worldly cares caused by the wealth of the Empire. In fact, St John Chrysostom warned his people that prosperity was more dangerous than persecution, for the real danger to spiritual life is the external victory of the church.[1] In other words, when Christianity is transformed into Christendom, we forget that we are merely pilgrims on earth and we lose sight of our heavenly goal.

Monasticism was a reaction against the worldly influence of the Christian Empire; it was an ascetic renunciation, which includes a complete abandonment of the world, of all social ties. But monastic life was never anti-social, Florovsky asserted; it was an attempt to build another 'City' in this material world. Besides, monasteries were not an integral part of the Christian Empire.[2] In fact, the monks attempted to escape from the material achievement of the Christian Empire. According to Origen, monasteries became an independent 'polis', where monks lived a life that was contrary to the values of the secular city. Not only were the monasteries outside the jurisdiction and control of the civil government, they also remained in some ways outside the episcopal authority. The founding of monasticism was special in that as history unfolded, the Christian world became polarized – it resulted in a conflict between the Empire and the desert, which culminated in the iconoclastic controversy.[3] During this controversy, it was the monks who defended the art, paintings, and sculptures, and saved them from destruction by the state.

---

1. Florovsky, 'Christianity and civilization', 15.
2. Ibid., 16.
3. Ibid., 17.

Monasticism was more successful than the Empire because the monks were able to preserve the true ideal of culture and learning, according to Florovsky. The spiritual creativity of the monks was nourished by a profound spiritual life: 'Christian holiness synthétises within itself all the fundamental and ultimate aspirations of the entire ancient Philosophy.' Monasteries were not just great centres of learning, but were also centres of culture: 'Monasticism in itself was a remarkable phenomenon of culture. It is not by chance that ascetic endeavour has been persistently described as "Philosophy", the "love of wisdom", in the writings of the patristic age. It was not by accident that the great traditions of Alexandrian theology were revived and blossomed especially in the monastic quarters.'[1] Christendom or a 'churchified' Empire, on the other hand, was a failure and fell into bloody conflicts and violence. But the desert was a success compared to the Christian Empire, as it was to remain a true witness to the flourishing of Byzantine theology, spirituality and art. The fall of the Empire thus led to the flowering of mystical contemplation on Mount Athos, and the revival of philosophy, which also aided the Renaissance in the West. Florovsky saw the fall of the Empire as the fulfilment of the desert.[2]

Monasticism was an attempt to escape the conflict and tension caused by the Christian Empire and the secular rulers. Florovsky wrote that 'the period of the bitter struggle between the Church and the Empire, under the Arianizing Caesars of the fourth century, was also the period of Monastic expansion.'[3] The monks were fleeing from the worldly pleasures that existed in the Empire. It was not an escape from responsibilities because life in the desert was not easy at all. Distrusting the christened empire, the monks wanted to leave the earthly kingdom to build the true Kingdom of God 'outside the gates', in the wilderness.[4] It was also not a search for extraordinary deeds, but for a simple life of living out their baptismal promise.

The monastic order was essentially a lay movement in that very few monks were ordained as priests. In fact, the taking of holy orders was not encouraged except by order of the abbots, most of whom were also laymen. The monastic state was clearly distinct from the clerical

---

1. Ibid., 17–18.
2. Ibid., 20.
3. Florovsky (1957), 'Empire and desert: antinomies of Christian history'. *Greek Orthodox Theological Review* 3, no. 2 (December), 146.
4. Ibid.

state. As priesthood was regarded as a 'dignity and authority', it was not considered compatible with the life of a humble monk. There were, of course, exceptions to this rule, especially when the monastic community needed someone to celebrate the liturgy. Eastern monasticism has preserved its lay character, as can be seen in the communities at Mount Athos, where only a few monks are ordained as priests. For Florovsky, 'This is highly significant. Monasticism cut across the basic distinction between clergy and laity in the Church. It was a peculiar order in its own right.'[1]

Hence, 'Monasticism was an instinctive reaction of the Christian spirit against that fallacious reconciliation with the present age which the conversion of the Empire might seem to have justified.'[2] It was a challenge to the Christian Empire to be faithful to the teaching of Christ. There were attempts to integrate the monastic movement into the life of the Empire and many concessions and immunities were given to the monks. But the giving of privileges did more harm than good, for it led to an 'acute secularization of Monasticism'.[3] As many monasteries were also outside the jurisdiction of the bishop, they enjoyed a certain independence and became a permanent resistance to the worldly dispositions that can creep into any society, be it Christian or secular.

## Critical Reflection

Georges Florovsky's neo-patristic synthesis, his insistence on making this method the norm for the church to renew itself, creates problems for inculturation or accommodation. If the Church Fathers employed the Hellenistic philosophical concepts and language of their time to articulate the scripture message to the Greco-Roman world, can we not use post-modern categories to promote the Gospel in our time? Florovksy's idea of making Christian Hellenism absolute is actually obsolete. This is because he ignored the context of individual culture or phenomenon. The fundamental weakness of his neo-patristic synthesis lies in his theoretical approach – abstract and idealistic. He paid little or no attention to praxis – the struggles and hardship of peoples. His neo-patristic synthesis was essentially an intellectual enterprise bereft of a concerted effort to improve the welfare of the people.

---

1. Ibid., 148.
2. Quoted in ibid., 149.
3. Ibid., 149.

Given this absolute method of returning to the patristic source, can we still regard Florovsky's theology as genuinely Orthodox, catholic or universal? If tradition is a living thing, guided by the Spirit, making a method absolute obviously does not make his theology Orthodox. It is fine to return to the ancient source of the Fathers, but this method cannot be taken as 'one size fits all'. In fact, some theologians believe that all theology is contextual and plurality is the norm. This suggests that 'The universal theologies . . . were in fact *universalizing* theologies; that is to say, they extended the results of their own reflections beyond their own contexts to other settings, usually without an awareness of the rootedness of their theologies within their own contexts.'[1] Therefore, we cannot claim one theological method as the norm for all Orthodox Christianity. Theologies must relate to different cultures, be attentive to local needs, and be ecumenical at the same time.

Be that as it may, given the understanding of inculturation in the twenty-first century, it is unfair to judge Florovsky on the basis of what we know now. We need to place him within the context of his own time, in the 1950s, when the call for a return to the Fathers was in vogue among Orthodox and Roman Catholic theologians.

We must acknowledge the significance of Florovsky's ecumenical effort and his vision of Orthodox theology characterized by a return to its spiritual heritage. His emphasis on prayer and contemplation, the encounter with God in Christ, as the determining factors in Orthodox theology, remain valid for all Christians. Rowan Williams writes: 'That style of religious thinking in Russia which . . . is developed with closer reference to Scripture, the Fathers and the ascetical tradition . . . is fundamentally non-philosophical. . . . It is very much a monastic theology, conscious, to a greater or lesser extent, of its roots in the liturgical and contemplative life.'[2] In many ways, Florovsky, as his writings show, adopted this style of religious thinking, which has been embraced by many devout Orthodox, Roman Catholics, and Protestants.

---

1. Robert J. Schreiter (1997), *The New Catholicity: Theology between the Global and the Local*. Maryknoll, New York: Orbis, p. 2.
2. Quoted in Sauvé, 'Florovsky's tradition', 237.

# Chapter 5
## Sergius Bulgakov

Son of an Orthodox priest, Sergius Nikolaevich Bulgakov was born in Livny, Russia, in 1871. He began his education at church-run schools, then entered Orel Orthodox Seminary in 1885. Typical of the many young Russians who turned away from the Orthodox Church in the late nineteenth century, Bulgakov experienced a crisis of faith early in life. He left the seminary and finished his studies at a secular school, Eletsk gymnasium. His attraction to Marxism led him to study law and economics at the University of Moscow (1890–1894) and he later started teaching in Moscow. Eventually, he became disillusioned by Marxist philosophy and returned to his childhood Orthodox faith. Influenced by his mentor, Pavel Florensky, he was ordained as a priest in 1918. He was forced to resign from the University of Moscow when the Bolsheviks came to power, and moved to Crimea where he taught at the University of Simferopol before the region was taken over by the communists.

In 1923, he was expelled from the Soviet Union, together with some members of his family. In 1925, the Russian Orthodox Theological Academy was founded in Paris and Bulgakov was hired as a professor of Dogmatics and dean of the new school. The years in Paris proved to be the most creative period of his life. Besides writing, he was involved in the Russian Student Christian Movement and in 1927 became one of the founders of the Fellowship of St Alban and St Sergius at High Leigh. During his time in Paris, he also participated in the Ecumenical Conference at Lausanne, Oxford, and Edinburgh and was active in the work of the Continuing Committee on Faith and Order.[1]

---

1. This brief biographical sketch is based on the following texts: Sergius Bulgakov (1976), *A Bulgakov Anthology*, ed. James Pain and Nicolas Zernov. Philadelphia: Westminster Press, ix–xvii, 4–9. Rowan Williams (ed.) (1999), *Sergii Bulgakov: Towards a Russian Political Theology*.

Bulgakov is regarded as the most prominent thinker of the Russian Silver Age, which began before the revolutions of 1917. Some have even compared Bulgakov to the brilliant Roman Catholic theologian, Hans Urs von Balthasar.[1] Although Bulgakov was critical of the dogma of papal infallibility, he was also sympathetic towards Roman Catholicism, with which he was infatuated for a time. In fact, it was his attraction to Roman Catholicism that led Bulgakov to examine critically the dogmas of papal infallibility and the Immaculate Conception of Mary. He was an original thinker and a controversial theologian, open to secular sciences and clearly a man ahead of his times. He died on 12 July 1944.

Sophiology forms the core of Bulgakov's theology: it is integral to his thought, and is in fact the instrument with which he unites and distinguishes divine and created realities. This chapter discusses Bulgakov's theory of Sophiology as a key to understanding three aspects of his vast theological work: Christology, Mariology, and ecclesiology. His kenotic Christology foreshadows Jürgen Moltmann's reflection on 'The Crucified God', his Mariology resonates with John Paul II's vision of faith and reason,[2] and his ecclesiology anticipates by more than thirty years some of the teachings of Vatican II.

### *Sophiology*

According to Bulgakov, Sophia (σοφία), the Greek word for 'wisdom', is both human and divine, created and uncreated, personal and 'more

---

Edinburgh: T & T Clark, 3. Paul Gavrilyuk (2012), 'Sergii Bulgakov' in Augustine Casiday (ed.), *The Orthodox Christian World*. London: Routledge, 345. See also Aidan Nichols, OP (2005), *Wisdom from Above: A Primer in the Theology of Father Sergei Bulgakov*. Herefordshire: Gracewing, 1–11. Some material in this chapter appeared as an article: Ambrose Ih-Ren Mong (2014), 'The Wisdom of Sergius Bulgakov'. *Ecumenical Trends,* vol. 43, no. 11, December, 1–12.

1.  'Sergius Bulgakov, widely regarded as the greatest Orthodox theologian of the twentieth century (calling him the von Balthasar of the East would not be wide of the mark), was the kind of religious thinker only that century could produce. A blend of martyr, mystic, and missionary, he sought to defend the deposit of faith while upending its traditional modes of expression.' Matthew Cantirino (2012), 'Sergius Bulgakov's religious materialism'. *First Things,* 19 April, http://www.firstthings. com/web-exclusives/2012/04/sergius-bulgakovs-religious-materialism.

2.  See Pope John Paul II (1998), *Fides et Ratio*, http://www.vatican.va/holy_ father/john_paul_ii/encyclicals/documents/hf_jp-ii_enc_15101998_ fides-et-ratio_en.html.

than personal'. It is the virtue required for the union between God
and Jesus Christ, and also for God's involvement with the world.
Bulgakov viewed the act of creation out of nothing (*creatio ex nihilo*)
as 'the ontological separation of divine and creaturely aspects of
Sophia'. Sophia is the original plan of God for humanity and exists
eternally in God, and it can become instantiated in creation, the
saints, and the Virgin Mary. By this theory, Jesus Christ redeemed us
in history, but in the metaphysical sense, our redemption means that
we return to the creaturely Sophia so as to be united with the divine
Sophia. For Bulgakov, this reunion takes place in the church, which
is 'the most significant manifestation of Sophia'.[1]

Sophia is the wisdom of God and as such, the sophiological point
of view can be applied to understanding fundamental aspects of the
Christian faith. What is this sophiological viewpoint? It is the doctrine
of God in and for the world. Bulgakov described it vividly here:

> Anyone who has visited the church of St. Sophia in
> Constantinople and fallen under the spell of that which it reveals,
> will find himself permanently enriched by a new apprehension
> of the world in God, that is, of the divine *Sophia*. . . . An ocean
> of light pours in from above and dominates the whole space
> below. It enchants, convinces, as it seems to say: I am in the
> world and the world is in me.[2]

Bulgakov claimed that the world is not only a world in itself, it is
also the world in God, for God dwells not only in heaven but also
on earth with human beings. Bulgakov insisted that Sophiology is
very much part of the patristic tradition of the church that has been
neglected as a result of Christianity's emphasis on the questions of
personal salvation, of faith and grace.[3] Sophiology can be seen as a

---

1. Gavrilyuk, *op. cit.*, p. 347.
2. Bulgakov (1976), 'The Wisdom of God' in Pain and Zernov (eds), *op.
   cit.*, p. 144. Aidan Nichols sums up Bulgakov's sophiology as follows:
   'The Wisdom of God is the divinity of God – not the personal existence
   of Father, Son and Spirit, but the living reality of the divine nature they
   share – the divine nature as a "world" that is wonderfully coherent in
   itself (all the divine attributes and divine ideas fitting perfectly with each
   other), a world that is at the loving disposal of the divine hypostases, on
   which they can draw, with which, in which and from which they can act.
   This is the "something real about God" that corresponds to the "Lady
   Wisdom" of the Old Testament.' Nichols, *op. cit.*, p. 25.
3. Tataryn asserts that 'Bulgakov's Sophia is reminiscent of the Logos-
   Sophia tradition of Clement of Alexandria.' Myroslaw Tataryn, 'Sergius

key to understanding Christian doctrines. As such, we can interpret Christology in relation to divine Sophia and Mariology in relation to creaturely Sophia. Sophiology can also be applied to understanding ecclesiology, for the church is both human and divine.

Sophiology deals primarily with the relationship between God and the world of human beings. Bulgakov argued that the synthesis of 'God-humanity' is the correct way to understand Christianity, a religion that has been poorly influenced by the extreme views of dualism and monism. This results in two opposite attitudes towards life: 'Manichaeism', a philosophy that separates God from the world, and 'secularism', an ideology, that embraces the world completely. Human beings, thus, are confronted with an 'either-or' situation: God or the world. Bulgakov argued that neither flight from the world nor submission to the world can be regarded as Christianity. Both tendencies are a form of modern atheism or paganism, a 'negation of Christianity'.[1]

The doctrine of the Incarnation, of the Word made flesh, as taught by the Council of Chalcedon in 451, is central to Christianity. According to Bulgakov, this dogma is 'derivative' in the sense that it proceeds from the 'primordial God-manhood.' Similarly, the dogma of Pentecost is also 'derivative' as it involves the descent of the Holy Spirit, which is linked to the Incarnation. Sophiology is the key to unlock the mystery of the Incarnation and Pentecost.[2] Sophia, as the revelation of the Logos, 'is the all-embracing unity which contains within itself all the fullness of the world of ideas'.[3] This means that Sophia is found not only in God, but also in all his creatures. For God withholds nothing in himself and does not limit his creatures in any way: '[A]ll things were made by him' (John 1:3).

Therefore, in Sophia, 'the fullness of the ideal forms contained in the Word is reflected in creation.' All creation is based on 'eternal, divine prototypes'.[4] Thus, the world of creation bears a 'certain imprint' of the world of God. In fact, creation shares in the fullness of divine forms or ideas. Creation here includes angels and human beings – heaven and earth – and they have their foundation in the divine Sophia. In Romans, St Paul says: 'For from him and through him and to him are all things' (Romans 11:36). The world, though

---

Bulgakov (1871–1944): time for a new look'. *St Vladimir's Theological Quarterly* 42, no. 3–4 (January), 318.

1. Bulgakov, *op. cit.*, pp. 150–1.
2. Ibid., p. 152.
3. Ibid., p. 154.
4. Ibid.

outside of God, exists only through his power: 'God confers on a reality which originates in himself an existence distinct from his own.' Bulgakov called this 'panentheism', a philosophy that states that though God is not all things, all things are in God.[1]

In Bulgakov's understanding of Sophiology, we perceive a unity that exists between the divine and creaturely Sophia even though they are distinct entities. One is eternal, the other is temporal; one is divine and the other participates in the divinity. For him, the whole of creation, in heaven and earth, is based on this unity and duality of Sophia in God. Regarding God's presence in the world, there is a profound affinity between Hans Urs von Balthasar's understanding of the Incarnation and Bulgakov's Sophiology. Von Balthasar wrote:

> It is in the cosmos of natural kinds that the fullness of the Being of the world must needs unfold and manifest itself, and man is the being in which this fullness becomes fulfilled and comes into its own. This is precisely the reason why God's absolute fullness of Being can choose man as the being and the vessel in which to reveal his own inner fullness to the world. God's 'turning to the creature as phenomenon' (*conversio Dei ad phantasma creaturae*) is so emphatically the very meaning of the interior perfection of all life and all form in the world that this 'turning' or *conversio* is necessarily anticipated in all attempts at a religious conception of the world.[2]

Further, von Balthasar claimed that it is only in faith that we can understand the reality of this union between the finite and the infinite. It is Christ, the God-human, who gives us the form to perceive the

---

1. Ibid., p. 155. See Nichols, *Wisdom from Above*, p. 34. It should be noted here that Bulgakov's speculative theory of Sophiology was regarded as almost heretical by his Orthodox contemporaries, including Vladimir Lossky. He was condemned by the local synod of the Russian Orthodox Church and the synod of the Russian Orthodox Church abroad. Protected by his bishop, Metropolitan Evlogii, and some professors at St Sergius, he was able to defend himself against charges of heresy. Gavrilyuk, *op. cit.*, p. 347. See also Bryn Geffert (2005), 'The charges of heresy against Sergii Bulgakov: the majority and minority reports of Evlogii's commission and the final report of the bishops' conference'. *St Vladimir's Theological Quarterly* 49, no. 1–2 (January), 47–66; and Barbara Newman (1978), 'Sergius Bulgakov and the theology of divine wisdom'. *St Vladimir's Theological Quarterly* 22, no. 1 (January), 39–73.
2. Hans Urs von Balthasar (1982), *The Glory of the Lord*, Vol. I. Edinburgh: T & T Clark, p. 171.

reality of the divine in the world and the reality of the world in the divine. According to von Balthasar, Jesus is not just a sign but a form, the 'determinant form of God' in the world, the 'Primal Image – the Archetype itself' that communicates God to us. We cannot distinguish between God's act of revelation and the content of his revelation; this revelation is both the interior life of God and the life of Jesus himself. The two cannot be separated although they are distinct: 'For the Word of God is *both* the divinity which expresses and reveals itself in the Trinity's eternity and in the economy of time *and* the human being Jesus Christ, who is the Incarnation of that divinity.'[1] It is within his kenotic theory that Bulgakov explored the theology of the Incarnation.

### *Kenotic Christology*

In *The Lamb of God* (1976), Bulgakov asserts that the salvation wrought by Christ is more precious than the world and that we attain this salvation through struggling with sin, subjecting our flesh to the spirit, and accepting the cross. This truth is understood clearly by Christians. However, the salvation of the whole church as Christ's kingdom in the world is not widely understood. The reason is that since the beginning of church history, Christianity has been challenged by a secularism that silently attempts to undermine the mystery of the Incarnation, Christ's human and divine natures. As such, we have heresies such as Docetism, Gnosticism, and Manichaeism, which seek to 'disincarnate the logos'.[2] These anti-Christ theories have led

---

1. Ibid., p. 183. Regarding Sergius Bulgakov and Hans Urs von Balthasar, Aidan Nichols writes: 'Each was a thoroughgoing Trinitarian thinker in his approach to modern theology, finding Trinity most fully displayed in the Cross and Resurrection of Christ.' Nichols, *Wisdom from Above*, p. 310. 'The question posed by this Swiss theologian is similar to that of Bulgakov: How is the absolute Being, who cannot exist except as Trinity, reflected in the being of the world? . . . Balthasar . . . suggests as did Bulgakov, that we leave the sphere of rational knowledge in order to speak in symbolic terms of the Father as the pure gift of self, as love free and without foundation. Balthasar writes: "To grasp that is impossible for me, except if one dares to speak with Bulgakov of the first inter- Trinitarian kenosis."' Antoine Arjakovsky and Michael Plekon (2005), 'The sophiology of Father Sergius Bulgakov and contemporary western theology'. *St Vladimir's Theological Quarterly* 49, no. 1–2 (January), 227–8.
2. Bulgakov (1976), 'The Lamb of God' in James Pain and Nicolas Zernov (eds), *A Bulgakov Anthology*. Philadelphia: Westminster Press, p. 114.

people to believe that Jesus has forsaken the world, that we can never attain the Kingdom of God on earth, and that therefore, we must be content with Christ's teaching as merely symbolic or ethical and we must escape into the 'desert of negation, indifference, and pride'.[1]

In other words, many doubt that Christ actually came to save us and to banish our sins and sufferings. The anti-Christ teaches that the world does not belong to Christ, but to itself. Even those who believe in Christ have their doubts: 'Who shall roll us away the stone from the door of the sepulchre, for it is very great?'[2] Bulgakov, however, believed that faith could move not only stones, but mountains. Quoting Revelation 5:11, 'Worthy is the Lamb that was slaughtered to receive power and wealth and wisdom and might and honour and glory and blessing', he argued that Christians must not run away from the world because Christ is coming to us, to the feast of 'deified humanity', as king and judge.[3] Therefore, we must not be afraid, but believe that Christ will truly come again. Our fear must be overcome by love.

Bulgakov emphasized that Christ's humanity was clearly seen on the cross; he was exhausted on the cross – 'his divine nature humbles itself to fit human creatures'. Although his divinity does not die, it 'bears the weight of his dying humanity'[4] and participates in his human death. Hence, his divine hypostasis participated in death because it is united with his human nature. Bulgakov wrote: 'Therefore it is the God-man in the integral unity of his complex being who dies, but dies differently in his respective natures: the human nature dies, and consequently its hypostasis, which is divine hypostasis of the Logos, passes with it through the gates of death to the depths of creaturely non-being.'[5] This means that when Christ died, the God-man also died, although the human nature and the divine nature died differently.

With reference to Psalm 22/Mark 15:34, 'My God, my God, why have you forsaken me? Why are you so far from helping me, from the words of my groaning?', Bulgakov claimed that Jesus' cry was indicative of 'a kind of sinking of the Son out of sight of the Father, his link with whom is thus known only in the pain of yearning.'[6] Jesus

1. Ibid., p. 115.
2. Ibid.
3. Ibid.
4. Ibid., 116.
5. Ibid.
6. Ibid.

was crying out of the depths of the 'creatureliness of his human nature'. Since the Father accepted his death on the cross, the Father also in some ways participated in this act of self-sacrifice. Bulgakov called the Father's involvement in the death of Jesus 'a spiritual participation in the vicarious sacrifice of love' even though the Father did not actually die.[1] In addition, the Father participated in the exhaustion of Jesus on the cross before he died. Jesus emptied himself, 'made discarnate in death', returning to God, his Father, who also took part in this humbling self-abasement of his Son. The Son's commitment to his Father signifies 'the deepest self-lowering of divinity'.[2] This also suggests that our spirits will return to God after we die.

Similarly, Bulgakov claimed that the Holy Spirit, just like the Father, also forsook Jesus when he died. This is because the Holy Spirit is the 'perceptible nearness of the Father, abiding in love'.[3] He is the actual love of the Father for the Son and thus, when the Father forsook the Son, the Holy Spirit also participated in this sacrificial act of abandonment. In fact, when the Holy Spirit descended upon Jesus when he plunged into the river of Jordan, it signified his coming death. At that event, the Holy Spirit willingly accepted the self-emptying of the Jesus and his exhaustion on the cross, and spent himself with Jesus.[4] This means that the Holy Spirit also has his kenosis, self-emptying, as he is dependent on the Son as the hypostatic love of Father and Son.

The Spirit is poured out in 'creation's process of becoming'.[5] He is the 'becoming of the world', 'the giver of life', and the Comforter who gives us joy and beauty. The Holy Spirit is the joy and triumph of sacrificial love. But, unlike the Son, the procession of the Holy Spirit is not a sacrificial act. It proceeds from the Father and rests on the Son. The kenosis of the Spirit consists in 'divesting himself of his hypostasis self and serving as a "bridge of love" between the Father and Son'.[6]

In *The Lamb of God* (1933), Bulgakov gives us a comprehensive kenoticism by expanding the scope of nineteenth-century kenotic theory. He applies the theory of *kenosis* to God's creative act and

1. Ibid.
2. Ibid., p. 117.
3. Ibid.
4. Ibid.
5. Sergii Bulgakov, '*The Lamb of God*: On the Divine Humanity (1933)' in Rowan Williams (ed.), *Sergii Bulgakov*, p. 195.
6. Gavrilyuk, 'Sergii Bulgakov' in Casiday, *The Orthodox Christian World*, p. 348.

to the inner life of the Trinity. According to him, the Trinity is the eternal act of self-giving as the Father gives himself entirely in begetting his Son. The Son also empties himself by submitting to be begotten of the Father through his obedience. Bulgakov also speaks of the 'supratemporal suffering' within the Trinity to capture the depth of this mutual sacrifice of the Father and the Son.[1] This mutual suffering was not the result of external limitations, because God is omnipotent; rather it was the expression of genuine love. Further, the cross, for Bulgakov, is not only a symbol of salvation, but also the power of mutual self-sacrifice and self-denial of the three divine persons: 'The historical Golgotha . . . was logically preceded by the metaphysical Golgotha.'[2] As such, Jesus' suffering was already pre-mediated before his Incarnation – it was a 'pre-temporal decision' to become human and to suffer. This suffering will eventually be overcome by the power of God.

In the creation of the world, the Son did what the Father willed. Though sent by the Father, the Son was not yet in hypostatic form, but 'only as the Word "spoken" about the world and "the utterances of the Word in this world". This coming forth of the Word from the Father and his coming into the world imply self-emptying of the Son, his *exinanitio*. He is sacrificed and humiliated in the creation of the world. The sending of the Son by the Father, "an outpouring of the Father's being" is the beginning of the "victim's oblation".'[3] In other words, it was a sacrifice for both parties when the Father decided to send his Son into the world. Further, in creation, God closed the ontological gap between himself and the world in an act of self-limitation. God freely chooses to limit his actions in the world by time and space so that humans can be free; the Son becomes a human being with all his limitations; the Holy Spirit restricts his activity in creation; and Pentecost is seen as the fulfilment of the Spirit's self-emptying, which began in creation and will end with the coming of God's kingdom.[4]

Bulgakov's kenotic theory is comprehensive, reaching beyond the Incarnation into creation and the inner life of the Trinity. Influenced by the German idealism of Fichte, Schelling, and Hegel, he saw the self-limitation of the Absolute as crucial in understanding the redemption wrought by Jesus Christ. Bulgakov was also faithful to

1. Ibid.
2. Ibid.
3. Bulgakov, *op. cit.*, p. 195.
4. Gavrilyuk, *op. cit.*, p. 349.

the traditional teaching of the church and attempted to formulate his kenotic theory in accordance with the Nicene Creed and the teaching of Chalcedon, which affirmed both Christ's divinity and humanity without separation. To this teaching, he added that the kenosis of Jesus involved all three persons of the Trinity. Therefore, to argue that the Father and the Holy Spirit did not suffer with Jesus is tantamount to destroying the unity of the Trinity. Bulgakov admitted that God himself cannot die, but suggested God can participate in human death. The Son's descent into hell is a continuation of his being forsaken by God. However, Christ's death is not the end; his resurrection and ascension belong to the final stages of his self-emptying.[1]

This last point is Bulgakov's special contribution to the theory of kenosis. The resurrection and ascension of Jesus by the power of the Father and the sending of the Holy Spirit at Pentecost will be the completion of Jesus' kenosis and his entry into divine glory. Bulgakov's emphasis on God's experience of forsakenness was taken up by the Lutheran theologian Jürgen Moltmann, who developed his dramatic trinitarian theology of the cross based partially on Karl Rahner's theory of immanent Trinity.

### The Crucified God

Moltmann asks: 'Has God himself suffered? Can God suffer and die?'[2] He looks at Christ's suffering for an answer when Jesus cries out 'My God, why hast thou forsaken me?' (Mark 15:34). In Moltmann's view, Jesus is actually saying, 'My God, why have you abandoned yourself?' Jesus is claiming that he and the Father are one; the Son acts for the Father. In other words, he is the God who suffers and dies. Jesus died because his God had forsaken him. This distinguishes Jesus' crucifixion from other crucifixions that were reserved for hardcore criminals in his time.[3] Thus, when

---

1. Paul Gavrilyuk (2005), 'The kenotic theology of Sergius Bulgakov'. *Scottish Journal of Theology* 58, no. 3 (January), 265.
2. Jürgen Moltmann (1972), 'The "Crucified God": a trinitarian theology of the cross'. *Interpretation* 26, no. 3 (July), 282. Kitamori puts it this way: 'The pain of God is in the infinitely deep background of the historical Jesus.' Thus the death of Christ means God has died. See Kazoh Kitamori (1965), *Theology of the Pain of God*. Virginia: John Knox Press, pp. 35, 44.
3. Moltmann, *op. cit.*, 285.

Jesus died, God died at the same time. It is the same with suffering; although God does not suffer like human beings, who are subject to sickness and death, this does not mean that he is in an absolute sense incapable of suffering.

Motivated by love, God allowed himself to suffer, Moltmann claims. This suffering of God was a voluntary sacrifice affected by his love for humankind. It was a suffering taken upon himself – the suffering of love. Moltmann argues that if God were incapable of suffering, he would be incapable of love. But God is love (1 John 4:8). He who loves is open to the sufferings that love brings; God suffers because he loves. In order to have a better grasp on this idea that God can suffer, Moltmann urges us to think of the Trinity as 'God's essence', as taught by Karl Rahner.[1] Rahner's teaching says that we must abandon the concept of two natures in traditional theology, which teaches that man is subject to change, but God is unchangeable; humans can suffer, but God cannot suffer.

In agreement with Moltmann, Roman Catholic theologian Walter Kasper teaches that the Early Fathers, in trying to differentiate the Christian God from the mythological understanding of a deity who could undergo change, made use of the Greek concept of impassability (*apatheia*) to describe the nature of divinity. As a result of Kasper's teaching, we tend to think of God as unmoved, without any feeling or emotion. However, Ignatius of Antioch asserted that the 'impassible one became capable of suffering for our sake'. Origen developed this further by saying that the Son felt compassion for our wretchedness and thus allowed himself to be crucified; he called this 'the suffering of love'.[2] This reveals that God is free to love and to suffer for us. Because God is love, he can suffer, and in his suffering he reveals his divinity. This means that the self-emptying cross does not lessen the divinity of God, but reveals his glory. His power lies in the fact that he can suffer and sympathize with us.

---

1. Moltmann, *op. cit.*, 288. Moltmann writes that Rahner stood by this paradox: 'The "unchangeable God" certainly has no fate and thus no death "in himself", but he himself (and not only the other) shares a fate with the other by means of the incarnation. . . . Thus precisely this death (and likewise the humanity of Christ) pronounces God.' This means that the death of Jesus is also the death of God because of the Incarnation. Jürgen Moltmann (1974), 'The crucified God: perspectives on a theology of the cross for today'. *Journal of Theology for Southern Africa* no. 9 (December), 12–13.
2. Walter Kasper (1993), *The God of Jesus Christ*. London: SCM Press, pp. 190–1.

In his attempt to construct a trinitarian theology of the cross as a way to understand the historic nature of Christ's being forsaken by God, Moltmann maintains that the 'Trinity is God's work on the cross, in which the Father lets the Son be sacrificed through the Spirit.'[1] In Romans, St Paul says, 'If God is for us, who is against us? He who did not withhold his own Son, but gave him up for all of us, will he not with him also give us everything else?' (Romans 8:31–3). If God did not spare his own Son to save evil persons, it must be love that made him do it. Moltmann thus concludes that when the Father sacrificed Jesus, he was actually sacrificing himself.

Further, Moltmann speaks of God's ultimate and complete self-humiliation in the crucified Jesus. In agreement with Bulgakov, he claims that God willingly enters into the limited and finite situation of human beings and embraces this human limitation as his own. Moltmann expresses his idea in this manner:

> If God's humiliation completes itself in the cross of Christ, then God not only enters into the finitude of man but also into the situation of his God-abandonedness. In Jesus, God does not die a natural death, but rather the violent death of a condemned person on the cross. At Golgotha he dies the death of complete God-abandonedness. The suffering in the suffering of Jesus is the abandonment, and indeed condemnation, by the God whom he called Father.[2]

As the result of this selfless act, the crucified God is near to us. He suffers the same loneliness and rejection as everyone else. No one is excluded from the 'pain of the Father, the love of the Son, and the life of the Spirit'.[3] On the cross of Christ, God himself died so that men and women could live again. God not only participates in our sufferings, but makes them as his own; he suffered the death of his

---

1. Moltmann, 'The "Crucified God" : a trinitarian theology of the cross', 291.
2. Moltmann (1974), 'Crucified God'. *Theology Today* 31, no. 1 (April), 14–15. Kasper also emphasizes the significance of the cross in his discussion on kenosis-Christology. He claims that God is truly human when he enters fully into the 'abyss and night of death'. This means that we must approach Jesus' divinity from the perspective of his death on the cross. At the same time we must understand that God is capable of self-emptying and suffering without losing his divinity. It is the humanness of God that we understand Jesus' suffering and death on the cross. Kasper, *op. cit.*, p. 189.
3. Moltmann, *op. cit.*, 15.

Son. Further, Moltmann claims that to understand the death of God, we must understand God as Trinity. The theology of the cross and Trinitarian theology are tied together under this concept:

> The event at the cross is an event within God. It is an event between the sacrificing Father and the abandoned Son in a power of sacrifice that deserves to be named the Spirit. In the cross, Jesus and the Father are in the deepest sense separated in abandonment, yet are at the same time most inwardly united through the Spirit of sacrifice. From the event between Jesus and his Father at the cross, the Spirit goes forth which upholds the abandoned, justifies the despised, and will bring the dead to life.[1]

Thus, the theology of the cross mirrors the doctrine of the Trinity. It is not a mere speculation that God suffers if we understand how he is related to the other two persons in the Trinity. God is concretely, historically present in the saving mission of Christ.

So far we have discussed the three persons in the Trinity: the Father, the Son, and the Holy Spirit. We will now discuss Bulgakov's understanding of Mary, the Mother of God, and Wisdom.

## Mariology

It should be noted that at the outset, Bulgakov's theological treatise on Mary, 'The Burning Bush', was a critique of the Roman Catholic understanding of Mary, particularly on the scholastic notion of 'pure nature', which viewed nature as untouched by God. This notion came from the Augustinian understanding of nature and grace. Bulgakov objected to this idea for he believed nature untouched by God to be un-Christian; if nature is created and loved by God, it must be profoundly touched by God.[2] His

---

1. Ibid., 16.
2. Andrew Louth (2005), 'Father Sergii Bulgakov on the Mother of God'. *St Vladimir's Theological Quarterly* 49, no. 1–2 (January), 153. Robert Slesinki writes: 'Acknowledging his polemical intent, Sergius Bulgakov initially conceived his dogmatic treatise on the Mother of God as a repudiation of the Catholic dogma of the Immaculate Conception, but soon realized he also needed to make a positive exposition of Orthodox doctrine at the same time. His point of departure for his critique is his reading of the late Scholastic teaching on the 'state of pure nature,' appealing to his understanding of

rejection of the notion of pure nature was a way of emphasizing the holiness of nature. Modern Roman Catholic theology has also repudiated this notion of 'pure nature'.

The Jesuit Henri de Lubac wrote against this notion in *Surnaturel* (1946).[1] In this work, de Lubac asserts that humanity was never created in a state of pure nature, independent of grace. On the contrary, humanity came to be within the supernatural sphere as a beloved or 'engraced' creature of God, a 'being in relation' with the Creator.[2] Similarly, Bulgakov argued that 'God came into the cool of the day to converse with man as with a friend, and this "conversation" was not some *donum superadditum* [a specially added gift] in relation to his incorrupt nature; to the contrary, this "speaking with God" was an intrinsic [right] given to it.'[3]

In 'The Burning Bush', Bulgakov speaks of Mary as the 'glory of the world' because she gave birth to God himself and thus she is

Catholic theological anthropology to corroborate his position. See Robert Slesinski (2007), 'Sergius Bulgakov on the glorification of the Mother of God'. *Orientalia Christiana Periodica* 73, no. 1 (January), 97–116. See also Nichols, *Wisdom from Above*, pp. 243–5.

1. 'Cardinal Henri de Lubac, one of the top theologians among the French Jesuits, died at the age of 95 in Paris. De Lubac was prohibited from teaching from 1946 to 1954 after the publication of his book *Surnaturel*. Rehabilitated in 1958, he took part in the [Second Vatican] Council at the request of John XXIII. His relations with Rome then became even more intensive during the reign of John Paul II, who, during a visit to Paris in 1980, interrupted a speech that he was giving when he saw the priest and said, "I bow my head to Father de Lubac."' Quoted in *Ignatius Insight*, http://www.ignatiusinsight.com/features2008/rvoderholzer_delubac_jan08.asp.

2. According to de Lubac, 'it is not the ancient concept of *natural pura*, but the system which has grown up around it in modern theology and profoundly changed its meaning, which it seems to me could be set aside without any loss.' He believed that a purely natural order has never in fact existed. In fact, de Lubac emphasized how 'the supernatural is a free gift . . . in relation to human nature in general as it may be abstracted from the observation of its concrete realization; but how it is so precisely in relation to the concrete human beings we are, in relation to all those who make up mankind as it is, mankind created by God to see him, or, as we sometimes say, "historic nature".' See de Lubac (1998), *The Mystery of the Supernatural*, trans. Rosemary Sheed and with an introduction by David L. Schindler. New York: Crossroad, pp. 32 and 55.

3. Slesinski, 'Sergius Bulgakov on the glorification of the Mother of God', 100.

higher than the angels. The glory of our material world is revealed in the glory of Mary. She is a 'personal revelation of the divine Wisdom, *Sophia*'. Bulgakov also regarded Sophia as Christ, the 'power and wisdom of God'. Christ's human nature originates in his mother. Christ represents both divine and creaturely Sophia and his mother is the 'created Sophia'.[1] Hence, there are two personal forms of Sophia: Jesus and Mary, which must be understood in relation to the doctrine of the Trinity. It follows that the Father, the first person, reveals himself in Jesus, the second divine person of the Trinity; the Father also reveals himself in the Holy Spirit, the third person, who proceeds from him and is active in the world. The Holy Spirit reveals himself to creatures, like Mary, 'through his action and gifts'.[2]

Attempting to connect Mary and Wisdom together, Bulgakov was convinced of the significance of Mary as the means to the ecumenical unity of the church. By separating divine wisdom from creature wisdom, Bulgakov succeeded in incorporating wisdom into his understanding of both God and Mary. He wanted to ensure that Mary was not transformed into a kind of goddess and emphasized that God is associated with divine wisdom and Our Lady is associated with creaturely wisdom. For Bulgakov, divine wisdom is part of God's nature, found only in the three persons of the Trinity.[3]

Although there is no personal incarnation of the Holy Spirit (like Jesus), there is one human being who becomes the vessel of the Spirit: the Blessed Virgin, who completely surrenders herself to the Holy Spirit. She becomes the Spirit's 'living receptacle, an absolutely Spirit-bearing creature, a Spirit-bearing human being'.[4] Bulgakov wrote:

> The Virgin is wholly deified, full of grace, 'a living temple of God.' Such a Spirit-bearing personality radically differs from the God-man, for she is a creature, but she differs as radically from the creation in its createdness, for she is raised and united to the divine life. And through this spiritualization is realized the image of God in man.[5]

1. Celia E. Deane-Drummond (2005), 'Sophia, Mary and the eternal feminine in Pierre Teilhard de Chardin and Sergei Bulgakov'. *Ecotheology* 10, no. 2 (August), 226.
2. Bulgakov (1976), 'The Burning Bush' in Pain and Zernov (eds), *A Bulgakov Anthology*, pp. 90–1.
3. Deane-Drummond, *op. cit.*, 223–4.
4. Bulgakov, *op. cit.*, p. 92.
5. Ibid.

Elevated to an intermediate position between creature and creator, Mary as a person is different from Christ, the God-man, and she is also radically different from the rest of humanity. Following the Orthodox tradition, Bulgakov taught that Mary is also 'wholly deified' and thus makes possible the divinization not only of people, but also of the world at large. According to him:

> The Mother of God, since she gave her son the humanness of the second Adam, is also the mother of the race of human beings, of universal humanity, the spiritual centre of the whole creation, the heart of the world. In her creation is utterly and completely divinised, conceives, bears and fosters God.[1]

According to Bulgakov, Mary's role is connected not only with the salvation of humankind but also with the restoration of the universe:

> As the glory of God and the glory of the world, as the manifested love of God for the world and the manifested love of the world for God, in her prayer she glorifies God. Her own prayer is glorification, eternally realised love, flaming and triumphant in its perfect joy – God's own love for himself in his creation. But as the foremost representative of the world and of all creation, the Mother of God also offers a prayer which is not her own, and yet is hers as the prayer of all of creation. She gives wings to its prayer; raising it to the throne of God, she gives it power; she is the intercessor raising her hands to God as a high-priestess (*orante*) and overshadowing the world with her veil.[2]

As the personal embodiment of the church, Mary is both the Mother and the Bride. She is the receptacle of the Holy Spirit, and she bears and gives birth to the Logos. She is *Theotokos*, Mother of God. As the church, Mary belongs to Christ, the Bridegroom and the Head of the Church. Emphasizing Mary as the church, Bulgakov asserted: 'The Church and Mary each bear the same relation alike to Christ and Christians.' As Jesus became the brother to all humankind when he taught us to call God Our Father, Mary is also the mother of all humankind. She is the 'praying Church', 'the universal Mother, defender and guardian'.[3]

Speaking of her mediatory significance, Bulgakov taught that Mary brought to her Son the world he has saved; 'its salvation is realized in and through her, and nothing in the world takes place

---

1. Quoted in Deane-Drummond, *op. cit.*, 224.
2. Bulgakov, *op. cit.*, p. 95.
3. Ibid.

apart from her.'[1] Similarly, von Balthasar claimed that 'The Marian experience of motherhood in the flesh, which is an experience of faith, as such remains unique . . . [but] open to all. It is open from within, from the womb of the Church, whence Christ's grace cannot radiate without traversing the experience of the womb.'[2]

It is also of great significance that the Mother of God was present at Pentecost at the very beginning of the church. She thus occupies a central place in the church; Mary is the Mother of the Church. Since Mary co-operates so well with the Holy Spirit, it is no wonder that many miracles happened through her intercession. Bulgakov claimed that the majority of miraculous revealed icons in Orthodox churches are icons of Our Lady. As she is so close to the church, the veneration of our Lady is the measure of churchliness. The church is the Holy Spirit who enables us to understand and revere the Mother of God.[3]

In the next section, we will discuss Bulgakov's ecclesiology as he expounded on the nature of the Orthodox Church.

## The Church

For Bulgakov, the Orthodox Church is the church of Christ on Earth. It is not an institution, but a new life with Christ guided by the Holy Spirit, in which the Spirit lives and works. Christ did not merely take on humanity but united with it to become the Body of Christ – the church under his authority. The church is also called the Bride of Christ, signifying the union between bride and bridegroom. This unity does not absorb but respects each other's differences. The church is also the life of Christ in us. It is the life in the Trinity, 'the love of the Father for the Son and that of the Son for the Father. . . . It is hypostatic. The love of God is the Holy Spirit, which proceeds from the Father to the Son, abiding upon him.' Bulgakov characterized the church as 'a blessed life in the Holy Spirit, or the life of the Holy Spirit in humanity'.[4] As we shall see, in Bulgakov's ecclesiology there is always the interplay between divine and human wisdom.

Since the fullness of the faith is too much to be held by any individual, tradition – the living memory of the church – contains the true doctrine through the ages: '[T]radition is a living power inherent

---

1. Ibid., p. 96.
2. von Balthasar, *The Glory of the Lord*, p. 343.
3. Bulgakov, *op. cit.*, p. 96.
4. Bulgakov (1976), 'The Orthodox Church' in Pain and Zernov (eds), *A Bulgakov Anthology*, p. 120.

in a living organism. In the stream of its life it bears along the past in all its form so that all the past is contained in the present and is the present.'[1] Although the period of the primitive church is different from the present, guided by the same Spirit, it is the same church that exists today. In other words, tradition is the living and binding force that keeps the church intact throughout history. In its external manifestation, tradition 'expresses itself by all that is impregnated with the Spirit of the Church'.[2] Its internal manifestation includes the church's literature, liturgy, and canonical texts.

Bulgakov asserted that, unlike the state, the church has only spiritual authority that comes from above in the form of ministry. The bishop works with the church and never above the church. Union with the church means that the bishop works closely with his people, the laity, who are not merely passive subjects, put people with gifts or charism, by virtue of their baptism. They too contribute to the Body of Christ. He wrote: 'The lay state should be considered as a sacred dignity; their baptism has made of them "a people of God, a royal priesthood". . . . As Christians having received baptism and the gift of the Holy Spirit through anointing, which may be conceived as a sort of ordination to the calling of Christians, the laity also are charismatic.'[3] Bulgakov's view of the laity is prophetic and enlightening as it anticipates the teaching of Vatican II in *Lumen Gentium*:

> The baptized, by regeneration and the anointing of the Holy Spirit, are consecrated as a spiritual house and a holy priesthood. . . . Though they differ from one another in essence and not only in degree, the common priesthood of the faithful and the ministerial or hierarchical priesthood are nonetheless interrelated: each of them in its own special way is a participation in the one priesthood of Christ.[4]

Bulgakov placed great importance on episcopal authority, but he had a misconception of Roman Catholic teaching on papal authority. He claimed that 'The pretension of the Pope to be the voice of the truth destroys the unity of the Church; it puts the Pope in the

1. Ibid., pp. 120–1.
2. Ibid., p. 122.
3. Ibid., p. 125.
4. Dogmatic Constitution on the Church – *Lumen Gentium* (1964), http://www.vatican.va/archive/hist_councils/ii_vatican_council/documents/vat-ii_const_19641121_lumen-gentium_en.html, no. 10.

place of the Church.'[1] Roman Catholics, however, see the pope as
a symbol of their unity. The pope does not replace the church, but
teaches through the magisterium, which also listens to the voice of
the faithful, to the *sensus fidelium*:

> In matters of faith the baptised cannot be passive. They have
> received the Spirit and are endowed as members of the body of
> the Lord with gifts and charisms 'for the renewal and building
> up of the Church', so the magisterium has to be attentive to the
> sensus fidelium, the living voice of the people of God. . . . The
> sensus fidelium can be an important factor in the development
> of doctrine, and it follows that the magisterium needs means by
> which to consult the faithful.[2]

Bulgakov's understanding of papal teaching was probably prevalent
in the Orthodox Church at that time, and the Roman Catholic
Church was still in the process of clarifying its understanding of papal
infallibility. His perception of Roman Catholicism was based on the
*Ultramontane* school, which he considered typical of the Western
Church.[3] As a result, he saw papal infallibility as a heresy, a spiritual
power to dominate others.

For Bulkagov, 'the soul of Orthodoxy is *sobornost*' – coming
together united in love. Opposed to the monarchical conception
of the church and authoritarianism, *sobornost* means a 'harmonious
sharing of authority'.[4] *Sobornost* suggests catholicity and ecumenicity,
where ideas are distinct but connected. It embraces people from all
over the world. Bulgakov claimed that Roman Catholics in the West
tend to see catholicity in quantitative terms, but in the East they
emphasize the qualitative aspect. Thus, each member of the church is

---

1. Bulgakov, *op. cit.*, p. 125.
2. International Theological Commission (2014), '*Sensus fidei* in the life of
   the Church', http://www.vatican.va/roman_curia/congregations/cfaith/
   cti_documents/rc_cti_20140610_sensus-fidei_en.html, no. 74.
3. 'Ultramontanism (from Medieval Latin ultramontanus, "beyond the
   mountains"), in Roman Catholicism, a strong emphasis on papal
   authority and on centralization of the church. The word identified
   those northern European members of the church who regularly
   looked southward beyond the Alps (that is, to the popes of Rome)
   for guidance.' *Encyclopaedia Britannica*, http://global.britannica.com/
   EBchecked/topic/613447/Ultramontanism. See Clarence Augustus
   Manning (1929), 'Bulgakov and the Orthodox Church'. *Anglican
   Theological Review* 11, no. 4 (April), 332–41.
4. Bulgakov, 'The Orthodox Church', p. 127.

'catholic' to the extent that he or she lives in union with the 'church invisible and in the truth'. This includes those who remain faithful to the truth in the midst of secular society. Catholicity also refers to the mystical or 'metaphysical depth of the Church'.[1] It has nothing to do with outward expansion because catholicity, in Bulgakov's opinion, has neither physical nor empirical traits. Under the guidance of the Holy Spirit, catholicity also means keeping in contact with the physical world and with the visible church.

Bulgakov suggested two different ways in which the unity of the churches might be realized: by Orthodox conciliarity, *sobornost*, or by submission to papal authority as promoted by Roman Catholicism. But submission to papal authority, he insisted, would make us not Roman Catholics, but papists. He noted that papalism has become unpopular and claimed that 'Catholicism is something greater than papalism.'[2]

Supporting catholicity in all its riches, Bulgakov had a different understanding of leadership and authority to Roman Catholics. He saw the hierarchy as a source of unity and believed it was chosen based on the teaching of the apostles. The highest authority is the General Council, the gathering of various churches, to consider matters related to the faith and to manifest their unity. Unlike with Roman Catholics, this unity does not involve having an external head of the church, like the pope. For Bulgakov, this unity was not an 'organization of power but a unity of life'.[3] He thus regarded the primacy of authority of the Roman pontiff as useless and harmful. The original unity lies in the apostles as a group, not just in Peter alone. Hence General Councils, though not considered infallible (in contrast to the pope), represent the highest decision-making body in the Orthodox Church. Bulgakov regarded this as the 'palladium of Orthodox liberty'.[4]

Furthermore, Eastern Christianity is more contemplative or mystical in its outlook, Bulgakov claims, while Western Christianity is more practical. Eastern Christianity regards John as its first apostle, while Peter heads the Roman Catholic Church and Paul the Protestant Church. Peter asked if two swords were enough and was concerned with the organization of the church; John, however, wished to rest on Jesus' breast. He was the one who received the Revelation on Patmos.[5] As for Paul, he preferred writing letters to the Christian communities.

---

1. Ibid., p. 128.
2. Ibid., p. 137.
3. Manning, *op. cit.*, 336.
4. Bulgakov, *op. cit.*, p. 129.
5. Ibid., p. 131.

In its monastic life, Eastern Christianity is basically contemplative and does not have the variety of orders that are found in the Roman Catholic Church. The Orthodox Church does not have active religious orders like the Jesuits or mendicant orders like the Franciscans and the Dominicans. Eastern monastic life emphasizes 'abandonment of the world for the service of prayer and ascetic practices, rather than fighting in the world'.[1] Bulgakov was particularly critical of the militant spirituality of the Society of Jesus.

Orthodoxy possesses the vision of 'ideal spiritual beauty', which is more aesthetic than ethical, a spiritual ideal that goes beyond good and evil. The ideal foundation of Orthodoxy is expressed not in ethics, but in 'religious sensibility.' Bulgakov admitted that such vision of spiritual beauty can only be gained by a few privileged people. Sometimes this 'spiritual aestheticism' can degenerate into indifference towards ethics and the discipline of the will.[2] Thus, he emphasized the need in Orthodoxy for humility, simplicity, and sincerity, qualities that are different from the proselytizing and domineering spirit of the Western Christian churches.

Although the Orthodox Church emphasizes religious sensibility, it is not indifferent to practical morality and philanthropy. Bulgakov believed that churches could organize joint ventures to alleviate poverty, injustice, and exploitation. As such ventures do not touch on doctrinal issues but work for the common good, they would be welcomed by most Christians. At a deeper level, Western Christianity can learn from the Eastern Church the contemplative dimension of its spiritual life and the East can learn from the West its organizational skills.[3]

Supporting the doctrine of apokatastasis, the final restoration of all people to God, a teaching advocated by Origen and Gregory of Nyssa, Bulgakov insisted that all baptized Christians are Orthodox in some ways. Orthodoxy has two circles, the outer circle and the inner circle, the court of the temple and the holies of holies. Unlike

---

1. Ibid., p. 132. Regarding the experience of faith, von Balthasar asserted that John's vision of Jesus is in itself contemplative, whereas Peter's eyewitness account is purely historical. There is not opposition between the bodily and spiritual sense since, from the beginning, John had heard, seen and touched the Word of Life with his physical senses. Because of this profound experience, John assumed that in love everything is possible. Von Balthasar, *The Glory of the Lord*, p. 358.
2. Ibid., p. 132.
3. Ibid., p. 133.

Roman Catholicism, Orthodoxy does not desire submission, but wishes to educate people. In other words, Orthodoxy does not insist on external submission, in contrast to the Roman Catholic Church, which demands submission to papal authority as the condition for reunion. Such submission is only necessary for the purpose of settling canonical matters.[1] For Bulgakov, the ideal reunion would have been for all Christian communities to embrace Orthodoxy. This would mean all the churches drawing together based on the 'maximum of their common heritage' – 'this maximum is Orthodoxy.'[2] The rationale for this is that the Orthodox Church is the true church and not merely one of the historical confessions. Bulgakov was convinced that the Spirit of God would lead people towards Orthodoxy because it possesses the truth and thus, the Orthodox Church does not need to proselytize.

Bulgakov observed that there is a modern tendency to restore tradition, which will eventually lead all Christian churches back to Orthodoxy. He found the Anglican or Episcopalian Churches in England and the United States to be making great progress in this direction. This return to the plenitude of tradition, he believed, would also liberate Roman Catholicism from its juridical excess.[3] Hopeful that in the near future the unity of East and West would be achieved, he pointed out that:

> [T]he most characteristic fact for the Church is the unbreakable union of the divine and human life, the fusion of form and content, without removal or dissolution of the human essence, endowed with a penetrability for the transformation of grace. Thus the Church is a union of the superworldly (transcendental) and the worldly (immanent) being. Such a unity is a mystery, surpassing the intelligence, and therefore the life of the Church is a mystery of the faith which is revealed only in the life experience of its members.[4]

This idea of union is an extension of the idea of the Incarnation where the divine become human. The two aspects, though distinct, always remain as one. In other words, in the church there exists both human and divine Sophia, which can only be perceived in faith.

1. Ibid., p. 135.
2. Ibid., p. 136.
3. Ibid., p. 138.
4. Quoted in Manning, 'Bulgakov and the Orthodox Church', 334.

In spite of his attack on the papacy, Bulgakov had something positive to say about the Roman Catholic Church:

It may well be said that the monarchy of the Vatican is a sort of a shell, beneath which is the living body of the Church. . . . In spite of the triumph of authority in any Christian confession, the true mind of the ecumenical Church continues to live in the depths and naturally tends to another unity – an inner unity. This is witnessed by all the living holiness so plentifully manifested in Catholicism, not by virtue of but in spite of papalism.[1]

In the concluding section we will see that Bulgakov was in fact for a short time attracted to Roman Catholicism, which he regarded as a temptation.

### Roman Catholicism

Sergius Bulgakov's life was marked by many interesting and complex stages. First he was attracted to theoretical Marxism and then he moved on to Kantian philosophy and German idealism, before returning to the faith of his childhood by entering the Orthodox priesthood. Even when he had embraced Orthodox Christianity, he remained critical and objective in his approach to the faith. It was said that he believed like a child, but tested his faith with the critical judgement of a philosopher and theologian.[2] He admitted that he had entertained thoughts of joining the Roman communion:

At that time there lived in Yalta a certain Lithuanian priest, persecuted by the Poles, a good Catholic, a convinced and enlightened papist, who had received his theological training in Rome. He provided me with the books I needed. . . . Under the impression of what was happening to the church in Russia and of my own studies I began inwardly, silently, and unbeknown to anyone, to incline more and more towards Catholicism. . . . I do not repent of my infatuation with Catholicism.[3]

1. Bulgakov, 'The Orthodox Church', p. 137.
2. Bulgakov (1959, republished 2008), 'The Vatican dogma', http://www. orthodoxchristianity.net/index.php?option=com_content&view=artic le&catid=14:articles&id=39:the-vatican-dogma. See also Winston F. Crum (1983), 'Sergius N. Bulgakov: from Marxism to sophiology'. *St Vladimir's Theological Quarterly* 27, no. 1 (January), 3–25.
3. Bulgakov, *op. cit.*

Nonetheless, he was very critical of the papacy, as revealed in his essays 'Peter and John, the Two Chief Apostles' and 'The Vatican Dogma'. His critical position in these works led people to think that he was against Roman Catholicism, which he denied unequivocally. In fact, he had great respect for Western Christianity and was ecumenical in his outlook. At the same time, he was realistic enough to realize that unity would not come soon because of the deep-seated psychological and historical wounds that have not been healed. He believed that only love is capable of closing the chasm between the two churches.[1]

According to Bulgakov, the chief obstacle to union between the Roman Catholic and the Orthodox Church is the Vatican dogma of papal infallibility. He acknowledged that Vatican I was of great significance to Roman Catholicism. He admired its immense power of discipline and organization, but lamented its lack of spiritual freedom. Although he insisted that Orthodoxy could not accept the papacy because it is a heresy, Bulgakov also admitted that the Orthodox Church can and should recognize the primacy of the Roman see. Bulgakov was hopeful that one day the two churches would be united because what is impossible to human beings is possible to God. All we need to do is to trust in providence, which directs us and governs the destiny of the church.

---

1.  Ibid.

# Chapter 6
# Vladimir Lossky

Vladimir Lossky was born on 8 June 1903 in Göttingen, Germany, and educated in St Petersburg, Prague, and Paris. It was in Paris that he spent most of his life, teaching, writing, and maintaining contact with the intellectual circles of Western Europe. Well acquainted with philosophy and the spirituality of the Church Fathers, Lossky was deeply rooted in the Orthodox tradition. In spite of his criticism of Western theology, he was an ecumenist interested in dialogue with other Christians. In Paris, he became a disciple of the Roman Catholic philosopher Étienne Gilson, who wrote a preface for his posthumously published thesis on the German mystic Meister Eckhart. Lossky's theological works were written in French, at the request of his Roman Catholic, Anglican, and other Protestant Church friends, in order to promote dialogue. According to his son, Nicholas, Vladimir Lossky would not tolerate the 'anti-ecumenism, anti-Semitism and above all crass anti-Catholicism' of some of his fellow Orthodox colleagues. In fact, he had very close ties with Roman Catholic theologians, such as Yves Congar, Jean Daniélou, Henri de Lubac, and others who were *periti* (experts) at the Second Vatican Council. These thinkers 'were his friends, after theological jousts conducted in the purest spirit of the mediaeval tournament, where the "adversaries" profoundly respected one another and always displayed perfect intellectual honesty.'[1] Sadly, Lossky died in Paris on 7 February 1958, before the start of the Council.

In his lifetime, Lossky published only one book, *The Mystical Theology of the Eastern Church* (1944). This work was the fruit of his lifetime theological reflection in which he participated deeply in the interior life of the Orthodox Church. Lossky was a penetrating scholar and also a devout Orthodox Christian who viewed Christian

---

1. Nicholas Lossky (1999), 'Theology and spirituality in the work of Vladimir Lossky'. *Ecumenical Review* 51, no. 3 (July), 293.

truth from the aspect of grace with emphasis on the doctrine of the Trinity. Steeped in the writings of the Greek Fathers, such as Pseudo-Dionysius and Gregory Palamas, Lossky stressed the apophatic character of Eastern theology. This chapter discusses some aspects of this negative theology relating to the knowledge of God, the Trinity, and divine energies. Although Lossky considered the Eastern method of divine contemplation superior to that of the West, this chapter attempts to show that within Roman Catholicism, apophaticism is also an important theme in the writings of Étienne Gilson, Meister Eckhart, and Henri de Lubac. We will begin with Lossky's understanding of theology in the Eastern tradition.

### Mystical Theology

Theology, Lossky asserted, is mystical to the extent that it reveals divine mystery. But mysticism is considered inaccessible to our understanding and therefore opposed to theology, which is supposed to be 'rational' in the Western tradition. Mysticism is viewed as an 'unutterable mystery', a 'hidden depth'; it is an experience to be lived rather than a subject to be studied. As an experience, mysticism goes beyond our mental perceptions. Combining the two, Lossky spoke of mystical theology as 'a spirituality which expresses a doctrinal attitude'.[1] He believed that if mysticism was separated from theology, religion would be static and lacking in dynamism, which is the core experience of the mystics. Lossky was also against the idea that mystical experience is reserved for a few privileged souls who have direct access to divine truth while the rest of humankind must rest content with blind obedience to the church's teachings. Such exclusive mentality has the tendency to set up a false dichotomy between mystics and theologians, saints and prelates, prophets and priests.

In the Eastern tradition, there has never been a sharp division between mysticism and theology, between personal experience of God and the doctrines taught by the church. The reason is that 'none of the mysteries of the most secret wisdom of God ought to appear alien or altogether transcendent to us, but in all humility we must apply our spirit to the contemplation of divine things.'[2] In other words, the dogmas of the church must be seen as revealed truths

---

1. Vladimir Lossky (1973), *The Mystical Theology of the Eastern Church*. Cambridge: James Clarke & Co., p. 7.
2. Quoted in V. Lossky, ibid., p. 8.

to be lived and we should try not so much to understand them as to experience them in their mystery. This means that theology and mysticism must support one another, because one is not complete without the other: 'If the mystical experience is a personal working out of the content of the common faith, theology is an expression, for the profit of all, of that which can be experienced by everyone.'[1]

In the West, there was a gradual separation between mysticism and theology, which influential French philosopher Henri Bergson observed. This kind of separation leads to two types of morality and religion, one static and the other dynamic. First, there is 'closed morality', which is common in civic societies; secondly, there is 'open morality', which transcends social groups, and is exemplified in the lives of saints. Closed morality is endorsed in 'static religion', and open morality is the product of 'dynamic religion', which Bergson identified with mysticism. But there is no connection between closed and open moralities and religions as each of them is distinctive, depending on their specific human constitutions and experiences.[2] More importantly, Bergson considered mysticism to be the essential element in dynamic religions:

> In our eyes, the ultimate end of mysticism is the establishment of a contact, consequently of a partial coincidence, with the creative effort which life itself manifests. This effort is of God, if it is not God himself. The great mystic is to be conceived as an individual being capable of transcending the limitations imposed on the species by its material nature, thus continuing to extend the divine action.[3]

This view is typical of Western spirituality – it tends to be individualistic. But for Lossky, mysticism and theology must be experienced and worked out within the context of the church. This ecclesial aspect is fundamental because, according to Lossky, when mysticism and theology are separated from the guidance of the church, our personal experience will be distorted by falsehood and uncertainty. Without ecclesiastical support, our spiritual experience will lack objectivity, and mysticism may be reduced to superstition. At the same time, the church would be static, lacking in dynamism

1.  Ibid., pp. 9–10.
2.  J. Deotis Roberts (1964), 'Bergson as a metaphysical, epistemological, and religious thinker'. *Journal of Religious Thought* 20, no. 2 (January), 110–11.
3.  Quoted in ibid., 113.

and creativity, if there was no inner and profound experience of divine truth. In other words, 'no Christian mysticism without theology . . . no theology without mysticism'. It is no wonder that in the Eastern Church, the three most important theologians are St John the Evangelist, St Gregory Nazianzen, and St Simeon – theologians who were also mystics. Mysticism is thus the 'perfecting and crown of all theology: as theology *par excellence*'.[1]

As Eastern theology is mystical, it transcends knowledge; it is a means towards union with God or deification: 'God became man that men might become gods' (St Athanasius). It was through its battles through the centuries against the various heresies that the church formulated its doctrines. For example, in its struggles against the Gnostics, the church stressed the deification of humankind; in its struggles against the Arians, the church affirmed that Jesus is truly God; in its condemnation of Nestorians, the church removed the wall that separated God from humankind; against the Apollinarians and Monophysites, the church affirmed the true humanity of Jesus Christ; and against the Monothelites, the church affirmed the union of divine and human wills for the salvation of humankind. Against the iconoclastic controversy, the church affirmed the possibility of expressing divine realities through a variety of media.[2] In all these conflicts, the church strived to protect its mystical core, which is expressed by its dogmas. The main objective of church doctrines is to help Christians achieve union with God, which is possible for all Christians and is not reserved for a few privileged individuals.

As mentioned earlier, Lossky insisted that spirituality and dogma, mysticism and theology cannot be separated in the life of the church. Therefore, it is important, indeed necessary, for Christians to practise their faith within the ecclesial context of Orthodoxy. Lossky lamented that the Eastern Church remains little understood: even the distinguished Roman Catholic theologian Yves Congar claimed that 'the East settled down in practice, and to some extent in theory, to a principle of unity which was political, non-religious, and not truly universal.'[3] Congar identified the non-theological factors that led to the schism between East and West in 1054, which include, among others, the removal of the capital from Rome to Constantinople and the political conflict between the Eastern Patriarchate and Rome. Iakovos, Metropolitan of Germany, confirmed that Congar's

1. V. Lossky, *op. cit.*, p. 9.
2. Ibid., p. 10.
3. Ibid., p. 14.

approach to Eastern Orthodoxy was 'friendly, objective and constructive. Although Congar uses the pattern of Western theology in his ecclesiology, he appreciates Eastern spirituality and mystical experience and wants his Church to grasp it.'[1]

To most Westerners, the Orthodox Church is made up of a federation of national churches and its political principle is based on the 'state-church'. Lossky said that such a generalization fails to take into account the canonical foundation and history of the Eastern Church. In fact, the Orthodox Church regards as heresy the view that the unity of local churches is based on political and cultural principles. This heresy is known as 'philetism'.[2] It is considered heretical because Orthodoxy is universal, present in many different cultures and not confined to a particular cultural form. Lossky asserted, 'the forms are different: the faith is one.'[3] In other words, the Orthodox Church has never considered any national culture as specifically Orthodox and hence it is able to spread throughout Russia, Asia, and North America, beyond the confines of its origin.

The Orthodox Church has very little biographical information on the experience of its great mystics. In contrast to the West, there is little record of autographical information that deals with the interior life such as those recorded in the lives of saints like Henry Suso and St Thérèse of Lisieux. In the East, mystical union with God is considered a secret and is not to be published, unless it is for the edification of others or as moral teaching.[4] The Eastern Church is always cautious of individual mysticism that lacks ecclesial support or guidance. It is no surprise that most of its mystics are monks or patriarchs.

Regarding East and West, Congar said, 'We have become *different men*. We have the same God but before him we are different men, unable to agree as to the nature of our relationship with him.' East and West have a different understanding of sanctity. The East emphasizes the importance of church dogma, which shapes a person's response to faith. Lossky wrote: 'For the inner experience of the Christian develops within the circle delineated by the teaching of the Church: within the dogmatic framework which moulds his person.'[5] This

1. Iakovos, Abp of the Greek Orthodox Archdiocese of North and South America (1970), 'Ecclesiology of Yves Congar: an Orthodox evaluation'. *Greek Orthodox Theological Review* 15, no. 1 (March), 103.
2. V. Lossky, *The Mystical Theology of the Eastern Church*, p.15.
3. Ibid., p. 17.
4. Ibid., p. 20.
5. Ibid., p. 21.

suggests that political or cultural factors are secondary to religious doctrines in moulding a person's faith. According to Lossky, there is a strong link between spirituality and dogma in the Eastern tradition. Hence, the difference between Eastern and Western spiritualities lies primarily in its dogmatic understanding.

Lossky's purpose in writing this work, *The Mystical Theology of the Eastern Church* (1973), was to promote mutual understanding between East and West. While remaining loyal to the dogmatic position of the East, Lossky was willing to learn from the West in order to understand on which points they differed from one another; he felt confronting differences rather than ignoring them was a better path towards unity. Like Karl Barth, Lossky believed that the union of churches is not constructed but discovered.[1] There is indeed a common heritage between the East and the West that needs to be rediscovered.

## Knowledge of God

There are two ways to practise theology, according to the Greek Father Dionysius: the cataphatic way (positive theology); and the apophatic way (negative theology). The cataphatic way affirms what we know about God and the apophatic way denies such positive knowledge. The first way is considered imperfect because our knowledge of God will always fall short of reality. The second way is considered perfect because it is true that we do not know what God is as his nature is unknowable. All knowledge has as its object 'that which is', but God is beyond all that is. Lossky put it this way: 'It is by *unknowing* that one may know Him who is above every possible object of knowledge. Proceeding by negations one ascends from the inferior degrees of being to the highest, by progressively setting aside all that can be known, in order to draw near to the Unknown in the darkness of absolute ignorance.'[2] In other words, we come to know God by ridding ourselves of our preconceived notions of him.

St Thomas Aquinas sought to synthesize these two opposed ways of knowing God by making negative theology a corrective to positive theology. He taught that we must deny the manner in which we understand God's divine nature. For example, we say that God is perfect or good, but we must be aware that God is such not in the same way that human beings can be perfect or good. According to Aquinas:

1. Ibid., p. 22.
2. Ibid., p. 25.

Since all things are comprised in the Godhead simply and without limit, it is fitting that he should be praised and named on account of them all. Simply because the perfections which are in creatures by reason of various forms are ascribed to God in reference to his simple essence: *without limit,* because no perfection found in creatures is equal to the divine essence, so as to enable the mind under the head of that perfection to define God as he is in himself.[1]

Critical of such scholastic method, Lossky questioned how far these 'philosophical gymnastics' of Aquinas correspond to the ideas of Dionysius. He believed that Dionysius favoured apophatic theology over affirmative theology. But for Aquinas, the two methods had equal merits. Insisting that apophaticism is the theological tradition in the Eastern Church, Lossky was determined to prove its superiority to Western positive theology. He provided the example of Dionysius, who taught us that it is necessary to renounce sense and reason so that we will be able 'to attain in perfect ignorance to union with Him who transcends all being and all knowledge'.[2] Dionysius regarded this as a purification of all thoughts, impure as well as pure, because even heavenly sounds and words can be an obstacle to union with God. This purification allows us to penetrate into the darkness wherein God dwells.

## 'Dark Night of the Soul'

Dionysius' divine darkness reminds us of St John of the Cross' *Dark Night of the Soul*: 'In darkness, and secure, by the secret ladder, disguised, – ah, the sheer grace! – in darkness and concealment, my house being now all stilled.'[3] In this work, John of the Cross narrates the journey of his soul to union with God as 'The Dark Night' because darkness represents the struggles and hardships that the soul has to experience in order to be detached from the world. It is a painful experience that people have to endure in order to reach spiritual maturity. According to Dionysius, this divine darkness is the home of God; for John of the Cross, it is the route that will bring us to mystical union with God.

1. Thomas Aquinas, *Quaestiones Disputatae de Potentia Dei*, Q. VII, Article V: 'Do These Terms Signify the Divine Essence?', http://dhspriory.org/thomas/QDdePotentia.htm.
2. V. Lossky, *The Mystical Theology of the Eastern Church*, p. 27.
3. St John of the Cross, *The Dark Night*, 'Stanzas of the Soul', https://www.ewtn.com/library/SOURCES/DARK-JC.TXT., nos. 73, 225.

Dionysius compared this journey to Moses' ascent to Mount Sinai to meet God. First, Moses purified himself from all that is unclean. Only when he was able to separate himself from the world could he reach the divine heights. Moses contemplated not God, who is invisible, but the place where God is. Lossky wrote:

> Moses is freed from the things that see and are seen: he passes into the truly mystical darkness of ignorance, where he shuts his eyes to all scientific apprehensions, and reaches what is entirely untouched and unseen, belonging not to himself and not to another, but wholly to Him who is above all. He is united to the best of his powers with the unknowing quiescence of all knowledge, and by that very unknowing he knows what surpasses understanding.[1]

According to Lossky, the apophatic way helps one to reach God by purifying the intellect of mental concepts – knowledge that is an obstacle has to give way to experience and in this case, to union with God. He regarded cataphatic theology as 'a descent from the superior degrees of being to the inferior' and apophatic theology as 'an ascent towards the divine incomprehensibility'.[2] Eventually, we must go beyond affirmation or negation, because God is wholly apart from all things.

Although there is similarity between Dionysian ecstasy and the Sixth Ennead of Plotinus on reaching the One, Lossky insisted that they are not the same. Dionysius was a Christian mystic and Plotinus was a Neo-platonist. The god of Plotinus is not incomprehensible by nature, but the God of Dionysius is. He 'makes darkness his secret place' and he is not the 'primordial God-Unity of the Neo-platonists'. Lossky claimed, 'the ecstasy of Dionysius is a going forth from being as such. That of Plotinus is rather a reduction of being to absolute simplicity.' Nonetheless, Dionysius, influenced by Neo-platonism, held that God is 'neither One, nor Unity.' Thus if the God of Revelation is not to be equated with the god of the philosophers, it is because of His 'fundamental unknowability' that distinguishes between the two basic conceptions.[3]

Defending the Church Fathers, Lossky claimed that the influence of Platonic philosophy on them is limited to external resemblances and superficial similarities. It did not form the basis of their

1.  V. Lossky, *op. cit.*, p. 28.
2.  Ibid.
3.  Ibid., pp. 30–1.

teachings as they were using Greek thought, which was prevalent at that time. Critical of the teaching of Origen, who is regarded as a religious philosopher rather than as a mystical theologian, Lossky cautioned against replacing the unfathomable nature of God with philosophical concepts. Regarding the relationship between Greek philosophy and Christianity, Lossky was influenced by the Roman Catholic philosopher Étienne Gilson.

Gilson insisted that the god of Plotinus is not a Christian God, nor is the world of Plotinus a Christian world, because Plotinus' universe is typically Greek, where God is neither the supreme reality nor the 'ultimate principle of intelligibility'. The first cause does not coincide with the philosophy of the One or the philosophy of being. The 'One' of Plotinus must necessarily beget that which has multiplicity: '[W]hile there is a radical difference of nature between the One, or Good, and all that which, because it is not the One, is multiple, there are but differences of degrees between all that which is not the One, and yet is, or exists.'[1]

Having the intellect or the soul, we also belong to the same metaphysical class, but in the Christian metaphysics of being, God is the Supreme Being who can only beget not another god, but persons. The Orthodox idea of deification was foreign to Gilson because only God 'who is' can enjoy his own fullness of perfection without the need to have other persons or things around him.[2] Thus human beings are radically different from God and might not have existed at all if God did not will it. They are finite and limited, and have their existence only because of God's freedom to grant them life. Gilson wrote:

> Such is, in fact, the Christian world of Saint Augustine. On the one side, God, one in the Trinity of a single, self-existing substance; on the other side, all that which, because it has but a received existence, is not God. Unlike the Plotinian dividing line which we have seen running between the One and all that is begotten by the One, the Christian dividing line runs between God, including his own begotten Word, and all that is created by God.[3]

As creatures, human beings are excluded from the divine order; we are not gods because between 'Him who is' and ourselves, there is a huge metaphysical gap that separates us. Except through divine will

---

1. Étienne Gilson (2002), *God and Philosophy*. New Haven: Yale Nota Bene, p. 51.
2. Ibid., p. 52.
3. Ibid., p. 53.

and pleasure, nothing can bridge the gap between human beings and God. Aware of such discrepancy between the divine and humankind, St Augustine knew that human reason is not able to reach the transcendent God whose 'pure act of existence' is vastly different from our 'borrowed existence'.[1] As such, even the philosophical methods of Plato and Plotinus were ineffective in assisting Augustine to contemplate the divine.[2]

## *Church Fathers*

Reason enables us to form concepts, and when we examine an object, we form concepts through such analysis. However, such analysis cannot exhaust the content of the object of perception. Lossky claimed that there will always be 'irrational residue' that escapes our examination and that it is the 'unknowable depth of things' that constitutes their real essence. Hence concepts conceal rather than reveal the essence of things. St Gregory of Nyssa posited that 'every concept relative to God is a *simulacrum*, a false likeness, an idol.'[3] This means that our understanding of God, the concept that we form regarding divinity, is essentially an idol. We can only stand in awe when we think of God – 'the wonder which seizes the soul when it thinks of God'. St Gregory Nazianzen said, 'It is difficult to conceive God, but to define Him in words is impossible.'[4]

As we can see, apophatic theology is highly regarded in the writings of the Church Fathers such as Gregory of Nyssa, Gregory Nazianzen, Clement of Alexandria, and John Damascene. This quotation from the fourteenth-century Byzantine theologian St Gregory Palamas sums up beautifully the meaning of apophaticism:

> The super-essential nature of God is not a subject for speech or thought or even contemplation, for it is far removed from all that exists and more than unknowable, being founded upon the uncircumscribed might of the celestial spirits – incomprehensible and ineffable to all for ever. There is no name whereby it can be named, neither in this age nor in the age to come, nor word found in the soul and uttered by the tongue, nor contact whether sensible or intellectual, nor yet any image which may

1. Ibid., p. 54.
2. Ibid., p. 55.
3. V. Lossky, *The Mystical Theology of the Eastern Church*, p. 33.
4. Ibid., p. 34.

afford any knowledge of its subject, if this be not that perfect incomprehensibility which one acknowledges in denying all that can be named. None can properly name its essence or nature if he be truly seeking the truth that is above all truth.[1]

Further, Lossky proposed that this radical form of apophaticism found in the Orthodox tradition is also an ecstatic quest that includes an inner purification. This purification means that we need to get rid of things that prevent us from reaching God – things that conceal the divine non-being as such. This includes a renunciation of things visible and created that obstruct our ascent to God. Above all, it is a question of union with God, which in Lossky's opinion will lead to deification or becoming a 'new person'. A theologian is someone who draws near to God, to be united with him: 'The way of the knowledge of God is necessarily the way of deification.'[2]

Lossky went as far as claiming that negative theology conforms to the truth and therefore, all true theology is apophatic. He believed that in cataphatic or positive theology, there is the danger of making our human concept into an idol of God. To avoid this, we must shift from positive to negative theology, where our speculation gives way to contemplation. This involves getting rid of concepts that shackle the spirit. Lossky claimed that 'the apophatic disposition reveals boundless horizons of contemplation at each step of positive theology.'[3] Ultimately, it is the experience of God, not knowledge, that matters. Christianity is not so much a philosophy for speculation as a communion with the living God – the Trinity.

## Trinity

Apophaticism in Eastern theology is not a kind of impersonal mysticism. In fact, the aim of negative theology is to lead one towards the Trinity. Even before the existence of the world, God has always been in Trinity – the Father, Son, and Holy Spirit. Critical of nineteenth-century German philosophy that uses phrases like 'procession of the persons', 'dialectic of the three persons', 'tragedy in the Absolute', Lossky emphasized that such language is inadequate and deficient to express the 'primordial mystery of revelation'.[4]

---

1. Ibid., p. 37.
2. Ibid., p. 39.
3. Ibid., p. 40.
4. Ibid., p. 45.

Apophatic theology is called into service to get rid of these human categories so that we can ascend towards the contemplation of the divine. The church has always strongly defended the mystery of the Trinity against various heresies; for example Sabellianism, which viewed the Trinity as three modes of manifestation, and Arianism, which divided the Trinity into three distinct beings.

Using the term *homooúsios* (ομοούσιος), Lossky pointed out that the church emphasizes the 'consubstantiality of the Three, the mysterious identity of the monad and of the triad; identity of the one nature and distinction of the three hypostases'.[1] The expression *homooúsios* is borrowed from Plotinus, and thus we must be aware of its limitation in explaining Christian truth, Lossky warned. In fact, to understand the Trinity, we need to undergo a change of heart or repentance, like Job, who, as a penitent, found himself face to face with God: 'I had heard of you by the hearing of the ear, but now my eye sees you; therefore I despise myself, and repent in dust and ashes' (Job 42:5–6). The mystery of the Trinity is accessible only if we are able to transcend human wisdom into the wisdom of God, which is foolishness to the Greeks.[2] This includes purifying Hellenistic ideas through Christian apophaticism and transforming rational thought into contemplation of the divine. Finding the right terms to express the unity and distinction within the Godhead is part of the process of purifying.

Due to their consubstantiality, Lossky argued that the only way to understand the relationship in the Trinity is through negation – 'that the Father is neither the Son nor the Holy Spirit; that the Son is neither the Father nor the Spirit; that the Holy Spirit is neither the Father nor the Son'.[3] Thus we understand their relation in terms of differences, but we are uncertain how this divine generation procession came about. In the West, they speak of the procession of the Holy Spirit – the Holy Spirit proceeds from the Father and the Son (*filioque*) – the principle that was the main cause of the split between East and West. The East opposed the *filioque* because it seems to weaken the monarchy of the Father: '[E]ither one is forced to destroy the unity by acknowledging two principles of God-head, or one must ground the unity primarily on the common nature, which thus overshadows the persons and transform them into relations within the unity of the essence.'[4] Further, Lossky argued

1.  Ibid., p. 49.
2.  Ibid., p. 50.
3.  Ibid., p. 54.
4.  Ibid., p. 58.

that the East has always supported the apophatic character of the procession of the Holy Spirit from the Father against 'a more rational doctrine' that makes the Father and the Son 'a common principle of the Holy Spirit'.[1] The *filioque* formula places their common nature above the persons.

As the mystery of the trinitarian God is incomprehensible, Lossky believed that this incomprehensibility could only be overcome with the help of apophatic theology. In fact, 'apophaticism finds its fulfilment in the revelation of the Holy Trinity as primordial fact, ultimate reality, first datum which cannot be deduced, explained or discovered by way of any other truth; for there is nothing which is prior to it.'[2] Apophatic thought, in denying all concepts or idea of divinity, finds its support only in God alone whose mystery is revealed in the Trinity.

In the Eastern Church, according to Lossky, God is always presented in the concrete, the God of Abraham, of Isaac and of Jacob, or the God of Jesus Christ. It is always the Trinitarian God – the Father, Son, and the Holy Spirit. The Western Church, on the other hand, tends to stress their common nature, thus developing a philosophy of essence. Hence, in the West, the Christian faith stresses personal relationship with Jesus Christ, and not so much with the Trinity. Christian life thus becomes Christocentric, with emphasis on the Incarnate Word. This emphasis, Lossky remarked, has become their 'anchor of salvation'. Critical of the doctrinal position of the Western Church, he thought that its emphasis on nature rather than persons would lead to a mysticism of 'the divine abyss' found in the writings of Meister Eckhart.[3] The mysticism in Eckhart's writings is a kind of impersonal apophaticism influenced by Neo-platonism, in Lossky's opinion.

## Meister Eckhart (c. 1260–c. 1327)

A German Dominican priest, Meister Eckhart was an immensely popular preacher in his own time. His writings form an important part of the foundation of Western mystical tradition. Although condemned by the Roman Catholic Church as heretical during his time, Eckhart's synthesis of Greek thought and Christian doctrines has now been widely accepted. In fact, today he is regarded as a trusted exponent of

1. Ibid., p. 62.
2. Ibid., p. 64.
3. Ibid., p. 65.

Christian mysticism and philosophical theology. Eckhart's mysticism had a great influence on thinkers like Hegel and Heidegger, which confirms his important position in European intellectual life.[1]

The controlling principle of Eckhart's theology is the concept of unicity or oneness, which he borrowed from the Greek Platonist, Plotinus. For Plotinus, redemption involves the ascent of the mind away from the multiplicity of this world to the primal oneness that can be achieved through an ecstasy of the mind. Using this idea, Eckhart attempted to construct a Christian metaphysics of the One within the framework of the Trinity and the Incarnation. For Eckhart, the notion of oneness comes close to capturing the essence of God without defining him with concepts that reveal more about our nature. Believing that names and concepts belong to the realm of created things, Eckhart placed the unity of God above all things, even at the expense of the multiplicity of God in the Trinity. This arose from his understanding that God is essentially 'fertile' and dynamic.[2] Thus we see in Eckhart's writings a bold attempt to reconcile Neo-platonic philosophy with Christian doctrines. Lossky, however, considered such an attempt 'a paradoxical circuit [by which] we return through Christianity to the mysticism of the Neo-platonists'.[3] But we shall see that Eckhart's theology of detachment comes close to the Orthodox understanding of deification.

Extolling detachment above any love, Eckhart believed that this is the one virtue that helps us to be united with God. A person's eternal happiness depends on God and himself becoming one and it is detachment that will enable God to come to him. The divine nature is unity and purity that come from detachment. In other words, detachment propels us to accept God. Thus Eckhart claimed that God comes only to those who are detached because they have nothing to distract them from receiving him who comes. Humility, an important Christian virtue, also leads to detachment, because it involves self-emptying.[4] This means stripping ourselves of material and immaterial comforts, including our concepts and ideas about God or other heavenly things.

---

1. For an introduction to his life, see Meister Eckhart (1994), *Selected Writings*, selected and translated by Oliver Davies. London: Penguin, pp. xi–xxxi.
2. Ibid., p. xxi.
3. V. Lossky, *The Mystical Theology of the Eastern Church*, p. 65.
4. Halcyon Backhouse (ed.) (1993), *The Best of Meister Eckhart*. New York: Crossroad, p. 89.

Quoting the Islamic philosopher Avicenna, Eckhart wrote: 'The mind detached is of such nobility that what it sees is true, what it desires comes about, and its wishes must be obeyed.' This is because when the mind is freed of attachment, 'it constrains God to itself.' In other words, God presents himself to the detached person who is carried away into eternity where nothing temporal can affect him. Detachment, in Eckhart's view, makes a person 'superlatively god-like' as he acquires from this virtue purity and simplicity.[1] Like the Orthodox idea of deification, Eckhart held that if a person is going to be like God, it will be by detachment, which will lead him to purity, simplicity, and eventually to immovability. All this is possible through grace, which draws human beings away from mere creatures to the fullness of God.

Deification is possible, according to Lossky, not through participation in divine essence, which is unknowable, but through God's uncreated energies. This is one of Lossky's unique contributions to Orthodox theology.

## Divine Energies

In order to establish the fact that God does communicate with his people, Eastern tradition teaches that there is a difference between divine essence and divine energies. Since we are called to participate in the divine nature, we need to be aware that in God there is a difference between his essence (nature), which is inaccessible, and his persons, which are accessible. Lossky viewed divine personhood as uncreated energies in which God communicates: 'The divine and deifying illumination and grace is not the essence but the energy of God,' a 'divine power and energy common to the nature in three'.[2] Divine nature is communicable only through its energy.

The exterior manifestation of God belongs to the realm of economy – it is the Logos or the Word that manifests the divinity of the Father. This Logos is the force, power, or energy of the Father or his operation. Thus we have the 'energies' or 'common operations' of the Trinity that allow us to get a glimpse of the divine mystery.[3] St Basil said it is by the energies that descended upon us that we know God, although his essence remains inaccessible.

1. Ibid., p. 91.
2. V. Lossky, *op. cit.*, p. 70.
3. Ibid., p. 71.

According to Lossky, energies are not the effects of divine operation as humans are. Uncreated, these energies or 'modes of existence' flow from the one essence of the Trinity.[1] In order to understand the procession of the divine persons and the creation of the world, 'We must . . . distinguish in God His nature, which is one; and three hypostases; and the uncreated energy which proceeds from and manifests forth the nature from which it is inseparable.'[2] Further, it is in creatures that these energies abide, thus showing forth the greatness and power of God. In 1 Timothy, St Paul says, 'It is he alone who has immortality and dwells in unapproachable light, whom no one has ever seen or can see' (1 Timothy 6:16). This eternal light, similar to divine energies, shines through the humanity of Christ who manifested his divinity to the apostles at the Transfiguration.

The concrete realities of divine energies are easily misunderstood by Christians. Regarding this misunderstanding, Lossky lamented that some Orthodox theologians had rejected this distinction between divine essence and energies; they accused Gregory Palamas of ditheism and polytheism.[3] In criticizing Orthodox theologians like Barlaam and Arkindynus for their inability to grasp the distinction between divine essence and energies, Lossky was in fact accusing the Western Church of a lack of understanding of the apophatic and antinomical spirit of Eastern theological tradition. Barlaam, having studied in Italy, and Arkindynus were both influenced by Aristotle and St Thomas Aquinas and thus rejected the Orthodox teaching of Palamas.

Divine energies are also presented to us as Wisdom, Life, Love, Being, etcetera. These are the innumerable names of God, according to the teaching of the Areopagite. Condemning Sergius Bulgakov, who equated Sophia (wisdom) with the divine essence, Lossky maintained that God is not determined by any of his attributes, including wisdom. Brandon Gallaher, however, claims:

> Despite major differences between the two thinkers (e.g. differing understandings of reason, the use of philosophy and the uncreated/created distinction), it is suggested that Lossky and Bulgakov have more in common than normally is believed to be the case. A critical knowledge of Bulgakov's sophiology

1. Ibid., p. 73.
2. Ibid., p. 74.
3. Ibid., pp. 76–7.

is said to be the 'skeleton key' for modern Orthodox theology which can help unlock its past, present and future.[1]

Lossky insisted that all determinations are inferior to God, 'logically posterior to His being in itself, in its essence'.[2] Thus when we say that God is Love or Wisdom, we understand these energies as subsequent to his essence, external to the nature of the Trinity; the Eastern Church never expresses the relationship between the persons in the Trinity in terms of attributes.[3]

The distinction between essence and energies forms the basis of the Orthodox doctrine of grace. This enables the Eastern Church to safeguard the meaning of St Peter's words: 'partakers of the divine nature' (2 Peter 1:4). This union with God in his energies helps us to participate in the divine nature without our essence becoming the essence of God. St Maximus teaches that 'in deification we are by grace (that is to say, in the divine energies), all that God is by nature, save only identity of nature.'[4] We thus remain as creatures, although by God's grace we become God, just as Christ remained God while becoming human in the Incarnation.

As we have seen, in his exposition of this fundamental aspect of Orthodox theology, the distinction between divine essence and energies, Lossky was critical of his fellow Orthodox theologian Sergius Bulgakov and Western theology in general. He accused Plotinus and Bulgakov of promoting a monistic idea of God. Critical of Thomas Aquinas and scholasticism, he saw Thomism as stained with monism. While Aquinas took a rational approach in his theology, Lossky argued that such an attempt to understand God through concepts and abstraction is futile. The Thomist approach is to link the knowledge of God to the created *nous* or the intellect. Lossky, however, was against 'isolating the locus for the union with God in the *nous*'.[5] Such an attempt at scholasticism, according to Lossky, is not an encounter with the living God, but a mental exercise of wrestling with an abstract knowledge of God.

1. Brandon Gallaher (2013), 'The "sophiological" origins of Vladimir Lossky's apophaticism'. *Scottish Journal of Theology* 66, no. 3 (January), 278-298, http://dx.doi.org/10.1017/S0036930613000136.
2. V. Lossky, *The Mystical Theology of the Eastern Church*, p. 80.
3. Ibid., p. 81.
4. Ibid., p. 87.
5. Aristotle Papanikolaou (2003), 'Divine energies or divine personhood: Vladimir Lossky and John Zizioulas on conceiving the transcendent and immanent God'. *Modern Theology* 19, no. 3 (July), 360.

Behind all his criticism of Western theology, it is Lossky's attack on the *filioque* that is most striking. Rowan Williams claims that Lossky's criticism of Western theology is unfair and inaccurate, but the main point Lossky raised has to do with how East and West approach the subject of knowing God – it is a 'question of rival conceptions of precisely how God is known, and how His activity is mediated in the world to created subjects'.[1] Regarding this issue, Henri de Lubac, in his work *Catholicism*, remarks that the 'Aristotelian logic' adopted in medieval theology is unsuited to organic and unitary ideas usually associated with Platonic philosophy. Aristotelian logic goes against mysticism because 'logical intelligence' seeks to analyse and clarify; it defines, isolates objects, and then connects them again artificially. In other words, logical thinking is 'impatient of any idea of mystery'.[2] De Lubac sought to present a corrective to a misunderstanding of Roman Catholicism, which can be seen as a corrective to Lossky's understanding of Western spirituality.

## *Roman Catholicism*

Writing against the nineteenth-century French philosopher Joseph Ernest Renan, de Lubac argued that his definition of Christianity as 'a religion made for the interior consolation of a few chosen souls' was a grave mistake. Perhaps it was a lack of 'Catholic mentality', 'admixture individualism', and the fear of 'pseudo-mysticism' that led Renan to believe that spiritual consolation is reserved for a few privileged souls.[3] De Lubac saw a creeping individualism in the Roman Catholic Church because of the need to achieve synthesis in its teachings. Quoting E. Masure, he wrote:

> Our academic teaching must be saved from individualism with which for the sake of clarity and the needs of controversy we seem to have allowed it to be associated since the sixteenth century. Our treatises on Grace and the Sacraments, on the Eucharist, even on the Church, are fashioned so as to give the impression that God the Redeemer is never faced with anything but an untold number of individuals, every one of them regulating on

1. Quoted in Papanikolaou, *op. cit.*, 360.
2. Henri de Lubac (1988), *Catholicism: Christ and the Common Destiny of Man*. San Francisco: Ignatius Press. pp. 307–8.
3. Ibid., pp. 305–7.

his own account the measure of his personal relationship with God . . . with no organic connection with each other. . . . In place of this conception we must bring back to the foreground the dogma of the Mystical Body in which the Church consists.[1]

Such an attempt, though challenging, would bring the Orthodox and Roman Catholic Churches closer to each other. Besides, Roman Catholic spirituality as understood by de Lubac resembles Orthodox mysticism because it focuses on the interior life, detachment, and solitude; in other words, it follows the narrow way. De Lubac warned against dissecting theology from mysticism and analysing mysticism through the categories of psychology and sociology:

> An interest in Catholic mysticism may prove disastrous for a certain spiritual aestheticism and for amateurs of psychological analysis, but it is only such parasites that it injures in this way. . . . The same correlation is found between 'experience' and 'thought,' and it would provide a further example of harmful 'specificism' to place them in opposition to each other, as if a choice must be made between personal experience without universal value and 'depersonalized' universal thought; as if self-awareness and reason had to be sacrificed to one another.[2]

The new person redeemed by Christ is both universal and personal. De Lubac believed that a synthesis between historical and reflective analysis can be achieved, as in St Augustine's *Confessions* or *City of God*. Joseph Maréchal, in his study of Roman Catholic mystics, wrote: '[T]he Catholic mystic is not merely a separated being in comparison with the rest of the faithful, an escapist in search of some hazy transcendence; that the mystic ascent is made up of "integrations" rather than "suppressions".'[3] This means that the Christian mystic is very much part of humanity, sharing its joys and sufferings. This brings us to Lossky's understanding of the spiritual life.

## The Spiritual Life

Lossky wrote that the purpose of Christian life in the Orthodox Church is simply to acquire the Holy Spirit, and only good works done in the name of Christ can give us the fruits of the Holy

1. Quoted in ibid., p. 320.
2. Ibid., pp. 347–8.
3. Ibid., p. 348.

Spirit. Hence, a work is good in so far as it brings us closer to
God. Virtues are not ends in themselves but visible signs of life
in Christ; they help us in acquiring grace. The notion of merit
is foreign to Orthodox theology and is seldom mentioned in its
spiritual writings. This is because in Orthodoxy, grace and human
freedom are not separated, but are seen as two sides of the same
reality. St Gregory of Nyssa wrote:

> As the grace of God cannot descend upon souls which flee
> from their salvation, so the power of human virtues is not of
> itself sufficient to raise to perfection souls which have no share
> in grace. . . . [T]he righteousness of works and the grace of the
> Spirit, coming together to the same place, fill the soul in which
> they are united with the life of the blessed.'[1]

Not a reward for meritorious acts, grace is given freely. Furthermore, in Orthodox theology, it is not a question of merit but a
synergy of divine and human wills, a harmony in which grace
becomes very fruitful. Although grace is the presence of God within
us, human effort is necessary, but this effort in no way determines
grace. Regarding this topic of grace and human freedom, Lossky
was critical of Pelagius and also of St Augustine, who used the same
rational method to dismiss Pelagianism.[2]

The spiritual life begins with conversion – 'an attitude of the will
turning towards God and renouncing the world'.[3] Renunciation of
the world means moving back into the interiority of the soul. It is
a 'concentration', a 'reintegration of the spiritual being in its return
to communion with God'.[4] Lossky saw the monastic life as ideal for
union with God as it trains the will towards him, for in the cloister
the wise and faithful monk is able to maintain his zeal and fervour
in seeking God.

Furthermore, in the ascetic tradition of the East, the heart is the
centre of all intellectual and spiritual pursuits. Without the heart,
the spirit is powerless because it is the centre of all activities.[5]
St Isaac the Syrian said, 'The very life of the Spirit being the
work of the heart, it is purity of heart which gives integrity to

---

1. Quoted in V. Lossky, *The Mystical Theology of the Eastern Church*,
   p. 197.
2. Ibid. p. 198.
3. Ibid., p. 199.
4. Ibid., p. 200.
5. Ibid., p. 201.

the contemplation of the spirit.'[1] As such, our activities must be constantly purified by the heart so that they are directed towards the spirit.

In the spiritual tradition of the Eastern Church, there is no clear-cut division between active and passive states in spiritual life. The human spirit is neither active nor passive, it is 'vigilant' under normal circumstances.[2] But the effects of sin will split the active and passive states leading to disintegration. Further, according to St Isaac the Syrian, there are three stages in the spiritual life: penitence, purification, and perfection. Penitence, or repentance, is the 'conversion of the will'; purification is the 'liberation from passions'; and perfection is the acquisition of perfect love, which is the 'fullness of grace'.[3] Penitence, or repentance, is not exactly a stage but an ongoing process. Lossky claimed that this understanding of repentance corresponds to the apophatic understanding of God: '[T]he more one is united to Him, the more one becomes aware of His unknowability, and, in the same way, the more perfect one becomes, the more one is aware of one's own imperfection.'[4]

'Hesychasm' is a method of interior prayer that is part of the ascetic tradition of the Eastern Church. Written down by St Symeon the New Theologian in the eleventh century, it was practised by St Gregory of Sinai at Mount Athos in the fourteenth century.[5] This method involves controlling one's breathing, having the right posture during prayer, and concentrating on the words of this short prayer: 'O Lord Jesus Christ, Son of God, have mercy on me a sinner.' This prayer is continually repeated at each breath until it becomes second nature to the practitioner. It may seem mechanical, but according to Lossky, this method of prayer is able to drive from the heart 'all contagion of sin' through the power of Jesus' name.[6] The practice of this spiritual exercise in the Eastern Church consists in opening

---

1. Ibid., p. 203.
2. Ibid.
3. Ibid., p. 204.
4. Ibid., p. 205.
5. According to Andrew Louth, 'The work ascribed to Symeon most popular among the hesychasts, the *Three Methods of Prayer*, is a somewhat later work. However, the libraries of the monasteries on the Holy Mountain provide evidence that many of the saint's works were known there in the fourteenth century.' Andrew Louth (2007), *Greek East and Latin West: The Church AD 681–1071*. New York: St Vladimir's Seminary Press, pp. 332–3.
6. V. Lossky, *The Mystical Theology of the Eastern Church*, p. 210.

our hearts to the indwelling of God's grace by constantly purifying our thoughts. It involves removing any particular image we have of the Godhead, freeing ourselves from any conceptualization of the divine. The fruit of prayer is divine love or energy, which inflames our souls and unites us with God by the power of the Holy Spirit.[1]

In the Orthodox tradition, the Holy Spirit is never thought of, as in the Roman Catholic Church, as the mutual love of the Father and the Son. Against the *filioque*, Lossky insisted that the Father is the 'sole hypostatic source of the Holy Spirit; the word "love" ($\alpha\gamma\acute{\alpha}\pi\eta$), when it is used of the Holy Spirit by the Eastern mystics, does not describe His "hypostatic character", His position in the Trinity, but always His nature as the giver of love, as the source of love within us, as He who enables us to participate in that supreme perfection of the common nature of the Holy Trinity.'[2]

For Lossky, the power of love communicated to the soul by the Holy Spirit is an uncreated energy and not an accidental effect, which Western theology seems to imply. As participants in the divine nature of the Holy Trinity, we also become partakers of the divine love of God, for God is love, as St John said. At the same time, St Basil said that we must have the correct human disposition to receive this love, 'a germ or potentiality for love'.[3] Eventually this love of God would lead us to love our fellow men and women. This involves knowledge or gnosis, co-operation with the Holy Spirit, and a firm determination.

To sum up, for Lossky, the final goal of Orthodox theology is union with God within the ecclesial context. In spite of changing historical circumstances, the church's mission is the same – helping its members to be united with God. The Fathers and Doctors of the church throughout history have had to defend dogmas to maintain this tradition as they witnessed to the same experience. Lossky

---

1. Ibid., p. 212. St Gregory Palamas (1296–1359) defended the Hesychasts when he 'upheld a doctrine of man which allowed for the use of bodily exercises in prayer, and he argued against Barlaam, that the Hesychasts did indeed experience the Divine and Uncreated Light of Thabor. . . . Gregory developed the distinction between the essence and the energies of God. It was Gregory's achievement to set Hesychasm on a firm dogmatic basis, by integrating it into Orthodox theology as a whole, and by showing how the Hesychast vision of Divine Light in no way undermined the apophatic doctrine of God.' Timothy Ware (1972), *The Orthodox Church*. Harmondsworth: Penguin, p. 76.

2. V. Lossky, *op. cit.*, p. 213.

3. Ibid., p. 214.

admitted that this tradition remains common to the East and the West regarding the Incarnation. But the teachings regarding Pentecost, the doctrine of the Holy Spirit, and grace and ecclesiology are no longer the same in the Orthodox and Roman Catholic Churches. There are two opposing traditions – represented by St Basil and St Augustine.[1]

The apophatic tradition of the Eastern Church is a witness to the Holy Spirit, who transforms divine darkness into light and who allows us to be in union with God. It is the Holy Spirit that reveals the mystery of the Trinity; without the Holy Spirit, dogmas would be merely abstract truth. In the Eastern Church, the day of Pentecost is called the Feast of the Trinity. Lossky considered this 'the absolute stability, the end of all contemplation and of all ascents, and, at the same time, the principle of all theology, primal verity, initial datum from which all thought and all being take their origin'.[2]

Following the Greek Fathers, Lossky identified the perfect knowledge of the Trinity with the Kingdom of God. The mystical theology of the Orthodox Church is always Trinitarian – union with the three divine persons. The apophatic theology of the Eastern Church safeguards the 'antinomy of the trinitarian dogma' against the Western formula of procession of the Holy Spirit from the Father and the Son.[3] Eastern theology emphasizes the procession of the Holy Spirit from the Father alone and thus maintains the hypostatic independence of the Spirit in relation to the Son. It upholds the fullness of the Paraclete at work in this world.

As we have seen, Lossky characterized Orthodox theology as apophatic, stressing divine incomprehensibility; he saw negation not as limitation, but the ability to transcend all concepts and speculation; he spoke of true gnosis (knowledge) and repentance, which lead to the contemplation of the Trinity. The apophatic way is the repentance of the human person in the presence of God. Lossky believed this to be the true tradition of the Orthodox Church. But as we have discussed, apophaticism and the importance of repentance are not entirely absent in the Roman Catholic Church. In the next chapter, we will discuss an Orthodox theologian who stood on different ground: Nicolas Berdyaev, whose writings anticipated the theology of liberation.

---

1. Ibid., p. 238.
2. Ibid., p. 239.
3. Ibid., p. 240.

# Chapter 7
## Nicolas Berdyaev

Born in 1874 into an aristocratic Russian family, Nicolas Alexandrovitch Berdyaev came from a long line of military men, and his father was an officer in the Imperial Guard. Not surprisingly, he was sent to the Military Cadet Corps for his education. But he disliked all things military and rebelled against regimentation. In 1894, Berdyaev enrolled as a law student at Kiev University and his concern with social justice led him to Marxism. In 1900, as a Marxist idealist, he began to write books and articles, a task he continued until his death in 1948. Berdyaev's participation in political revolts led to his expulsion from the university. Never gaining a degree, he read widely and independently. He was attracted to Marxism, but the writings of Ibsen and Dostoyevsky helped him recognize Marxism's philosophical weaknesses.[1]

In 1901, after his return from exile, Berdyaev met a young professor, Sergius Bulgakov (1871–1944), who influenced him to embrace Orthodox Christianity. Bulgakov had been a Marxist and taught economics in Kiev. The two became lifelong friends. In 1903, Berdyaev went to Germany to study for a semester at the University of Heidelberg. Upon his return to Russia, he met and married Lydia Yudifovna and settled in St Petersburg.[2]

Moving to Moscow in 1908 to join the Religious Philosophy Society there, Berdyaev met a group of religious thinkers who had experienced the same religious struggles that he was undergoing.

1. Fuad Nucho (1966), *Berdyaev's Philosophy: The Existential Paradox of Freedom and Necessity*. New York: Anchor Books, Doubleday & Co., pp. 11–12. Some material in this chapter appeared as an article: Ambrose Ih-Mong (2013), 'Towards an Orthodox theology of liberation: an examination of the works of Nicolas Berdyaev'. *International Journal of Orthodox Theology* 4, no. 2, 43–73.
2. Nucho, *op. cit.*, p. 12.

Their open discussion of religious philosophy aroused his interest in Russian Orthodoxy and his own philosophical ideas began to take shape. It was around 1905 that Berdyaev took Orthodox Christianity seriously and became friendly with some famous Orthodox theologians. Conscious of his faith as a Christian, he turned from Marxism to Christianity.[1]

A faithful son of the Orthodox Church, Berdyaev valued the freedom that exists in this great family of Eastern Orthodox. Built on the principles of self-government, both the clergy and the laity share in building the church, the body of Christ. As a result, the Orthodox Church is closely related to the people and culture of the place. A national church, the Orthodox Church was first to resist the claims of the papacy. The simplicity in Orthodox theology, as well as the freedom, attracted Berdyaev. He felt at home in the Orthodox Church because it was not authoritarian and absolute in its teachings and practices; as he said, 'I have not known authority . . . most particularly, in my religious life.'[2]

Well acquainted with many theological works, Berdyaev attempted to study the nature and essence of Orthodoxy, Roman Catholicism, and Protestantism. He came to the conclusion that Orthodoxy is 'less susceptible to definition and rationalization than either Catholicism [or] Protestantism.' This feature of Orthodoxy gives the church more freedom, and thus, in his opinion, it is superior to the other branches of Christianity. Though not a typical Orthodox believer, he insisted that he had never severed his link with the Orthodox Church. However, he was not totally satisfied with it and did not consider his church as the only true one.[3] Upon his arrival in Paris in 1923, Berdyaev took part in ecumenical gatherings of Orthodox, Roman Catholics, and Protestants.[4] Thus it was no surprise that when Berdyaev died, on 23 March 1948, his Orthodox funeral service was attended by Roman Catholics and Protestants, a sign of true ecumenical observance.[5]

As a Russian philosopher, Berdyaev is not well known in Western circles. The influence of the Orthodox Church has a peculiar influence

1. Nicolas Berdyaev (1950), *Dream and Reality*. London: Geoffrey Bless, p. 180.
2. Ibid., p. 48.
3. Ibid., p. 177.
4. Ibid., p. 258.
5. Donald A. Lowrie (ed. and trans.) (1965), *Christian Existentialism: A Berdyaev Anthology*. London: George Allen & Unwin, p. 23.

on the Russian mind. There are also differences between Western and Eastern Christianity and the societies they formed.[1] But, as we shall see, when it comes to dealing with the pain and anguish of humanity, the plight of the poor and oppressed, there are striking similarities in the way theologians of both traditions interpret their situations in the light of scripture.

In this short biographical sketch above, it is clear that Nicolas Berdyaev prized freedom more than other things on earth. He was called the 'philosopher of freedom'. In fact, he himself wrote, 'I do indeed love freedom above all else. . . . From my early childhood I was wedded to freedom'[2] and 'the problem which preoccupied me above every other was that of freedom.'[3] He continued, 'Freedom, unconditional and uncompromising freedom, has been the fountain-head and prime mover of all my thinking.'[4] In view of his struggle for freedom throughout his life, Berdyaev was critical of the shortcomings of both capitalism and socialism. Nonetheless, his tendency was towards supporting socialism as the basis of government because of his concern for social justice.

## Liberation Theology

Started in the 1950s and 1960s in Latin America, the theology of liberation was a response to the plight of the poor, marginalized, and dehumanized sectors of society caused by social injustice in the region. The term was used by Gustavo Gutiérrez, a Peruvian Roman Catholic priest, in his seminal work, *A Theology of Liberation*, published in 1973. His theological approach was a sincere attempt to bring about a just society.

Liberation theology interprets the teaching of Christ with the aim of helping the poor to free themselves from unjust economic, political, and social conditions. Its methodology is to practise theology from the point of view of the economically poor and downtrodden members of the community by identifying with their struggles and hope. This means that the church must concentrate its effort on liberating people from poverty and oppression and must fight for their rights. Gutiérrez puts it simply: 'The theology

1. David Bonner Richardson (1969), *Berdyaev's Philosophy of History*. The Hague: Martinus Nijhoff, p. xvii.
2. Berdyaev, *Dream and Reality*, p. 46.
3. Ibid., p. 24.
4. Ibid., p. 158.

of liberation tries – in ecclesial communion – to be a language about God. It is an attempt to make present in this world of oppression, injustice and death, the Word of life.'[1]

Liberation theology has its roots in the long biblical tradition in which God liberated his people not only from sin and eternal damnation, but also from social and political oppression. Orthodox Christians, also deeply rooted in biblical tradition, were oppressed and marginalized in Russia. They were also involved in political conflicts in Greece, Romania, Bulgaria, and elsewhere in Europe. It is therefore surprising to find Orthodox Christians, who are no strangers to liberation struggles, reluctant to adopt and develop the theology of liberation.

This chapter seeks to examine the Orthodox Church's reticence to embrace liberation theology in spite of the fact that its members have experienced much poverty, oppression, vulnerability, and suffering, as in Latin America and the Caribbean. Notwithstanding the Orthodox Church's lack of enthusiasm to accept liberation theology, there were Russian thinkers who displayed socio-critical strands in their writings reflecting the themes of liberation. However, the term 'liberation theology' cannot be used to describe the religious-revolution movements in Russia at the end of the nineteenth and beginning of the twentieth centuries. In view of this, we will discuss the writings of Nicolas Berdyaev, who focused his writing on issues related to Gustavo Gutiérrez's theology of liberation. As we shall see, in spite of their different backgrounds, there are striking similarities in their theological, social, and political analysis in the light of biblical tradition. In many ways, the theological and socio-political commentaries of Berdyaev anticipate the theology of liberation. First, we will examine some of the reasons why Orthodox Christians find the teaching of liberation theology unacceptable.

## Contextual versus Universal

Heavily influenced by the material condition and culture of society, liberation theology is based on praxis and context. Since liberation theology is concerned with abolishing oppressive structures, it is directed neither by classical manuals nor tradition, but by present

---

1. Gustavo Gutiérrez (1999), 'The Task and Content of Liberation Theology' in Christopher Rowland (ed.), *The Cambridge Companion to Liberation Theology*. Cambridge: Cambridge University Press, p. 37.

realities and future possibilities. Its commitment to social change is based on the Gospel values seen through eyes of the poor and marginalized.[1] Liberation theology takes a critical and clear attitude towards economic, social, and cultural issues in society. It is critical not just of society, but of the church as well, in so far as they fail to establish a more equitable society based on Gospel values. Liberation theology takes its inspiration not only from revelation and tradition, but also from historical process. Because it is open to historical process, 'truths' that have been established once and for all are considered 'static' and, in the long run, 'sterile'.[2] Not denying orthodoxy, liberation theology seeks to balance and even to reject the exclusiveness and primacy of Christian doctrine. Furthermore, liberation theology regards the obsession with orthodoxy as nothing more than fidelity to an outdated tradition.[3]

Unlike liberation theology, with its focus on context and praxis, Orthodox theology strives to be universal and contemplative. It seeks to formulate a 'universal theology' that can unite all Christians and regards its tradition as living, developing, and normative.[4] Vladimir Lossky argues that 'theology must be of universal expression. It is not by accident that God has placed the Fathers of the Church in a Greek setting; the demands for lucidity in philosophy and profundity in gnosis have forced them to purify and to sanctify the language of the philosophers and of the mystics, to give to the Christian message, which includes but goes beyond Israel, all its universal reach.'[5] While liberation theology emphasizes the immanence of God and the humanity of the suffering Christ, Orthodox theology, profoundly soteriological, emphasizes the transcendence of God and the divinity of Christ.[6]

For the Orthodox, faith is 'a personal adherence to the personal presence of God Who reveals Himself'. Theology 'as word and

1. See Stephen B. Bevans (2002), *Models of Contextual Theology*. Maryknoll, New York: Orbis, pp. 70–3.
2. Gutiérrez (1973), *A Theology of Liberation*. Maryknoll, New York: Orbis, p. 13.
3. Ibid., p. 10.
4. Stephen Hayes (1990), 'Orthodoxy and liberation theology'. *Journal of Theology for Southern Africa*, no. 73 (December), 13.
5. V. Lossky (2001), *Orthodox Theology: An Introduction*. Crestwood, New York: St Vladimir's Seminary Press, pp. 30–1.
6. Peter Bouteneff (2012), 'Liberation: challenges to modern orthodox theology from the contextual theologies'. *Union Seminary Quarterly Review* 63, no. 3–4 (January), 27.

as thought must necessarily conceal a gnostic dimension, in the sense of the theology of contemplation and silence.'[1] Although it acknowledges the importance of theological teaching as part of historical work here on earth, with careful consideration to space and time, Orthodox theology stresses contemplation: 'Nourished with contemplation, it does not become established in silence but seeks to speak the silence, humbly, by a new use of thought and word.'[2] Faith is regarded as an 'ontological relationship between man and God'.[3] This Orthodox understanding of faith as contemplation is a far cry from the action-packed theology of liberation that seeks to overthrow unjust social and political structures, with violence if necessary.

Another reason why the Eastern Church is reluctant to adopt the Latin American model of liberation theology is the understanding that Orthodox theology is 'liberation theology' as it is. The Incarnation, death, and resurrection of Jesus Christ lead to our liberation from the bondage of sin and damnation. Christ rescues us from the clutches of sin and thus liberation is at the heart of the Gospel.

## *Western Influence*

In spite of the fact that liberation theologians are highly critical of European thought, and deny that their theology is European, they have actually assimilated many of those Western ideas in one way or another. Here I would like to mention the German theologian Jürgen Moltmann, who has exerted a profound influence on liberation theologians and others. In his *Theology of Hope*, Moltmann criticizes the static eschatological concept in Christianity. Moltmann writes: 'To believe means to cross in hope and anticipation the bounds that have been penetrated by the raising of the crucified . . . the man who thus hopes will never be able to reconcile himself with the laws and constraints of this earth. . . . Hope finds in Christ not only a consolation *in* suffering, but also the protest of the divine *against* suffering.'[4] Believing that Christian mission is not just to spread the faith and the hope that goes with it, Moltmann insists that evangelization must be involved in the 'historic transformation

1. Vladimir Lossky, *op. cit.*, p. 13.
2. Ibid., p. 14.
3. Ibid., p. 16.
4. Jürgen Moltmann (1967), *Theology of Hope*. New York: Harper & Row, pp. 20–1.

of life'.[1] Here it means that the Gospel challenges us to bring about a more equitable world, to close the gap between the sorry state of affairs now and the promised future.

Echoing Karl Marx, Moltmann writes, 'The theologian is not concerned merely to supply a different *interpretation* of the world, of history and of human nature, but to *transform* them in expectation of a divine transformation.'[2] Influenced by Moltmann and at the same time critical of his work, Gutiérrez argues that 'The hope which overcomes death must be rooted in the heart of historical praxis; if this hope does not take shape in the present to lead it forward, it will be only an evasion, a futuristic illusion.'[3] In other words, Christianity is moving towards the future and beyond, but those who are too concerned with the 'beyond' run the risk of neglecting to work for a just society and to struggle for liberation from unjust economic and political structures.

Marxism, another strand of European thought, exerts a powerful influence on the theology of liberation. Liberation theologians make use of Marxist categories in their social analysis with the hope of changing the unjust social and political structures in Latin American society. Like Marx, these theologians recognize that economics plays a crucial role in the historical process. They embrace the Marxist notion of class struggle and believe that the oppressed must shape their own history by taking up the liberating praxis of the Gospel. Gutiérrez acknowledges the influence of Marxist thought as a positive force, with its focus on praxis and the transformation of the world. He considers the confrontation between contemporary theology and Marxism as 'fruitful'.[4] Appreciating Marx's analysis, Gutiérrez writes: 'Pointing the way towards an era in history when man can live humanly, Marx created categories which allowed for the elaboration of a science of history.'[5]

Framed in Marxist categories, liberation theology is rejected by the Orthodox Church. Latin Americans who live under unjust social and political structures may find communism, influenced by Marx, enlightening and liberating. In fact, Latin American liberation theologians take pride in using Marxist analysis as it is scientific and respectable in the Western world. But Orthodox Christians living in the former Communist states of the Soviet Union and Eastern Bloc

---

1. Ibid., p. 330.
2. Ibid., p. 84.
3. Gutiérrez, *op. cit.*, p. 218.
4. Ibid., p. 9.
5. Ibid., p. 30.

countries find Marxism extremely repulsive because it is associated with oppressive regimes and dictatorship. In Europe, communism has collapsed, and in the so-called communist countries, preserving Marxism is only an excuse for those in authority to remain in power. In China we have 'socialism with Chinese characteristics', which basically means relentless capitalism coupled with dictatorship by the Communist Party. The military in China is characteristically called 'The People's Liberation Army'.

Orthodox critical perception of Marxism is echoed by Joseph Ratzinger, who claims that 'where the Marxist ideology of liberation had been consistently applied, a total lack of freedom had developed, whose horrors were now laid bare before the eyes of the entire world.'[1] Commenting on the issue of orthodoxy and orthopraxy, a crucial theme in liberation theology, Ratzinger has pointed out that orthopraxy means 'right action', which is related to the code of rites, and orthodoxy means right way of worshipping and glorifying God (*doxa*) as understood by the early Eastern Churches.[2]

In spite of the Orthodox distrust of Marxism, there were Christian thinkers in Russia, among them Sergius Bulgakov and Nicolas Berdyaev, who attempted to assimilate Marxist thought in their theology. Marxism actually became an inspiration for some theologians who were anxious to create a more just and humane society in Russia.

## Back in the USSR

The 1917 revolution in Russia culminated in the overthrow of the Tsarist imperial regime and the establishment of a new socialist state. Before this event, throughout those years of oppression, political groups like the Mensheviks (pure Marxists), the Bolsheviks (neo-Marxists), and other socio-political groups emerged that influenced both secular and religious groups, including some well-known theologians. According to the Ukrainian scholar, Alexander Negrov, 'The Russian religious philosophy of that period was devoted to the goals of a practical transformation of life and society and to a recognition of God as the substantial factor.'[3] Advocates of this philosophy accused

1. Joseph Ratzinger (2004), *Truth and Tolerance*. San Francisco: Ignatius Press, p. 116.
2. Ibid., pp. 124–5.
3. Alexander I. Negrov (2005), 'An overview of liberation theology in orthodox Russia'. *Hervormde Teologiese Studies* 61 (1&2), 330.

the Orthodox Church of being too concerned with the afterlife and thereby neglecting to make the message of Christ relevant to the needs of people in this present life. They wanted the Orthodox Church to be more involved in the lives of the common folk, in the social, economic, and political transformation of the country.

Regarding this transformation, Nicolas Berdyaev put it succinctly when he wrote: '[T]he light, which comes upon the highest leaders of organized religion, must shine toward the lower horizons of the society.'[1] In other words, the Orthodox Church must make a shift from insisting on religious piety to implementing concrete pastoral programmes for the people. Its theology, then, must reflect and respond to the specific situations and issues in Russia. In light of this, Marxism became an inspiration and a challenge for Orthodox Christians like Berdyaev, whose philosophical and theological writings were critical of the ecclesiastical, social, and political structures of Russian society.

A significant feature of Russian theology in the twentieth century was the focus on the Kingdom of God – regnocentrism. There was an intense seeking of the Kingdom of God which led some Orthodox theologians to call for the 'Christianization of the world and for the activity of humans in the world'. Negrov claims that 'Russian theological thought at the end of the nineteenth century was very social in its focus. . . . Hidden behind these social utopias was the search for the Kingdom of God. Russian thinkers attempted to find a path for Russia which might avoid the development of capitalism with its inevitable triumph in the spiritual, moral and socio-economic spheres.'[2] Berdyaev, for example, called upon Christians to be creative in changing and improving the social order. He also reminded us that nothing is eternal, neither socialism nor capitalism. Our history points towards the realisation of the Kingdom of God and this implies that we do not have a perfect society on earth, but we can improve society for the betterment of humankind. A perfect society can come about only through the 'transfiguration of the world', which is the coming of the Kingdom of God, the new Jerusalem.[3]

Some Russian Orthodox thinkers were convinced that socialism could help to create a more equitable society. They believed that socialism was not all together incompatible with Christianity and

---

1. Ibid., 331.
2. Ibid., 333.
3. Berdyaev (1945), *The Destiny of Man*. London: Geoffrey Bless, pp. 231–2.

that it could lead to the realisation of social justice, whereby the exploitation of human beings would no longer be allowed. This means that Christians should promote a socialisation of society that would guarantee people's right to work, to live life to the full, and to promote justice. According to these thinkers, only the church, because of its spiritual orientation, is able to create the New Man that Marxism promotes. Nicolas Berdyaev was one of those thinkers who believed that it was possible for a Christian to be a socialist. In fact, Berdyaev insisted that a Christian 'ought to be a socialist'.[1]

## Capitalism and Socialism

Critical of both capitalism and socialism, Berdyaev argued that in the struggles for workers' rights, both systems regard the person merely as a function of society. Nineteenth-century capitalism in Marx's analysis means the desire to maximize profit rather than the desire to meet real human needs. The workers are alienated in capitalist society because they are regarded not as individuals with positive human traits, but as a source of manpower to be exploited in the pursuit of wealth. Berdyaev equates socialism with Marxism. Although Christian ethics is opposed to the ideologies of capitalism and socialism, Berdyaev believed that there was partial truth in socialism and that the 'morally objectionable aspects of socialism have been inherited by it from capitalism'.[2] As such, he was more concerned with the struggle against capitalism than with socialism in the liberation of workers. For Berdyaev, the struggle against the injustice of capitalism meant the 'struggle for the economic rights of the individual, for the concrete rights of the producer and not for the abstract rights of the citizen'. Liberation of the worker is the liberation of the person from the oppressive clutches of capitalism.[3]

Social problems are related to that of private property, and thus, according to Berdyaev, socialism is right to question the institution of private property. Obviously, an unlimited and absolute right of property would result in some people being impoverished. In other words, uncontrolled private property breeds 'evils and iniquities of feudalism and capitalism'. It also leads to 'unendurable social inequality, proletarianization of the masses and the loss by the workers of the means of production'. Such a situation can only

1. Ibid., p. 334.
2. Ibid., pp. 213–14.
3. Ibid., p. 216.

increase 'envy, malice and vindictiveness [so] that the oppressed lose all human semblance', becoming a 'non-person', as it were. At the same time, Berdyaev did acknowledge that there is a right to private property because it is connected to the principle of personality. The person must be given some power over the material things in this world and the state has no right to deprive them of such things, including the freedom of thought, conscience, and speech, and the right to move freely. This means that the right to private property is related to freedom. If the state is the sole owner of all the material goods in society, the people will be enslaved: 'Economic dependence deprives man of freedom, whether it be dependence upon capitalists or upon the community and the state.'[1]

Berdyaev argued that the problem of absolute private property cannot be solved by transferring this right from a few owners to the state. This would only lead from one tyranny to another – from a few rich individuals, such as bankers and owners of factories, to the community or the state. This would result in more restriction of freedom. For Berdyaev, true liberation consists of denying unlimited power to anyone. It is 'godless or anti-Christian' to believe that some people can have absolute ownership of the material world. Absolute right of property belongs to God only. Therefore the right of owning property must be shared between the individual and the society, and this right must be limited and functional as well. Berdyaev argued that property helps the human being realize his freedom, but that it can also be a means of exploitation and tyranny. This evil can be avoided when God becomes the absolute owner and man acts as his steward. Believing that the desire for limitless wealth is the basis of capitalist society with its deceptions and contradictions, Berdyaev called for self-control and self-limitation in acquiring properties.[2]

Though Berdyaev was critical of both capitalism and socialism, he favoured socialism as the basis of government. He believed that capitalism destroys the reality of property. In struggling against capitalism, Berdyaev spoke of the need to 're-establish the spiritually personal attitude to the world of things and material goods, the ultimate bond between personality and the world in which it is called upon to act.' While he believed in unlimited freedom in the spiritual realm, Berdyaev called for restricted freedom in the economic realm. Economic freedom must be reduced to the minimum or it will lead

1. Ibid., p. 217.
2. Ibid., p. 218.

to great abuses, as when people are deprived of their daily bread. In this respect, Berdyaev upheld socialism. He insisted that it is the responsibility of the state to protect one social class, usually the poor and marginalized, from the oppression of another, namely the rich and powerful. The ideal situation would be to develop the professional middle class.[1]

Some of the issues raised by Berdyaev above are reflected in the theology of liberation as they affect the lives of the poor and marginalized. We shall now examine some specific topics in the works of Gutiérrez and Berdyaev. In spite of their different cultural, historical, and even religious backgrounds, there are striking similarities in their discourses. These topics concern Christian anthropology, praxis, Marxism, history, and eschatology.

## *Christian Anthropology*

Gustavo Gutiérrez argues that the point of departure for contemporary theology since the Age of the Enlightenment has been the challenge raised by the modern secular spirit. The West has been affected by aggressive secularism that denies the existence of God or relegates religion to the private sphere. However, in South America and in the Caribbean, the challenge comes not from the non-believers, but from the 'non-persons', who have been deprived of their status as human beings. Gutiérrez claims that 'the "non-person" questions not so much our religious universe but above all our economic, social, political and cultural order, calling for a transformation of the very foundations of a dehumanizing society.'[2]

The notion of personhood, 'personality', features significantly in Berdyaev's writings. Berdyaev was very much aware of how society can deprive a person of his or her dignity as a human being, making him or her into a 'non-person' in Gutiérrez's sense. He condemned the champions of capitalism who wanted to justify and preserve the form of economic slavery known as free labour. The capitalist and socialist societies do not recognize 'personality' as an ultimate value. The value of personality is overtaken by the value of material wealth. In other words, what you have is more important than who you are. Instead of 'personality' in Berdyaev's sense, which values the dignity of the human person, the bourgeois capitalist society encourages 'individualism', which destroys and dehumanizes people.

---

1. Ibid., p. 219.
2. Gutiérrez, 'The Task and Content of Liberation Theology', p. 28.

Stressing the importance of the human person, Berdyaev wrote: 'Personality is the image and likeness of God in man and this is why it rises above the natural life. . . . The value of personality is the highest hierarchical value in the world, a value of the spiritual order. . . . [T]he idea of personality lies at the basis of ethics.'[1] In other words, the theology of liberation demands that we give a 'non-person' back their 'personalities'. Further, he argued that 'The so-called individualism, characteristic of the bourgeois capitalist society and connected with economic freedom and unlimited right of private property, has nothing to do with personality and is hostile to it.'[2] Believing that the individualism of capitalist society destroys the dignity of the human person, Berdyaev sought to uphold the sacredness of 'personality' that is related to the inherent value of the human person who is made in the image of God.

Influenced by Kant and Christianity, Berdyaev taught that human personality is 'the highest hierarchical value in the world'. This means that all exploitation by an economic system, a state, or a society is a denial of this fundamental Christian truth. In exploitation and oppression, the human being is treated like an object, a means, or a thing. But in reality, according to Berdyaev, the human person is 'a greater value than society, nation, government, although he is often crushed by society, nation, and government which make themselves idols of the objectified, fallen world'.[3] Personality is 'resistance, an unbroken creative act'.[4] Therefore it is important for the personality not to submit to unjust and oppressive structures, but to resist.

### Reflection on Praxis

In practicing a theology of liberation, according to Gutiérrez, the first step is to contemplate God, to discover and put into practice his will for us. This means that the veneration of God and doing his will come together. The consequence of prayer is the commitment towards the poor in which we find the Lord (cf. Matthew 25:31–46). In 'The Task and Content of Liberation Theology', Gutiérrez writes: 'Contemplation and commitment in human history are fundamental dimensions of Christian existence; in consequence,

---

1. Berdyaev, *The Destiny of Man*, p. 55.
2. Ibid., p. 213.
3. Matthew Spinka (1949), *Nicolas Berdyaev: Captive of Freedom*, p. 139.
4. Berdyaev (1944), *Slavery and Freedom*. London: Geoffrey Bless, p. 49.

they cannot be avoided in the understanding of faith.' The first act is solidarity with the poor in which the mystery is revealed. The second act is reasoning.[1] In other words, theology, as a critical reflection in the light of the Word, helps us to understand the relationship between our life of faith and the need to build a more equitable and humane society.

Hence, an act of faith is the starting point of all theological reflection. Gutiérrez insists that it is not just an intellectual assent to the message, but 'a vital embracing of the gift of the Word as heard in the ecclesial community, as an encounter with God, and as love of one's brother and sister. It is about existence in its totality.' To receive the Word is to make it happen: it is a 'concrete gesture'. At the same time, authentic theology is always spiritual, as taught by the Church Fathers.[2] Here we have theology as a critical reflection of praxis.

Gutiérrez teaches that performing acts of charity lies at the heart of the Christian life. In fact, this conforms more to the biblical view of the faith, as St Paul said: '[L]ove is the nourishment and the fullness of faith.' The gift of one's self to God implies the gift of oneself to others – this is the foundation of the *praxis* of Christian's active presence in history.[3] This means that faith is not just a mere affirmation or assent; it is also a commitment. Gutiérrez cautions us that this is not just a horizontal approach to faith, but a 'rediscovery of the indissoluble unity of man and God'.[4]

As we have seen, Gutiérrez acknowledges that the confrontation between theology and Marxism has been enriching as theologians have begun to search for theology's own sources, to understand the transformation of this world and the historical stage in which the drama of human existence takes place. This confrontation with Marxism enables theology to understand the meaning of faith in its historical context and what it means to transform the world in the light of the Gospel.[5]

Another important feature of liberation theology is the rediscovery of the eschatological dimension, which has led its practitioners to consider the central role of historical praxis. For Gutiérrez, 'human history is above all else an opening to the future.' This means that man must orient and open himself 'to the gifts which gives history

1. Gutiérrez, *op. cit.*, pp. 28–9.
2. Ibid., p. 29.
3. Gutiérrez, *A Theology of Liberation*, pp. 6–7.
4. Ibid., p. 8.
5. Ibid., pp. 9–10.

its transcendent meaning: the full and definitive encounter with the Lord and with other men.' Here the importance of action is stressed in Christian life: 'To do the truth.' Christians are called to transform the world, to establish brotherhood and communion in the world.[1] In other words, Christian life is about concrete service to others and not just an acceptance of doctrines or an assent to an intellectual faith.

To practise theology, according to Gutiérrez, means to have a critical attitude towards economic and socio-cultural issues. It necessarily includes a criticism of society and the church in the light of the Gospel. 'Theology is reflection, a critical attitude.'[2] This means that pastoral service must come first, followed by theological reflection. In *A Theology of Liberation*, Gutiérrez writes: 'Critical reflection thus always plays the inverse role of an ideology which rationalizes and justifies a given social and ecclesial order.'[3] Critical analysis of social, economic, and political systems is also an important feature of Berdyaev's philosophical writings. Praxis or faith in action includes the struggle for social justice, a topic on which Berdyaev wrote in the light of his Orthodox faith and the situation in his homeland.

## *Social Justice*

In view of humans' tendency to exploit one another in a capitalist society, Nicolas Berdyaev insisted that it is not enough to engage only in spiritual struggle against sin. We must not accept every social system as inevitable. In other words, we must fight for social justice. Traditionally, Christians have been prepared to defend and justify unjust social structures, believing that original sin made human beings bad and thus that it is impossible to eradicate social injustice. Berdyaev argued that such an attitude is simply 'hypocritical and sociologically false'. Besides original sin, Christianity also teaches about seeking the Kingdom of God and striving for perfection, just as the heavenly Father is perfect. Although the bourgeois capitalist system is the result of original sin, Berdyaev argued, this does not mean that we cannot change it. Social reforms and improvements are possible in spite of sinful humanity. It is also important to note that the will to create the greatest possible social justice does

1. Ibid., p. 10.
2. Ibid., p. 11.
3. Ibid., p. 12.

not mean that we are capable of creating an earthly paradise. But Christians must do their best 'to realize Christian truth in the social as well as in the personal life'.[1]

Berdyaev warned us that if Christianity continues to refuse to take social justice seriously on the grounds that original sin makes us incapable of any good, then this task will be taken on by others and the idea of justice will distort. We find this in revolutionary movements, in socialism and communism.[2] In other words, Berdyaev urged Christians to take up the cause of social justice and not to leave this task to unbelievers, because without God as the foundation, justice will be distorted or perverted.

Christianity is realistic about human nature and therefore it will not allow a false utopia to develop. However, Christianity demands that we seek in concrete ways the realisation of social justice in our society. Distinguishing the Christian idea of social justice from materialistic socialism, Berdyaev taught that Christian ethics does not accept the materialistic view of the world and also does not recognize 'the metaphysics of equality which denies personality with its spiritual life and devastates reality'.[3] As mentioned earlier, by 'personality' Berdyaev means the spiritual and ethical dimensions of the human person. A personality has absolute value because he or she is made in the image and likeness of God and the human soul is more valuable than all the kingdoms of the world. A person may sacrifice his/her life but not his/her personality, which is a 'spiritual-religious category'.[4] As such, Berdyaev insisted that the social question 'of the spiritual enlightenment of the masses, without which no justice can be achieved'[5] could only be solved with a 'spiritual regeneration'.

Berdyaev posited that the Christian understanding of wealth and poverty cannot be translated into social categories because the truth of Christianity points to the Kingdom of God. The question of creating a more equitable society is a secular issue and not a spiritual issue. However, it would be wrong for Christians to be indifferent to social life and to accept social injustice and exploitation. In other words, Christians must not bow down before social structures created by others.[6]

---

1. Berdyaev, *The Destiny of Man*, p. 221.
2. Ibid., pp. 222–3.
3. Ibid., p. 223.
4. Berdyaev (1955), *The Origin of Russian Communism*. London: Geoffrey Bless, p. 178.
5. Berdyaev, *The Destiny of Man*, p. 224.
6. Ibid., p. 231.

Based on economic freedom, capitalism actually promotes a new kind of slavery, which is even more inhumane than the slavery of old, according to Berdyaev. Although socialism does not recognize the value of freedom and personality, he still believes it is a more humane system than capitalism. This brings us to two topics related to socialism – communism and Christianity – on which Berdyaev offered some important insights that were developed by later scholars.

## Marxism and Christianity

Nicolas Berdyaev highlighted the messianic root of Marxism. He recognized that beyond the doctrine of historical and economic materialism, Marxism is 'a doctrine of deliverance, of the messianic vocation of the proletariat'. This points to a future perfect society in which people will no longer depend on economics. For Berdyaev, this was the soul of Marxism – a utopia. He believed that man's complete dependence on economics is due to the sin of the past, but that in the future all this can be changed. This attempt to create a perfect world, which is an attempt to establish the Kingdom of God on Earth, is 'a secularization of the ancient Hebrew messianic consciousness'.[1]

Scottish philosopher Alasdair MacIntyre characterizes Marxism as a Christian heresy. Deeply influenced by French socialists who appealed to Christian principles, Marxist philosophy and the idea of alienation have roots in Judaism and Christianity. Marxism also has a strong 'apocalyptic force' that is similar to Christian eschatology. Marx was inspired by Jewish and Christian messianic hopes to establish a secularized version of a utopic classless society utilizing the Hegelian idea of dialectical materialism. Hegel's theory of evolution implies that through contradictions and their resolutions, we move to a higher phase of development.[2]

In this connection, Berdyaev viewed the theory of evolution as a false religion seeking to replace Christianity. He felt that, no matter how valid it may be, the theory of evolution cannot be identified with the Christian eschatological concept. Secular theory of progress can have no meaning because it has no goal – it lacks true teleology.[3]

1. Berdyaev, *The Origin of Russian Communism*, p. 98.
2. Owen Chadwick (1975), *The Secularization of the European Mind in the Nineteenth Century*. Cambridge: Cambridge University Press, pp. 68–9.
3. Spinka, *Nicolas Berdyaev: Captive of Freedom*, p. 179.

Furthermore, there are dynamic principles of history that determine the destinies of humankind and that eventually produced that world history that coincides with the Christian history.[1] Here, Berdyaev was of the opinion that true progress must be seen in the Christian perspective with the coming of the Kingdom of God. Any other religious theory of progress is necessarily an imitation of the Christian ideal. As we shall see, Gutiérrez also believes that 'history is one' – world history and Christian history coincide and Christ is the Lord of history.

Berdyaev wrote that in Russia, communism seeks to replace Christianity and the functions of the church are transferred to the state. Communism embraces the whole of one's life; it seeks to answer religious questions and to give meaning to life. Communism acts like a religion. It is concerned with the salvation of the souls of its citizens and preaches one saving truth: 'the truth of dialectic materialism'.[2] The communist government views the church as the cause of slavery and exploitation. In view of this, Berdyaev saw communists as very ignorant and unenlightened about religious matters. At the same time, he was also critical of Christians who condemn communists for their persecution because Christians themselves are not innocent of atrocities. In fact, Christians have done little for the realisation of social justice and the promotion of the brotherhood of man. How can they accuse the communists for failing to do so? Berdyaev wrote:

> The sins of Christians, the sins of the historical churches, have been very great, and these sins bring with them their just punishment. Betrayal of the covenant of Christ, the use of the Christian Church for the support of the ruling classes, human weakness being what it is, cannot but bring about the lapse from Christianity of those who are compelled to suffer from that betrayal and from such a distortion of Christianity.[3]

Christians are not innocent in Berdyaev's thinking. In fact, the Christian faith has been manipulated to serve the establishment of the Kingdom of Caesar, to defend the ruling class, the rich and powerful. The poor and marginalized have been told to accept their sufferings and hardships as part of their lot in life and to submit meekly to

1. Berdyaev (1936), *The Meaning of History*. New York: Charles Scribner's Sons, p. 111.
2. Berdyaev, *The Origin of Russian Communism*, p. 169.
3. Ibid., p. 171.

every social evil. Christian humility has been falsely interpreted to deny human worth. In view of this, Berdyaev saw communism as a challenge to the Christian world: 'In it is to be seen the Highest Tribunal and a reminder of duty unfulfilled.'[1] He lamented that since the time of Constantine, the church has not so much as overcome the Kingdom of Caesar as has been subjected to it.[2] Christians have failed in their duty and commitment. Communism thus challenges Christians to be faithful to the Gospel values that they profess.

## Great Mentor of Christianity

As a supporter of classless society, Berdyaev came close to being a communist. However, at the same time, he was also a supporter of 'the aristocratic principle as a qualitative principle in human society'. This noble principle depends not on one's class or property, but on one's character or personal quality. Berdyaev supported a 'Christian personalism',[3] but not an individualism opposed to the principle of personality and communion. Influenced by Orthodox Christian anthropology, he spoke of the idea of 'God-humanity'. As in Jesus Christ, the God-man, the incarnation of God in Man, there is also in humanity a collective incarnation of God. 'God-humanity is the continuation of the incarnation of God.'[4] Communism claims to have created not just a new society, but a new mankind. But Berdyaev believed that communism deprives mankind of its depth and turns the individual into 'a flat two-dimensioned being'.[5] For him, a new mankind can only come about when the individual is regarded as of supreme value in life, not just as a commodity in the structure of society. This implies the Christian idea of rebirth into the new Adam.

In spite of his severe criticism of communist philosophy, Berdyaev believed that the social system of communism could be reconciled with Christianity. In fact, he was more critical of the capitalist system, which, he believed, 'crushes personality and dehumanizes life', turns human beings into commodities and 'article[s] of merchandise', and subjects humans to the power of economics and money. Communism at least attempts to solve the problem of food distribution. Here is a famous saying of Berdyaev regarding the question of bread for the hungry:

1. Ibid., p. 172.
2. Ibid., p. 174.
3. Ibid., p. 179.
4. Ibid., p. 180.
5. Ibid., p. 182.

The question of bread for myself is a material question, but the question of bread for my neighbours, for everybody, is a spiritual and a religious question. Man does not live by bread alone, but he does live by bread and there should be bread for all. Society should be so organized that there is bread for all, and then it is that the spiritual question will present itself before men in all its depth.[1]

This means that the struggle for spiritual interests, for spiritual revival, is not enough because a large part of humanity is without food. Christians must first respond to the basic necessities of the vast majority of people. In other words, we must preach with our actions.

Communism is 'a great mentor for Christians', Berdyaev claimed, because communism reminds Christians of the prophetic message of Christ in the Gospel.[2] While the capitalist system urges people to follow their personal interests in order to promote economic development for the community, Berdyaev argued that the economic system of communism urges people to serve the common good, which is closer to the Christian ideal.[3] He also believed that communism has the potential to challenge and 'stimulate the awakening of the Christian conscience'. Christian truth lies in promoting justice and emancipation from social slavery.[4] This implies the idea of 'conscientization' or developing the power of the poor and oppressed to transform society, developed by Paulo Freire in his seminal work, *Pedagogy of the Oppressed* (1968).

## History and Eschatology

Following biblical tradition, Gutiérrez presents eschatology as the 'driving force of salvific history radically oriented toward the future'. Eschatology becomes the key to understanding the Christian faith. Like the prophets in the Old Testament, our life in Christ must be directed towards the future, although our concern is with the present.[5] This means that the full meaning of God's action in history is understood only in its eschatological perspective. It is the revelation of the final meaning of history that gives value to the present.[6]

---

1. Ibid., p. 185.
2. Ibid.
3. Ibid., p. 186.
4. Ibid., p. 188.
5. Gutiérrez, *A Theology of Liberation*, p. 162.
6. Ibid., p. 165.

In the same way, for Berdyaev, history has meaning because it is moving towards a fulfilment; it comes to an end. Otherwise life or history is meaningless if there is no closure. He concluded that the 'true philosophy of history is eschatological in nature'.[1] Thus the historical process must be understood in the light of its final end. Berdyaev adopted a Christian-Judaic understanding of history.

Originating from the Jewish idea of historical fulfilment, Berdyaev's concept of history is different from the Greek understanding, which is cyclical in nature. The Jewish consciousness looks towards the future, in expectation of some great event about to happen in the destinies of Israel and other nations as well. 'For the Jews the idea of history turns upon the expectation of some future event which will bring with it a solution of history.'[2] This Jewish understanding of history is closely linked to eschatology.

Eschatology concerns the final destiny of humankind – death and judgement. It is also the goal of history and its fulfilment. The Greeks had no such concept, but for the Jewish people, Berdyaev wrote, 'It is absolutely essential for conception and elaboration of the idea of history, as a significant progression or movement capable of fulfilment. No conception of history is feasible without the idea of fulfilment because history is essentially eschatological.'[3]

Another important feature of Berdyaev's understanding of history is messianism, which is also of Jewish origin. Growing out of Judaism, Christianity is essentially messianic. In the synoptic gospels, the focus is on the preaching of Jesus Christ on the coming of the Kingdom of God. Berdyaev stressed that the 'true messianic belief is the messianism which looks for a new era of the Spirit, for the transformation of the world and for the Kingdom of God'. As such, he rejected all attempts to establish an earthly utopia or theocracy because 'To a notable degree history is the history of crime, and all the dreams of idealists about a better state of society have ended in criminal deeds.'[4]

Even though we have not realized the Kingdom of God, Berdyaev argued that all is not lost because 'The great testing trials of man and the experience of the seductive lures through which he lives have a

1. Berdyaev, *Dream and Reality*, p. 294.
2. Berdyaev, *The Meaning of History*, p. 28.
3. Ibid., p. 32.
4. Quoted in C.S. Calian (1968), *Berdyaev's Philosophy of Hope: A Contribution to Marxist-Christian Dialogue*. Minnesota: Augsburg, p. 108.

meaning.'[1] This means that the freedom of man must be tested and proven. It will be an 'empty freedom' when it is not 'unaware of resistance, when it is too easy'. It is in conflict that freedom is tempered and fortified. Berdyaev characterized bourgeois freedom as empty and egoistic. Without resistance and sacrifice, 'freedom disintegrates'. So it is the conflicts and failures of history that compel human beings to push forward towards the Kingdom of God, according to Berdyaev. For the realisation of the Kingdom of God, what we need is 'not change *in* this world, but a change of this world'.[2]

Critical of a passive understanding of the apocalypse, Berdyaev believed that the end of the world depends on the activity of man: 'The revolutionary apocalyptic consciousness actively and creatively turns to the realization of human personality and to the society which is linked with the principle of personality.'[3] Spiritual and social revolutions cannot be wrought by human beings alone, but with the 'outpouring of the Spirit, which changes the world'. Berdyaev wrote: 'Active eschatology is the justification of the creative power of man. Man is liberated from the sway of the objectivization which had enslaved him.'[4] This suggests that man must rebel against the slavery of history in order to take history into his own hands.

The above reflection by Berdyaev suggests, in the words of Gutiérrez, that 'history is one' and there is only 'one human destiny' assumed by Christ, the Lord of history. Our human history is the history of our salvation. We have moved from an abstract, essentialist approach to 'an existential, historical, and concrete view which holds that only man we know has been efficaciously called to a gratuitous communion with God'.[5] The liberation of the Jewish people from the bondage in Egypt recorded in the Old Testament is both a historical fact and a biblical story. In view of the liberation of the Jews, Gutiérrez argues that it is by transforming the world, breaking out of servitude, establishing a just society, and assuming our destiny in history that we becomes truly ourselves. This can also mean the flourishing of the personality in Berdyaev's sense.

In spite of the Orthodox Church's lack of interest, for reasons that we have discussed, in the theology of liberation as practised in Latin America, there were voices in Russia in the late nineteenth

1. Berdyaev, *Slavery and Freedom*, p. 263.
2. Calian, *op. cit.*, pp. 108–9.
3. Berdyaev, *op. cit.*, pp. 264–5.
4. Ibid., p. 265.
5. Gutiérrez, *A Theology of Liberation*, pp. 153.

and early twentieth centuries that were critical not only of the social and political structures, but also of the ecclesiastical hierarchy. In the tradition of St John Chrysostom, they recognized the poor and downtrodden as the ones favoured by God and spoke against their wealthy oppressors. Nicolas Berdyaev was one of such modern prophets whose writings have influenced many people, not least the liberation theologian Juan Luis Segundo.

In this chapter, I have attempted to relate the works of Berdyaev to the themes of liberation theology taught by its founding father, Gustavo Gutiérrez. The similarities in their writings on Christian personalism, social justice, Marxism, history, and eschatology suggest that there is potential for ecumenical dialogue between Roman Catholic and Orthodox Christians on these issues. Berdyaev would agree that our mission now is not so much to work for the unity of the churches as for the unity of humankind journeying towards the Kingdom of God. As an existentialist philosopher, critical of both capitalism and communism, and upholding the Orthodox Christian faith, he has taught us the need to struggle for freedom and justice. Like most liberation theologians, he was in favour of some form of socialism. Berdyaev was in many ways a liberationist and his works foreshadowed the theology of liberation.

# Chapter 8
## Jaroslav Pelikan

It is commonly believed that all writing is autobiographical. In this regard, the writings of Jaroslav Pelikan reveal the spiritual journey that brought him to the bosom of the Orthodox Church, which he aptly described as a 'the logical culmination of a development in my mind and spirit that has been going on for decades'.[1] A Lutheran pastor and theologian for most of his life, Pelikan ended his life as an Orthodox layman as he finally became convinced, as a result of many years of historical study, that the Orthodox Church was the most faithful custodian of the apostolic faith.

In exploring Pelikan's 'homecoming' to Orthodoxy, this chapter seeks to examine his understanding of Christian doctrinal development, his sympathetic yet critical view of Roman Catholicism, and his encounter with Hellenism, which eventually led to his reception into the Orthodox Church. Unlike Adolf von Harnack, who believed that the Hellenization of the Christian faith was a corruption, Pelikan believed that for Christianity the turning towards Greece was indeed necessary and providential. Even as early as the 1970s, when he published the first and second volumes of *The Christian Tradition: The Emergence of the Catholic Tradition (100– 600)* in 1971 and *The Spirit of Eastern Christendom (600–1700)* in 1974, the writings of Pelikan reveal his love for and affinity with the Eastern Church.

---

1. From an open letter from Pelikan to members of Bethesda Lutheran Church, New Haven, Connecticut, the Evangelical Lutheran Church in America congregation to which Pelikan had belonged, quoted in 'Pelikan to Orthodox church', *The Lutheran*, May 1998, http://www. thelutheran.org/article/article.cfm?article_id=1897. Some material in this chapter appeared as an article: Ambrose Ih-Mong (2014), 'Return to Orthodoxy: an examination of Jaroslav Pelikan's embrace of the Eastern faith'. *International Journal of Orthodox Theology*, 5, 1, 59–83.

Regarding the second volume, Robert Louis Wilken, a former student and friend of Pelikan, claimed that there was little evidence in his public life that Pelikan was moving towards Eastern Orthodoxy. However, if writing is autobiographical, one can trace his attraction to the Eastern Church from his critical yet optimistic assessment of both the Hellenization of Christianity and of the Greek Fathers. But it took quite a long time before Pelikan landed on the shore of Orthodoxy. It was only on 25 March 1998, at the age of 75, that Jaroslav Pelikan was chrismated in the Orthodox Church. To the bishop who received him, he said: 'Any airplane that circled the airport for that long before landing would have run out of gas.'[1] His reasons for moving towards the Orthodox Church were both personal and theological, but it was not so much a conversion as a return to where he truly belonged.

Both the Orthodox Church and the Roman Catholic Church have a long history, with their roots going back to the apostolic tradition. Compared to Protestantism, they have more to offer to their adherents in terms of dogmatic teaching and tradition. That Pelikan chose the Orthodox Church over the Roman Catholic Church revealed his own Slavic background, which is more at home in Eastern Orthodoxy. An ardent admirer of Martin Luther, Pelikan believed that 'one could be catholic and orthodox without being papal'.[2] Though he ended his life as an Orthodox Christian, his devotion to Luther and love for the spirit of catholicity remained. This chapter concludes that Pelikan was indeed a true ecumenist who loved the Christian traditions he interpreted and who gave much thought to the importance of the ecumenical cause – the unity of Christians.

### *Slavic Heritage*[3]

Born in Akron, Ohio on 17 December 1923, Jaroslav Pelikan described his home as a place where there was an abundance of

---

1. Spoken to His Beatitude Metropolitan Theodosius regarding his late entry into the Orthodox Church. Pelikan (2005), 'A Personal Memoir: Fragments of a Scholar Autobiography' in Hotchkiss *et al.*, *Orthodoxy and Western Culture: A Collection of Essays Honoring Jaroslav Pelikan on His Eightieth Birthday*. New York: St Vladimir's Seminary Press, p. 44.
2. Pelikan (1974), *The Spirit of Eastern Christendom (600–1700)*. Chicago: University of Chicago Press, p. 2. A person of the church, he was also at home with the Benedictine monks in St John's Abbey in Collegeville, Minnesota. Patrick Henry and Valerie Hotchkiss (2005), 'Was wir Ererbt Haben' in Hotchkiss *et al.*, *op. cit.*, p. 17.
3. See Pelikan, 'A Personal Memoir' in Hotchkiss *et al.*, pp. 29–44.

'good food . . . music, books, languages, and above all tradition and faith'. Pelikan was of European Slavic descent; his father was from Slovakia and his mother from Yugoslavia. From his mother he acquired a 'seriousness about the conduct of life' and from his father 'a deep and all-but-pantheistic sense of affinity with Nature'. Both his father and grandfather were Lutheran pastors who could preach eloquently and powerfully in their native Slovak as well as in English. Pelikan claimed that unlike many of his academic peers, he never had serious doubts about the fundamentals of Christianity because he possessed that simple 'Slavic piety'. His father said that Jaroslav 'combined German Lutheran scholarship and Slavic orthodox piety – and fortunately not vice versa'.[1]

Conscious of his minority status as a Slovak in the United States, he was determined to master German and other languages, such as Latin, Greek, Hebrew, Czech, Serbian, and Russian, besides Slovak and English. Alongside his gift for languages, evident from an early age, Pelikan's ability to work long hours and to fall asleep instantly, combined with his monkish temperament, made him an ideal scholar. As a result he was able to complete both his BD at Concordia Seminary and his PhD at the University of Chicago (in 1946) by the age of 23. As a church historian, Pelikan stood in the tradition of Adolf von Harnack, who wrote the *History of Dogma* (1896–1899), but he sought to offer a different understanding of Christian doctrinal development. Pelikan warned his readers, 'we shall ignore Adolf [von] Harnack at our peril',[2] so it is important to have some understanding of Harnack's fundamental ideas on early church history and the development of dogma.

## *Adolf von Harnack (1851–1930)*

The decline of the Christian faith, according to von Harnack, is a result of the transformation of the Gospel by Greek philosophy, which led to the formulation of dogma. A definite stage in Christian history, dogmatic Christianity stands between Christianity as the religion of the Gospel, which implies personal experience, and Christianity as a sacramental and cultic religion. The Christian faith aligned

1. John H. Erickson (2005), 'Jaroslav Pelikan: The Living Legend in Our Midst' in Hotchkiss *et al.*, *op. cit.*, p. 7.
2. Pelikan (1961), 'Introduction to the Torchbook Edition' in Adolf von Harnack, *The Mission and Expansion of Christianity in the First Three Centuries*. New York: Harper Torchbooks, p. vi.

itself with either one or the other. It is obvious that von Harnack favoured primitive Christianity based on personal experience. When Christianity becomes intellectual, he asserted, 'there is always the danger . . . that as knowledge it may supplant religious faith, or connect it with a doctrine of religion, instead of with God and a living experience.'[1] This intellectualization of the Christian faith eventually leads to the secularizing of Christianity.

The formation of dogma, von Harnack argued, was the work of the 'Greek spirit on the soil of the Gospel'. The Gospel was expressed in Greek thought in order to make itself more intelligible to the Gentiles and it was through this Hellenization of the Christian faith that the church spread its influence and power over the ancient world and formed its peoples. Although von Harnack acknowledged it as a triumph of the Christian spirit, he insisted that the Gospel itself is not dogma, 'for belief in the Gospel provides room for knowledge only in so far as it is a state of feeling and course of action that is a definite form of life'.[2] Contrary to von Harnack, as we shall see, Pelikan argued that it was Hellenistic culture that had been influenced by the spirit of the Hebrew scripture and the Gospel, and not the other way around.

It was inevitable, in von Harnack's opinion, that primitive Christianity would disappear and become dogmatic Christianity so that it could compete with Greek rationalism. For example, in the second century, Christian apologists attempted to equate Logos with Jesus Christ.[3] This was to render the Christian faith as the rationalism of Greek thought and 'thus marked out the task of "dogmatic" and, so to speak, wrote the prolegomena for every future theological system in the Church'.[4] Clearly von Harnack was against this dogmatization of the living faith because if Christianity is wedded to only one system of metaphysics, it limits its own relevance and life span. The Gospel, on the other hand, is timeless and universal.

Favouring Augustine, von Harnack believed that the doctor from Hippo was able to penetrate dogma to present a moral psychology of faith. Augustine based his theology on his personal experience of faith rather than intellectual abstraction, and thus, he can be

---

1. Adolf von Harnack (1961), *History of Dogma*, Vol. I, trans. Neil Buchanan. New York: Dover, p. 16.
2. Ibid., pp. 17–18.
3. von Harnack (1957), *What is Christianity?*, trans. Thomas Bailey Saunders. New York: Harper & Row, pp. 202–3.
4. von Harnack (1961), *History of Dogma*, Vol. II, trans. Neil Buchanan. New York: Dover, p. 224.

considered to be the origin of classic Protestantism. Von Harnack wrote that Augustine 'rescued religion from its communal and cultus form and restored it to the heart'.[1] Martin Luther, originally an Augustinian priest, was brought up in that tradition.

If Christianity is interpreted through the lens of one philosophical system, namely the Greco-Roman model, according to von Harnack, it will outlive its usefulness. Robert Wilken proposed a different viewpoint when he said that we should now speak of the 'Christianization of Hellenism'. We should not forget the debt owed to Jewish thought and the Jewish Bible, but we should also acknowledge the positive effect of Greek philosophy on the Christian faith, especially in its emphasis on virtues and the moral life. In *Spirit of Early Christian Thought: Seeking the Face of God* (2003), Wilken writes: '[O]ne observes again and again that Christian thinking, while working within patterns of thought and conception rooted in Greco-Roman culture, transformed them so profoundly that in the end something quite new came into being.'[2] This idea of Wilken, supported by Pelikan, represents a turning away from von Harnack's thesis, which dominated the nineteenth- and early twentieth-century interpretation of Christian history.

Unlike von Harnack, who believed that the development of church dogma represented a hardening of the Gospel message, Pelikan insisted that Christian doctrines are more than just ideas and concepts; they are 'what the Church believes, teaches, and confesses as it prays and suffers, serves and obeys, celebrates and awaits the coming of the kingdom of God'. It is also an expression of the broken state of Christian faith and witness, the most patent illustration of the truth of the apostolic admission in 1 Corinthians 13:12: 'Now we see in a mirror dimly. . . . Now I know in part.'[3] Christian doctrines thus help us to get a glimpse of divine reality that no words can fully express. At the same time, it is also important to understand that Christian doctrines did not descend directly from God, but, according to John Henry Newman, developed and evolved through time in an organic fashion. Both Pelikan and Newman believed in the importance of dogma in Christian faith.

1. von Harnack (1959), *Outlines of the History of Dogma*. Boston: Beacon Press, p. 336.
2. Robert Louis Wilken (2003), *Spirit of Early Christian Thought: Seeking the Face of God*. New Haven: Yale University Press, p. xvi.
3. Pelikan (1969), *Development of Christian Doctrine: Some Historical Prolegomena*. New Haven: Yale University Press, pp. 143–4.

## *Development of Christian Doctrine*

As an advocate of creedal Christianity, Pelikan, like Newman, maintained that Christian doctrine is the principle of religion. As such, religion cannot last long when its dogmatic principles are denied because these principles give the faith its essence and impulse. In other words, religion cannot survive by emotions or ethical principles alone. For Pelikan, Christian doctrine refers to what the Church of Jesus believed, taught, and confessed based on the Word of God. Be that as it may, Christian doctrine has also been a source of fierce contention among Christians and has led to the separation of churches. In fact, Newman identified the development of doctrine as the point of contention between Roman Catholics and Protestants. In 1845, in order to prove that nineteenth-century Roman Catholicism was the closest to the Church of Athanasius in the fourth century, Newman wrote his *Essay on Development of Christian Doctrine*. Although Newman understood that the dogmatic principle written in human language was imperfect, he insisted that it was necessary because dogmas are divinely revealed. Dogma is the church's manner of expressing its tenets and must be held in faith. Seeking to critique Newman, Pelikan gave his own reflection on this topic from a Protestant point of view.

Following Newman's criteria of authenticity, Pelikan first commented on 'The Preservation of Type or Idea'. Any development in the Roman Catholic Church has to preserve the basic idea of the church – thus catholicity must be used to distinguish genuine development from corruption. Protestants like von Harnack and Sebastian Franck believed that the development of the ecclesiastical hierarchy, creed, and canon in the Roman Catholic Church was a corruption of apostolic Christianity. This is what divides some Protestants from other Protestants, and Protestants from all Catholics.[1]

Newman held that in spite of the variety of doctrines, one can still discover a continuity of principles, and the truth and authenticity of these doctrines is based on fidelity to these continuing principles. But many Protestants argued that the continuity of the church is based not on dogmatic principles but on Christian experience, the 'realm of inner experience'. Supporting Friedrich Schleiermacher and Newman, Pelikan asserted that the authenticity of doctrinal development depends on its 'congruence with inner experience'.

---

1. Ibid., p. 14.

It is experience within 'the setting of the Church – its memory, its witness, its celebrations', and not just any idiosyncratic emotions.[1]

The church, Newman taught, has the power to assimilate extra-Christian sources for the purpose of evangelization; it is able to adopt pagan philosophy, existing rites and customs of the people, for its own Christian development. As we have seen, von Harnack had a contrary view regarding the church's power of assimilation – he saw it as a betrayal, a sell-out to the process of Hellenization. Although the von Harnack school of thought has lost some of its prestige, Pelikan acknowledged that its position is still influential in some circles. In fact, Karl Barth, another great Protestant theologian of the twentieth century, was totally against Christian assimilation of alien elements.[2]

Protestantism teaches that any doctrinal development must be based on explicit reference to the scripture – *sola Scriptura*. Otherwise it is a corruption. Looking at specific doctrinal issues, Newman taught that: 'Scripture must be said to contain implicitly the doctrines that the later doctrinal development of the Church has made explicit in creed and dogmatic decree.'[3] In other words, we must pay attention to traditions apart from the Bible. In an apparent move to support Newman's idea, Pelikan argued that different Protestant denominations have different understandings of *sola Scriptura*. The Reformers used tradition in their reading of scripture to support their position. Further, *sola Scriptura* has itself become an indispensable tradition for Protestants in their theological works.

There is a logical sequence in doctrinal development, according to Newman. For example, the doctrine of the Incarnation leads to the understanding that Mary is the Mother of God. There is a systematic connection between these two doctrines and this proves that the development is genuine. Luther, however, objected to this because a theologian need not be a logician: 'In vain does one fashion a logic of faith. . . . No syllogistic form is valid when applied to divine terms.'[4] Supporting Luther's view, Pelikan argued that the authenticity of Christian doctrine is to be found in its biblical source and not in the structure of the doctrinal system. In 1969, reflecting on Newman's understanding of doctrinal development, Pelikan revealed the Reformer's principle with his stress on *sola Scriptura* and the inner experience of our Christian faith.

1. Ibid., pp. 15–16.
2. Ibid., pp. 17–18.
3. Ibid., p. 19.
4. Ibid., p. 21.

Regarding 'preservative additions', Newman argued that dogmas are needed to preserve the faith that the church confesses and therefore, if one is obedient to the church, one must uphold its dogmas. But classic Protestant teaching, according to Pelikan, maintains that 'dogmas were merely summaries of scriptural doctrine'. The church's role is a passive one in the formulation of dogmas. Christians subscribe to doctrines contained in the Creed not because they are in the Creed, but because they are also in the scriptures. In fact, Protestants believe that there has been no development of Christian doctrine since the apostolic times and therefore, other than the doctrines taught by the apostles in the scriptures, everything else is error and destructive to the faith.[1]

Some theologians maintain that the fact that the Roman Catholic Church has endured for such a long time, expressed by Newman as 'chronic continuance', shows that its doctrinal development has been authentic. But Protestants, like von Harnack, believe that primitive Christianity has disappeared to give way to institutional Christianity represented by the Roman Catholic Church. Chronic continuance, in the Protestant view, reveals the inauthentic nature of doctrinal development.[2]

In presenting the Protestant response to Newman's essay on doctrinal development, Pelikan also insisted that theologians are merely 'spokesmen' for the church, not 'corporate popes'. At the same time, his Roman Catholic affinities were revealed when he wrote: 'It was the sacramental life of the community, not the speculation of its theologians that brought forth Cyprian's doctrine of original sin. Similarly, the religious life . . . was responsible for the evolution of the doctrine of Mary in the thought of Athanasius.' Pelikan acknowledged that Newman's emphasis in his writings on the church as community 'provided a much-needed corrective to the emphasis of German Lutheran *Dogmengeschichte* on the great ideas of the great theologians – an overemphasis that has had as its almost unavoidable corollary a preoccupation with discontinuity.'[3] This statement reflects Pelikan's intention to move away from von Harnack's theory of the early church, characterized by discontinuity. It also reveals his affinity with Roman Catholicism or, more concretely, with the spirit of catholicity, which he believed all genuine Christian traditions possess. In *The Riddle of Roman Catholicism*, Pelikan presents a sympathetic and yet

---

1. Ibid., pp. 22–3.
2. Ibid., pp. 23–4.
3. Ibid., pp. 144.

critical account of the Roman Catholic Church. In my opinion, it is as sympathetic as it could possibly be, written by a theologian from a Lutheran perspective in the United States in the late 1950s.

## The Western Church

First of all, Pelikan considered the development of catholic Christianity to be valid. For him, catholicity meant 'identity plus universality'; identity here means that it is distinct from the world and universality means that it embraces all humankind.[1] Christianity became catholic when it moved out of the confines of Judaism towards the non-Jews. The ministry of Jesus was not a nationalistic message, but a universal salvation for all peoples. Pelikan also claimed that the church became catholic when it established an episcopal ministry with priests and bishops. In the New Testament, Jesus instituted the apostolic office.[2] The development of the sacraments and liturgy also helped to make the church catholic as they seek to satisfy the longing of people for forgiveness and immortality.[3]

In theology, catholic Christianity clarifies its identity and universality. Pelikan maintained that theology helped the church to define and defend its teaching against the distortions of heretics, and thus, catholic means orthodox. In many ways, heresies helped the church to clarify and define precisely the core of its teachings, namely creation, redemption, and revelation. Pelikan's partiality towards the East was revealed when he considered Origen (more on him later) as 'the catholic theologian' because he was able to combine the defence of the faith with a profound knowledge of the scriptures, which few could do then and even now.[4]

The primacy of Rome was questioned by Pelikan, who insisted on the uniqueness and prestige of Jerusalem as narrated in the New Testament. For him, Jerusalem should be regarded as the mother church as acknowledged by Paul himself. In the early church, all

---

1. Pelikan (1959), *The Riddle of Roman Catholicism*. New York: Abingdon Press, p. 22.
2. Ibid., p. 25.
3. Ibid., pp. 27. McGrath notes that in the twentieth century, Western theologians were very interested in the notions of 'catholicity' which were dominant in the Orthodox churches. 'Catholicity' is often expressed in Russian as '*Sobornost*', which generally means 'universality'. Alister E. McGrath (2006), *Christianity: An Introduction*. Oxford: Blackwell, p. 265.
4. Pelikan, *op. cit.*, pp. 29–30.

matters were settled in Jerusalem. Although Pelikan questioned the
authority of Rome, he also acknowledged the primacy of Peter –
Peter comes first in the apostolic college.[1] But what made Rome
prestigious was the orthodoxy of its bishops. Throughout the history
of doctrinal development in the church, Pelikan wrote, the popes
'manifested an astonishing capacity to select and formulate – or to take
credit for – the orthodox solution to thorny theological questions'.[2]
In doctrinal disputes, Rome showed its ability and orthodoxy. It was
not just because Rome had better strategy in the worldly sense, but
that Rome was able to put forward intrinsically valid theological
formulas that were accepted by the orthodox majority. Aided by
scripture and tradition, Rome had this uncanny ability to distinguish
the core of the faith from its speculative elements. In short, Pelikan
argued that Rome enjoyed a unique position among the patriarchates
because of its orthodoxy, location, and freedom.[3]

In spite of his sympathetic and favourable review of the Roman
Catholic Church, Pelikan was also critical of the attempt by the
Roman Church to dominate the Eastern Church after the Siege of
Constantinople by the Fourth Crusade in 1204. Supporting Eastern
Orthodox writers, he was of the opinion that it was the Crusaders'
brutality that led to the split between Rome and the East. Pelikan
also pointed out that in modern times, Roman Catholic leaders
have admitted their mistakes in trying to Latinize Eastern liturgical
traditions, but unfortunately Rome has refused to be merely first
among equals.[4] Unlike Protestantism, which Rome does not consider
as part of the church, the churches of the East remained churches.
Hence Rome is keen to achieve unity with Eastern Orthodoxy
and is willing to let the Eastern Churches retain their own rites,
traditions, and patriarchs. Unfortunately, Pelikan lamented, due to
bad experiences in the past, very few Orthodox leaders take Rome's
friendly gestures seriously. This brings us to Pelikan's discussion of the
Eastern Orthodox tradition, which finally became his spiritual home.

### The Eastern Church

In order to grasp Jaroslav Pelikan's profound affinity with the
Orthodox spirit later in his life, it is necessary to understand his

1. Ibid., p. 35.
2. Ibid., p. 39.
3. Ibid., pp. 39–42.
4. Ibid., p. 43.

nuanced and in-depth view on the Hellenization of Christianity based on his reading of the Cappadocian Fathers and others. A clear indication that Pelikan had a deep love for Greek culture and language can be found in the dedication of his work, *Christianity and Classical Culture*: 'To my daughter, Miriam, who has deepened and enriched my own encounter with Hellenism.' Pelikan regarded the fact that the New Testament was written in Greek and not in Hebrew or Aramaic as a great convergence of mind and spirit in human history. This means that any other translation of the Christian scripture has to take into consideration its understanding of Greek semantics and syntax. Not only scripture, but also Christian doctrine was expressed with precision in Greek, revealing the superiority of Eastern theology. Furthermore, not even Latin words can match the sophistication of Greek in expressing the various doctrinal controversies. In fact, the Orthodox Christians believed that the Light comes from the East – *Ex Oriente Lux* – 'an affirmation of the special destiny of the East', and thus they disparaged the West as a symbol of the 'godless souls in the deep hell of ignorance'.[1]

The Christian thinkers despised the Greek religious beliefs but upheld their philosophical outlook. For example, Clement of Alexandria called upon his colleagues to combine scripture with the writings of Homer: 'Philosophy is a long-lived exhortation, wooing the eternal love of wisdom, while the commandment of the Lord is far-shining, "enlightening the eyes".' Clement was a Christian apologist steeped in Platonic doctrine that taught the pre-existence of the soul and at the same time he was also against Gnosticism.[2] Thus we see that the borrowing of Greek concepts was not a straightforward process. In fact, Henry Chadwick argued that it would be misleading to consider Clement a Hellenizer because he was very attached to the church.[3] The same can be said of other Christian apologists; they quoted scripture to support philosophy, which in turn was modified to fit scripture.

Contrary to many Western scholars who believed that there was not much doctrinal development in the East, Pelikan, in the second volume of *The Christian Tradition: The Spirit of Eastern Christendom (600–1700)*, attempted to show that there was indeed lively doctrinal development in the Orient. His affinity with Orthodox theology and

---

1. Pelikan, *The Spirit of Eastern Christendom*, pp. 2–3.
2. Pelikan (1971), *The Emergence of the Catholic Tradition (100–600)*. Chicago: University of Chicago Press, pp. 47–8.
3. Ibid., p. 55.

piety is obvious in his detailed analysis of the theological controversies that occurred in the Eastern Church. It would also be a mistake, Pelikan argued, to think that there is no one as brilliant and as creative as Augustine of Hippo among the Greek theologians. He considered Origen of Alexandria to be Augustine's equal in his theological writings.

## Origen of Alexandria

Origen was a 'consistent Hellenizer': in his writings we see the constant tension between biblical and philosophical doctrines. Dismissing the literal resurrection of the body, Origen insisted that this literal doctrine was allegorical because 'in the body there lies a certain principle which is not corrupted from which the body is raised in corruption.'[1] Acknowledging the doctrine of the immortality of the soul, he believed that the soul existed before time. In Origen's work, both biblical doctrine and philosophical speculation form part of his theologizing. As mentioned earlier, Pelikan considered Origen to be the 'catholic theologian' and a church's man, to be judged according to the intellectual climate of his time.

## The Cappadocian Fathers

Besides Origen, the three Cappadocian Fathers, Basil of Caesarea, his brother Gregory of Nyssa, and Gregory of Nazianzus, in their joint accomplishment as Christian thinkers in the Eastern Church, also matched Augustine's influence in the Latin West. They were Hellenists, having studied classical Greek literature and philosophy, but they were not uncritical of its influence in their theological expositions.[2] In fact, Pelikan claimed that they were constantly engaging with the monuments of Greek culture, its thought processes and concepts, in order to refine their own understanding of natural theology and Christian revelation. In *The Emergence of the Catholic Tradition*, Pelikan's bias towards the Greek Fathers is evident in his treatment of the doctrine of the Trinity: he focuses much more on the teaching of the Cappadocians than on Augustine's *De Trinitate*. Unlike von Harnack, who considered Augustine a monumental figure in the history of Christianity, Pelikan emphasized the writings of the Greek Fathers.

---

1. Ibid., p. 48.
2. See Pelikan (1993), *Christianity and Classical Culture: The Metamorphosis of Natural Theology in the Christian Encounter with Hellenism*. New Haven and London: Yale University Press, pp. 3–9.

The Cappadocians taught that Greek culture is not to be shunned but cultivated, because a believer can benefit from pagan learning, just as Moses' training in Egyptian culture enabled him to become a great teacher and leader. Likewise, Basil became the champion of Christian Hellenism and he was at the same time critical of some of its aspects. An example of Hellenistic influence is the sophisticated style of writing that the Cappadocians learned in their classical education. Having benefited greatly from reading pagan books, Basil, in his educational treatise, *Ad adolescentes, de legendis libris Gentilium*, gave a positive assessment of Greek classical learning. It would be a grave mistake, Basil warned, to abandon classical learning as an excuse for embracing the Christian faith. In their opposition to the emperor Julian the Apostate, who wanted to break the alliance between Christianity and Greek culture, the Cappadocians insisted on speaking, writing, and thinking in Greek in their theological treatises and exhortations.[1] According to them, it is obvious that one can be Hellenistic without embracing the Greek deities and myths.

In spite of their admiration for Hellenistic classical learning and culture, especially the Greek language, these theologians never failed to extol the simplicity and beauty of the Hebrew scripture and faith that they believed to be far superior to Greek wisdom.[2] In other words, the Cappadocians adopted a rather ambivalent attitude towards Greek classical learning: they loved the Greek language but were very critical of Greek myths, religion, and various aspects of Hellenistic philosophy. An example of their love for the classical language, Pelikan remarked, is the fact that much of the vocabulary used in Christian liturgy was borrowed from classical Greek, for example '*panēgyrizein* (to celebrate) and *heortazein* (to keep a festival)'.[3]

Against Greek religious belief, worship, and myths, the Cappadocian teachers aligned themselves with pagan Greek thinkers in natural theology and rationalistic philosophy, for they were conscious of the distinction between Greek religious belief and their critical thinking. It is in natural theology, Pelikan argued, that fruitful exchange between Hellenism and Christianity took place. Quoting Werner Jaeger, he wrote: '[T]he Greek spirit reached its highest religious development, not in the cults of the

1. Ibid., pp. 10–12.
2. Ibid., p. 12.
3. Ibid., p. 23.

gods . . . but chiefly in philosophy, assisted by the Greek gift for constructing systematic theories of the universe.'[1] It is through Greek philosophical-scientific concepts and not their religious ideas that Christian thinkers developed their own natural theology. Formulated by Gregory of Nyssa, it was a method that made use of scripture and human reasoning, joining divine and human knowledge, to formulate doctrines against heretical teachings. The Cappadocians also believed that it was faith that gives us the fullness of understanding.[2] Here we see another attitude towards Greek influence.

In spite of his praise and admiration for the use of Greek language in scripture and theology, Pelikan cautioned that the term 'Hellenization' is too simplistic to describe accurately the process and relationship between Greek culture and orthodox Christian doctrine. Christian doctrine expressed in Greek 'bears the marks of its struggle to understand and overcome pagan thought'. The Christian apologists' attitude towards ancient culture is 'contradictory': on the one hand, they try to bring out the contrast between Christianity and pagan thoughts, and on the other hand, the deeper contrast has been absorbed into Christian concepts. The apologists wanted to show that Christ was 'the revealer of true philosophy' and at the same time that he was also the fulfilment of ancient pagan philosophy.[3] They bring to our attention the constant tension and struggle in the encounter between Hellenism and Christianity. In short, it was not a simple and straightforward process.

Pelikan taught that the development of Christian doctrine was a process of 'de-Hellenization' of the theology that was developing in the early church by placing limits on Greek speculative thought. Contact with Greek culture was an important development, a theological necessity, as it helped to preserve Christian orthodoxy by engaging with the pagan philosophy. The Hellenization of Christianity was a complex and contradictory process. Pelikan believed that the struggle and tension that Greek influence caused in the development of Christian doctrine was not a compromise with secularism as taught by von Harnack, but part and parcel of God's plan to reach his people. Regarding this issue, Joseph Ratzinger, Pope Emeritus Benedict XVI, has said:

---

1.  Ibid., p. 24.
2.  Ibid., pp. 26–7.
3.  Pelikan, *The Emergence of the Catholic Tradition*, pp. 45–6.

The encounter between the Biblical message and Greek thought did not happen by chance. The vision of Saint Paul, who saw the roads to Asia barred and in a dream saw a Macedonian man plead with him: 'Come over to Macedonia and help us!' (cf. Acts 16:6-10) – this vision can be interpreted as a 'distillation' of the intrinsic necessity of a rapprochement between Biblical faith and Greek inquiry.

This inner rapprochement between Biblical faith and Greek philosophical inquiry was an event of decisive importance not only from the standpoint of the history of religions, but also from that of world history – it is an event which concerns us even today.[1]

The fact remains: Christianity originated in Palestine, but developed in the East before it emerged in the West.

## The Orthodox Tradition

As a church historian, Pelikan appreciated the fact that the Orthodox Church has a long history compared to the Roman Catholic and Protestant traditions.[2] It has preserved its ancient practices and traditions more fully than the other Christian churches. It is a tradition that is not fossilized but is fully alive, as Pelikan famously put it: 'Tradition is the living faith of the dead, traditionalism is the dead faith of the living.'[3] This means that Orthodox Christianity is a living faith connected with the past as well as with the present and future.

1. Pope Benedict XVI (2006), 'Faith, Reason and the University', lecture at the University of Regensburg, 12 September, http://www.vatican. va/holy_father/benedict_xvi/speeches/2006/september/documents/hf_ben-xvi_spe_20060912_university-regensburg_en.html.
2. Jacobsen claims that the Orthodox Church has the 'longest history' of the four major Christian traditions, Orthodox, Catholic, Protestant, and Pentecostal. McGrath asserts that by the end of the first century, Christianity seemed to have established itself throughout the eastern Mediterranean world. Of the three important theological centres in the early church, Alexandria, Antioch, and Western North Africa, the first two were Greek-speaking and the third was Latin-speaking. See Douglas Jacobsen (2011), *The World's Christians: Who they are, Where they are, and How they got there*. Oxford: Wiley-Blackwell, p. 13; and Alister E. McGrath (2006), *Christianity: An Introduction*. Oxford: Blackwell, pp. 182 and 184.
3. Pelikan (1984), *The Vindication of Tradition*. New Haven: Yale University Press, p. 65.

Regarding the issue of salvation, Orthodoxy's understanding is broader compared to that of Roman Catholics and Protestants. It stresses the idea of *theosis* or deification of humanity and creation: 'I have said, you are gods; and all of you are children of the most High' (Psalm 82:6). Athanasius said, 'God became man so that man might become a god.'[1] This means that we participate in God's divine life, not that we are his equals.

Accordingly, Orthodox theology possesses a much more positive attitude towards human nature than Roman Catholicism and Protestantism. In Orthodox theology, human beings are weakened by sins, but they are not totally lost or depraved and thus, salvation is seen as a recovery from sickness.[2] It is logical to think that God, as creator of the universe, desires to save the whole world, humans as well as all that is in it. This understanding of universal salvation in Orthodox tradition is known as apokatastasis. I believe it is this aspect of Orthodox teaching, this broad vision of universal salvation, that Pelikan took to heart, as he was a person who truly loved the Christian traditions such that he studied and interpreted as a church historian and theologian. In short, Pelikan was an ecumenical scholar who seriously sought the unity of all Christians.

## Orthodoxy and Vatican II

Pelikan claimed that the Orthodox Church has had an influence on the Roman Catholic Church, especially in the area of ecclesiology. This is demonstrated by the direction the Second Vatican Council took regarding the nature of the church and its relation to other Christian communities as well as members of other religions. One of the main ideas that the Roman Catholic Church has learned from the Eastern Church is the concept of *sobornost*. Other areas of Orthodox influence on the Roman Catholic Church include the centrality of worship, liturgy, the emphasis on the Eucharist, and pneumatology.

In the twentieth century, there was the theological rediscovery of the doctrine of the church, closely tied to the rediscovery of the reality of the church itself. The doctrine of the church as the supreme expression of the social character of Christianity was sensitive to both

---

1. Cf. St Athanasius, *De Incarnatione* or *On the Incarnation*, 54:3, PG 25:192B; also *Catechism of the Catholic Church*, paragraph 460, http://www.vatican.va/archive/ENG0015/__P1J.HTM; and http://www.philvaz.com/apologetics/a124.htm.
2. Jacobsen, *op. cit.*, p. 18.

the community and individual experience. According to Pelikan, Eastern Orthodoxy became influential in this area and the term *sobornost*, 'spiritual unity and harmony', was adopted by western theologians. *Sobornost* for the Eastern Orthodox Church means that authority lies in the church as opposed to a 'papal monarch' in Roman Catholicism and the *sola Scriptura* in Protestantism.[1] Pelikan considered this to be a period of intense ecclesiological renewal and believed that the Christian East had a lot to contribute in this area.

Pelikan also argued that the principle of 'the rule of prayer should lay down the rule of faith' influenced the renewal of ecclesiology during the twentieth century greatly.[2] This was a time of new attention given to the centrality of worship in both life and doctrine. It became an ecumenical tool for understanding the distinctiveness of individual churches and for a path towards unity; it also led to redefining the essence of the church. Twentieth-century Roman Catholic ecclesiology emphasized 'the harmony of spirit between liturgy and chant' and 'the common sacrificial action of priest and people,' and also warned against 'an excessively external definition of the church'.[3] The Second Vatican Council also reiterated the importance of liturgy, defining it as the summit and fountain from which the power of the church flows. The primary aim of the liturgical renewal was to recover the objective expression of corporate faith and worship in the Eucharist. Here we clearly see the influence of Orthodoxy on Roman Catholicism.

During the twentieth century, the development of 'biblical theology' as a distinct field of study led to an examination of metaphors such as 'people of God', 'bride of Christ', and 'body of Christ' for their special contribution to the total biblical picture of the Christian community. Because of its eucharistic associations, 'the body of Christ' became an important metaphor in theological vocabulary. According to Pelikan, the concept of 'the mystical body of Christ' became prominent with the promulgation of the papal encyclical *Mystici corporis Christi* – the term 'mystical' is used to distinguish the church as '"body of Christ" in relation to his "physical" or "natural" or "eucharistic body"'.[4]

---

1. Pelikan (1989), *Christian Doctrine and Modern Culture since 1700* (Vol. V of *The Christian Tradition*). Chicago: University of Chicago Press, p. 287.
2. Ibid., p. 294.
3. Ibid., p. 295.
4. Ibid., p. 302.

Pelikan argued that in the twentieth century churches often allowed themselves to be separated by secular forces in spite of the blurring of confessional differences that occurred at this time. The historical relativism that was a product of the eighteenth and nineteenth centuries made people recognize that doctrines such as justification had been conditioned by historical events in the church and also individual psychology during the Reformation. There was an agreement that Christian doctrine needed to stand on its own beyond the relativities of history; theologians also needed to set themselves apart from their secular counterparts by 'articulating "the relativism of faith"'.[1]

The church in the late nineteenth and twentieth century also saw the possibility of constructing a more humane and just social order. Pelikan praised Christians for taking the lead in the campaign against slavery. The 1891 encyclical of Pope Leo XIII, *Rerum Novarum*, became the charter of Roman Catholic social teaching. The law of social solidarity, the 'solidaristic conception of sin' and the social gospel in general were gaining popularity:[2] 'To those whose minds live in the social gospel . . . the kingdom of God is a dear truth.'[3]

While continuing to affirm its saving mission by converting the world to the Gospel of Christ, the Second Vatican Council also considered the doctrinal meaning of the status of non-Christians in their own right. According to Pelikan, this was in contrast to the conventional view of the uniqueness and exclusivity of the Gospel revelation that found support in the Gospel of John's pre-existent Logos. Another traditional view was the application to the new awareness of the primacy of Christian revelation – salvation only in Christ. There was also the commitment to the particularity of Christian revelation with an affirmation of the universal salvific will of God in Christian revelation: 'God's revelation is not confined to the church, although the church has, in the scriptures and in its experience, the means of interpreting God's continued revelation,' according to the Lutheran Bishop Nathan Söderblom.[4]

Related to this concern with 'progressive revelation' was the recognition in the Decree on Religious Liberty of the Second Vatican Council that all nations of different cultures are coming to closer unity and relationship. This insight had come only through

---

1. Ibid., p. 307
2. Ibid., p. 319.
3. Ibid., p. 321.
4. Ibid., p. 333.

development of doctrine and a deeper development in the church's understanding of revelation through the centuries. Pelikan argued that this could also lead to 'a further clarification of the relation between particularity and universality, and thus of the relation between Christianity and other religions'. The Council also extended to non-Christian religions an acknowledgement of positive values in their traditions, 'a recognition of a supreme Divinity and a supreme Father': '[T]he Catholic Church rejects nothing that is true and holy in these religions.'[1]

The Second Vatican Council expressed for the church of the twentieth century a doctrinal foundation. The unity of the church was a divine gift to be received with gratitude and it is the task of all Christians to restore that unity. The Council looked beyond the needs of any particular church to a vision of catholic universality and the *sobornost* that all men and women will embrace. This brings us to the issue of ecumenism.

## The Ecumenical Cause

According to Pelikan, the ecumenical cause is important to the church. The unity we have is in Christ, and this gives hope to our ecumenical efforts. Further, all Christians – Orthodox, Roman Catholics, and Protestants – believe that the church is holy, catholic, and apostolic, although they disagree on the definitions of each of these terms. Emphasizing that the holiness of the church is a gift of God, Pelikan maintained that even if Roman Catholics and Protestants cannot agree on the meaning of holiness, they have at least admitted that they fall short of the holiness that is expected of them. Hence we have a unity of weakness.[2]

As we have seen, Pelikan defined catholicity as identity plus universality, which is the ideal of both Roman Catholics and Protestants. But he also reminded us that both churches cannot achieve this ideal if they remain separated because Protestants 'need Roman Catholicism to prove their own catholicity. Protestants are catholic if they realize that Roman Catholicism is Christian.'[3] The presence of the Eastern Churches, Pelikan argued, shows that it is wrong to equate catholic with Roman Catholic. This understanding may form the basis of our effort to be united.

---

1. Ibid., p. 334.
2. Pelikan, *The Riddle of Roman Catholicism*, p. 184.
3. Ibid., p. 186.

Regarding the apostolic nature of the church, Roman Catholics trace their roots to the promise that Jesus gives to Peter: 'And I say also unto thee, That thou art Peter, and upon this rock I will build my church; and the gates of hell shall not prevail against it' (Matthew 16:18). Protestants, on the other hand, insist that they are faithful to the apostolic scripture of the New Testament.[1] This means that apostolic origin is to be found in fidelity to the Bible and not in the authority of the popes who can and did err. Not stating explicitly who he considered to have the better argument, Pelikan insisted that apostolic does not mean uniformity as the New Testament testifies to the variety of its witness in Peter, Paul, and Apollos – none of them alone makes the church apostolic. Pelikan wrote: 'The church will be apostolic when it finds its unity in the one Lord and one faith confessed by the apostles at the same time that it cultivates the unity-in-diversity manifested by the apostles.'[2] This means that the church can remain together in spite of conflicts and disagreements in doctrines and customs as the clash between Peter and Paul in the early church has shown.

Besides focusing on areas of commonality, Pelikan looked at sources of ancient Christian faith for the purpose of furthering the cause of Christian unity. These are scripture, tradition, Early Fathers, the Reformation, and liturgy. Although the interpretation of scripture has been one of the main sources of conflict and disagreement among Christians, Pelikan suggested that historical-critical study of the Old Testament has the potential to bring Roman Catholics and Protestants together. Further, he claimed that Protestants were beginning to pay more attention to the question of tradition, which is an authoritative voice for Roman Catholics as well as Orthodox.[3]

Regarding the legacy of the Early Church Fathers, Pelikan was delighted to see Catholic theologians gaining fresh insights from their study of Greek-speaking theologians from the East. Catholic theologians have interpreted Origen, for example, not according to the later standard of orthodoxy, but according to the importance of his writings at that time.[4] Thus the importance of historical–critical studies of scripture and the Church Fathers has drawn Christians from different traditions closer together. Pelikan believed that if church leaders started to take this kind of study seriously, we could achieve further unity at the official level.

---

1. Ibid., p. 187.
2. Ibid., p. 188.
3. Ibid., pp. 191–3.
4. Ibid., p. 195.

Regarding the legacy of the Reformation, Pelikan insisted that Roman Catholics take seriously the gravity of this historical event and do not dismiss it as another heresy or as the greatest apostasy in church history. For Pelikan, the Reformation was both tragic and necessary: it was tragic because both sides lost something valuable in the process; and it was necessary because the reformers wanted the best and highest in Roman Catholicism. Thus, Pelikan called upon his fellow Protestants to understand that the Reformation makes no sense apart from the Roman Catholic context in which it happened.[1] Martin Luther, an Augustinian and scripture scholar, was brought up in the great tradition and piety of the Roman Catholic Church. Nothing can change this fact. This means that Protestants must take pride in the catholicity of their reformers and come to appreciate the beauty and genius of Roman Catholicism at its best.

Through ecumenical contact with Roman Catholicism, Protestant Christians can learn to appreciate and adopt the forms and rites of Roman Catholic liturgy. Roman Catholics can also learn from Protestants the 'evangelical forces' of preaching and hymn singing. Pelikan was of the opinion that liturgical exploration can be used as a method to understand more profoundly what divides and what unites Christians from different traditions.[2]

Finally, Pelikan called upon all Christians to bear the burden of separation through mutual support and 'mutual responsibility to and for each other'.[3] Our common faith in the Lord must lead us to examine the strengths and weaknesses of our differences and to learn from one another. Pelikan maintained that neither Protestantism nor Roman Catholicism possesses the fullness of the Christian tradition. This means that we must seek to incorporate as much as possible of the total Christian tradition into our own church. Thus Protestants must learn to strengthen their catholicity and Roman Catholics must become more evangelical in their worship.[4] Deeply aware of the deficiencies and weaknesses of both Protestantism and Roman Catholicism, Pelikan at last found what he believed to be the ideal Christian community for him – the Orthodox Church.

As an ecumenist, Pelikan chose to embrace Orthodoxy at the end of his life because it has a long historical tradition going back to apostolic times; it possesses solid formulation of faith found in its

1. Ibid., p. 197.
2. Ibid., pp. 199–200.
3. Ibid., p. 215.
4. Ibid., pp. 222–3.

ancient doctrines; it emphasizes an inner experience in its religious devotion; and it has splendid and solemn liturgical rites as well as an established monastic tradition with its stress on the mystical life. All these can be found in one way or another in Roman Catholicism and Protestantism. But it is in the Orthodox Church, Pelikan believed, that they find their deepest and fullest expressions, and it is here that he returned to rest.

# Conclusion

We have seen that Orthodox theology, like other mainstream theology, has its sources in scripture, tradition, and the works of the Church Fathers. But it is the way Orthodox theologians interpret these sources that gives them a distinctive character. Orthodox theology is by no means uniform. In fact, Orthodox thinkers display a certain pluralism in their approach to various theological issues, as we have seen in studying the works of these eight theologians. Nonetheless, at the official level, there are fundamental basic beliefs that both the Orthodox and Roman Catholic Churches hold as non-negotiable. To conclude this study, we will look at some of the common declarations and a joint commission report issued by both churches to help us better appreciate the common heritage that both churches possess. Human factors, such as pride, rivalry, and the inability to forgive, have kept the two sister churches apart. Hence the title of this work emphasizes the idea of purification of memory as a way to move forward towards unity.

At the official level, the foundations have been laid for further dialogue on theological issues as well as mutual co-operation in pastoral and educational work. A study of three common declarations arising from the meeting between the Roman Catholic and Orthodox Churches and of the joint commission report will reveal to us some of our common beliefs. The first declaration was made by Pope Paul VI and His Holiness Mar Ignatius Jacob III in 1971. His Holiness Mar Ignatius Jacob III, Syrian Orthodox Patriarch of Antioch and all of the East, paid an official visit to Rome from 25 to 27 October 1971. The pope and the patriarch acknowledged the spiritual communion that existed between the two churches, namely in the celebration of the Eucharist, the profession in the Lord Jesus Christ, and the apostolic traditions that form part of their heritage. These traditions include the Fathers and Doctors of the Church, such as St

Cyril of Alexandria, who are recognized as common teachers in the faith. In spite of conflicts due to human failings, the Holy Spirit is active in the churches. Mutual denunciations have now given way to reconciliation with the hope that 'the burden of history which still weights heavily upon Christians' will eventually be removed.[1]

Pope Paul VI and the Patriarch Mar Ignatius Jacob II recognized their common faith concerning the 'mystery of the Word of God made flesh', in spite of different theological expressions in their respective traditions.[2] With this acknowledgement of common faith, obstacles can gradually be removed to achieve full communion between the Eastern and Western Churches. They also stressed the importance of mutual respect between the two churches and openness to the action of the Holy Spirit. Theologians from both sides were exhorted to delve deeper into the mystery of Christ while remaining faithful to the apostolic tradition. The two leaders also appealed to leaders in the Middle East, especially in the Holy Land, to work towards peace, justice, and religious freedom for all the inhabitants there.

The second declaration of Paul VI and Shenouda III took place in 1973. As a gesture of goodwill, the Roman Catholic Church returned the relics of St Mark to Egypt in order to deepen its relationship with the Church of Alexandria. In the common declaration, the two churches first affirmed the three early ecumenical councils regarding the teaching on the Trinity: '[W]e confess one faith in the One Triune God, the divinity of the Only Begotten Son of God, the Second Person of the Holy Trinity, the Word of God, the effulgence of His glory and the express image of His substance, who for us was incarnate, assuming for Himself a real body with a rational soul, and who shared with us our humanity but without sin.'[3]

Affirming the divinity and humanity of Christ, the declaration states: 'In Him His divinity is united with His humanity in a real, perfect union without mingling, without commixtion, without confusion, without alteration, without division, without separation. His divinity did not separate from His humanity for an instant, not for the twinkling

---

1. 'Relations with the Churches of the East: Syrian Orthodox Church', http://www.vatican.va/roman_curia/pontifical_councils/chrstuni/anc-orient-ch-docs/rc_pc_christuni_doc_19711025_syrian-church_en.html.
2. Ibid.
3. *Common Declaration of Pope Paul VI and of the Pope of Alexandria Shenouda III* (1973), http://www.vatican.va/roman_curia/pontifical_councils/chrstuni/anc-orient-ch-docs/rc_pc_christuni_doc_19730510_copti_en.html.

of an eye.'[1] In short, Jesus is truly God and truly man. Further, the declaration affirms the seven sacraments and the veneration of Mary, the Mother of God. To a large extent, the two churches share the same understanding regarding ecclesiology, which includes the role of the ecumenical and local councils. The spirituality of the two churches is expressed in the celebration of the Eucharist. They observe the fasts and feasts of the church, and the veneration of the relics of the saints, and trust in the intercession of the angels and saints.

Recognizing the sins and mistakes of the past, the two churches admitted that they share responsibility for the existing division that has been widened by theological and non-theological factors since 451. They acknowledged that in spite of these differences, the churches share a common heritage that can serve as a basis for them to achieve the 'fullness and perfection of that unity' that is God's gift.[2]

In order to carry out this task, the churches agreed that they would set up a joint commission for the study of patristics, liturgy, theology, and history. They also planned to seek ways to co-operate and resolve practical problems in a spirit of mutual respect. In other words, they agreed to 'reject all forms of proselytism, in the sense of acts by which persons seek to disturb each other's communities by recruiting new members from each other through methods, or because of attitudes of mind, which are opposed to the exigencies of Christian love or to what should characterize the relationships between Churches'.[3] Thus Roman Catholics would remain Roman Catholics and Orthodox would remain Orthodox – there was to be no poaching of members in this encounter. Instead, they made plans to consult, co-operate, and deepen clarity in the various theological and academic disciplines.

Regarding the need to learn from each other, Aidan Nichols asserts: 'One strategy open to Rome is, evidently, to call up from the vasty deep the spirits of Christian East – for in the struggle for the conservation of a classical understanding of doctrine, liturgy, spirituality, ethics, and (for the most part) Church government, the East can stand with Rome over against Neo-Modernist, or Neo-Protestant tendencies in the West.'[4] He concludes that 'the energies of authentic Roman Catholicism can only be increased by the inflow

1. Ibid.
2. Ibid.
3. Ibid.
4. Aidan Nichols, OP (2010), *Rome and the Eastern Churches*. San Francisco: Ignatius Press, pp. 12–13.

of Orthodox faith and holiness: the precious liquid contained within the not seldom unattractive phial of Orthodoxy's canonical form. Can this greatest of all ecclesiastical reunions be brought off? The auguries are not good, yet, the Christian lives in hope in the unseen.'[1]

Finally, the two churches condemned the manipulation of religions for political purposes in the Middle East, which has led to the suffering and homelessness of thousands of Palestinians. They hoped and prayed that the crisis in the Middle East could be resolved in a peaceful and just way. This message is even more relevant and significant today given the tense and painful situation in the Gaza Strip.

The third common declaration, of His Holiness John Paul II and His Holiness Moran Mor Ignatius Zakka I Iwas, took place in 1984. In this encounter, the two religious leaders confessed the faith formulated in the Nicene Creed and insisted that the conflicts and separations between the two sister churches in the past do not affect the substance of their faith, since these came about because of differences in terminology adopted by various theological traditions. The two leaders assured each other that there is no basis for this division and schism today as they reaffirmed their profession of common faith in the Incarnation of Jesus Christ. Besides the belief in the Incarnation, the two churches also share the same view regarding the sacraments, such as the Eucharist, baptism, confirmation, reconciliation, and anointing the sick. In short, the Roman Catholic Church and the Syrian Orthodox Church of Antioch hold the same beliefs regarding the sacraments of the church.[2]

Unfortunately, there is still a lack of the complete identity of faith and therefore the two churches cannot concelebrate in the holy Eucharist. Nonetheless, they can still collaborate in various pastoral works. In case of emergency, the faithful of each church can ask for the sacraments of penance, Eucharist, and anointing of the sick from priests of the other sister church. They can also collaborate in priestly formation and theological education. All this is done with the hope of full visible communion between the Roman Catholic Church and the Syrian Orthodox Church of Antioch in the near future.[3]

These common declarations are reflected in the International Joint Commission for Theological Dialogue's *Nature, Constitution*

1. Ibid., pp. 381–2.
2. *Common Declaration of His Holiness John Paul II and His Holiness Moran Mor Ignatius Zakka I Iwas* (1984), http://www.vatican.va/roman_curia/ pontifical_councils/chrstuni/anc-orient-ch-docs/rc_pc_christuni_ doc_19840623_jp-ii-zakka-i_en.html.
3. Ibid.

*and Mission of the Church*, published on 29 January 2009. This joint commission for theological dialogue between the Roman Catholic Church and the Oriental Orthodox Churches included, on the one side, the Roman Catholic Church and, on the other, the family of Oriental Orthodox Churches. In the report, the two churches are described as sharing the following elements of communion: they both confess the apostolic faith as expressed in the tradition, scriptures, and the first three ecumenical councils (Nicaea (325), Constantinople (381), and Ephesus (431)) and the Nicene-Constantinopolitan Creed. They share the same belief in the Incarnation of Christ as true God and true man, venerate Mary, the Mother of God, and both celebrate the seven sacraments. Finally, regarding the Eucharist, they both believe that bread and wine become the true Body and Blood of Jesus Christ.[1]

The Roman Catholic Church and the Orthodox group both embrace the concept of church as communion. The report states that the term *koinonia*

> comprises two essential dimensions: the vertical-transcendent communion of all the faithful with God the Father in the Lord Jesus Christ by the Holy Spirit and the horizontal communion of all the faithful in all time and all space with each other, a special aspect of which is the communion of the one Church on earth and in heaven. Without either of these dimensions the Church would not be the Church.'[2]

Regarding the attributes of the church, Roman Catholics and Orthodox both believe that 'the Church is called one not because she is in one place, but she is one in faith and in her calling in one hope, in one mother, and in her birth from the womb of the one baptismal font, in one food of the divine books, in one body and blood of the Saviour, in one head and crown and cloth that we put on: Christ.' This bond of unity in the church is guaranteed by the profession of the one faith handed down from the apostles. In fact, the church never lost the unity that is its essence, in spite of the divisions and conflicts that occurred over the centuries between various factions in the Body of Christ.[3]

---

1. International Joint Commission for Theological Dialogue (2009), *Nature, Constitution and Mission of the Church* (29 January), http://www.vatican.va/roman_curia/pontifical_councils/chrstuni/anc-orient-ch-docs/rc_pc_christuni_doc_20090129_mission-church_en.html.
2. Ibid.
3. Ibid.

The church is catholic because of the presence of Christ. Catholicity here means '*according to the totality* or *in keeping with the whole*'. Catholicity, however, is not to be confused with uniformity; 'rather, putting down roots in a variety of cultural, social and human terrains, the Church takes on different theological expressions of the same faith and different appearances in ecclesiastical disciplines, liturgical rites and spiritual heritages in each part of the world. This richness shows all the more resplendently the catholicity of the one Church.' Further, the church is also apostolic because it is founded upon the teaching of the apostles. It continues to be taught and guided by the ecclesiastical hierarchy of bishops, priests, and deacons.[1]

Both churches agree that full communion means unity in faith, sacramental life, and apostolic ministry. Unfortunately, they do not have complete agreement on the nature of eucharistic and ecclesial communion and therefore, they cannot have a common Eucharist. However, through dialogue between the two churches, progress has been made towards a common understanding regarding constitutive elements of the faith, especially in Christology. The Joint Commission is hopeful that further convergence of belief, which will eventually allow a common celebration of the Eucharist, is possible in the near future. All agree that the present state of division is 'a scandal' that wounds the Body of Christ. Therefore Christians are called upon to heal the wounds of division and to respond fervently to the prayer of the Lord Jesus 'that they all may be one' (John 17:21).[2]

In examining the official declarations of the two churches and the report of the joint commission, it becomes apparent that there is goodwill on both sides to come closer to each other. Therefore it is important that they return to the source and deposit of faith to rediscover their identities and unity. Returning 'home', as it were, may assist Orthodox and Roman Catholics to re-examine and to re-define their own tradition in view of dialogue and eventual reunion. Just as some Orthodox and Roman Catholic theologians are returning to the writings of the Church Fathers of the East and the West to revive their own tradition within the context of the early church, both sides can return to the same patristic source in search of unity. Before this undertaking, there must be the purification and healing of memories in the community as well as at the personal level of both churches.

---

1. Ibid.
2. Ibid.

# Bibliography

Afanasiev, Nicholas (1992), 'The Church which Presides in Love' in John Meyendorff (ed.), *The Primacy of Peter: Essays in Ecclesiology and the Early Church*. New York: St Vladimir's Seminary Press.

— (2003), 'The Eucharist: The Principal Link between the Catholics and the Orthodox' in Michael Plekon (ed.), *Tradition Alive: On the Church and the Christian Life in Our Time/Readings from the Eastern Church*. Lanham: Rowman & Littlefield.

— 'Una sancta' (2003), in Michael Plekon (ed.), *Tradition Alive: On the Church and the Christian Life in Our Time/Readings from the Eastern Church*. Lanham: Rowman & Littlefield.

Arjakovsky, Antoine and Plekon, Michael (2005), 'The sophiology of Father Sergius Bulgakov and contemporary western theology'. *St Vladimir's Theological Quarterly* 49, no. 1–2 (January), 219–35.

Athanasius, St, *De Incarnatione* or *On the Incarnation* 54:3, PG 25:192B.

Backhouse, Halcyon (ed.) (1993), *The Best of Meister Eckhart*. New York: Crossroad.

Balthasar, Hans Urs von (1982), *The Glory of the Lord*, Vol. I. Edinburgh: T & T Clark.

— (1990), *Mysterium Paschale*, trans. and with an introduction by Aidan Nichols, OP. Edinburgh: T & T Clark.

Berdyaev, Nicolas (1936), *The Meaning of History*. New York: Charles Scribner's Sons.

— (1944), *Slavery and Freedom*. London: Geoffrey Bless.

— (1945), *The Destiny of Man*. London: Geoffrey Bless.

— (1950), *Dream and Reality*. London: Geoffrey Bless.

— (1955), *The Origin of Russian Communism*. London: Geoffrey Bless.

Bevans, Stephen B. (2002), *Models of Contextual Theology*. Maryknoll, New York: Orbis.

Boeve, Lieven and Mannion, Gerard (eds) (2010), *The Ratzinger Reader*. London: T & T Clark.

Bordeianu, Radu (2009), 'Orthodox-Catholic dialogue: retrieving Eucharistic ecclesiology'. *Journal of Ecumenical Studies* 44, no. 2 (March), 239–65.

Bouteneff, Peter (2012), 'Liberation: challenges to modern orthodox theology from the contextual theologies.' *Union Seminary Quarterly Review* 63, no. 3–4 (January), 24–33.

Breck, J., Meyendorff, J., and Silk, E. (eds) (1990), *The Legacy of St. Vladimir: Byzantium, Russia, America*. Crestwood, New York: St Vladimir's Seminary Press.

Bulgakov, Sergius (1959, republished 2008) 'The Vatican dogma', http://www.orthodoxchristianity.net/index.php?option=com_content&view=article&catid=14:articles&id=39:the-vatican-dogma.

— (1976) *A Bulgakov Anthology*, ed. James Pain and Nicolas Zernov. Philadelphia: Westminster Press.

— (1976), 'The Burning Bush' in James Pain and Nicolas Zernov (eds), *A Bulgakov Anthology*. Philadelphia: Westminster Press.

— (1976), 'The Lamb of God' in James Pain and Nicolas Zernov (eds), *A Bulgakov Anthology*. Philadelphia: Westminster Press.

— (1976), 'The Orthodox Church' in James Pain and Nicolas Zernov (eds), *A Bulgakov Anthology*. Philadelphia: Westminster Press.

— (1976), 'The Wisdom of God' in James Pain and Nicolas Zernov (eds), *A Bulgakov Anthology*. Philadelphia: Westminster Press.

— (1999), '*The Lamb of God*: On the Divine Humanity (1933)' in Rowan Williams (ed.), *Sergii Bulgakov, Towards a Russian Political Theology*. Edinburgh: T & T Clark.

Calian, C.S. (1968), *Berdyaev's Philosophy of Hope: A Contribution to Marxist-Christian Dialogue*. Minnesota: Augsburg.

Cantirino, Matthew (2012), 'Sergius Bulgakov's religious materialism'. *First Things*, 19 April, http://www.firstthings.com/web-exclusives/2012/04/sergius-bulgakovs-religious-materialism.

Casiday, Augustine (ed.) (2012), *The Orthodox Christian World*. London: Routledge.

Chadwick, Henry (2003), *East and West: The Making of a Rift in the Church: From Apostolic Times until the Council of Florence*. Oxford: Oxford University Press.

Chadwick, Owen (1975), *The Secularization of the European Mind in the Nineteenth Century*. Cambridge: Cambridge University Press.

Chrysostomos, Abp of Etna (2001), 'Evaluating the fourth crusade'. *Orthodox Tradition* 18, no. 2 (January), 27–44.

Congar, Yves M.J. (1964), *Tradition and the Life of the Church*. London: Burns & Oates.

— (1983), *I Believe in the Holy Spirit*, Vol. II, trans. David Smith. New York: Seabury Press.

Cottier, Georges (2004), 'The purification of memory'. *Nova Et Vetera* 2, no. 2 (September), 257–66.

Crum, Winston F. (1983), 'Sergius N. Bulgakov: from Marxism to sophiology', *St Vladimir's Theological Quarterly* 27, no. 1 (January), 3–25.

de Lubac, Henri (1986), *Christian Faith: The Structure of the Apostles' Creed*, trans. Illtyd Trethowan and John Saward. London: Geoffrey Chapman.

— (1988), *Catholicism: Christ and the Common Destiny of Man*, trans. Lancelot C. Sheppard and Sr Elizabeth Englund OCD. San Francisco: Ignatius Press.

— (1998), *The Mystery of the Supernatural*, trans. Rosemary Sheed and with an introduction by David L. Schindler. New York: Crossroad.

— (2006), *Corpus Mysticum: The Eucharist and the Church in the Middle Ages*, trans. Gemma Simmonds CJ with Richard Price and Christopher Stephens, ed. Laurence Paul Hemming and Susan Frank Parsons. London: SCM.

Deane-Drummond, Celia E. (2005), 'Sophia, Mary and the eternal feminine in Pierre Teilhard de Chardin and Sergei Bulgakov'. *Ecotheology* 10, no. 2 (August), 215–31.

DeVille, Adam A.J. 'On the Healing of Memories: An Analysis of the Concept in Papal Documents', http://www.koed.hu/sw249/adam.pdf.

Dulles, Avery, SJ (1996), 'The Church as Communion' in Bradley Nassif (ed.), *New Perspectives on Historical Theology: Essays in Memory of John Meyendorff*. Grand Rapids, Michigan: William B. Eerdmans.

Eckhart, Meister (1994), *Selected Writings*, selected and trans. Oliver Davies. London: Penguin.

Erickson, John H. (1970), 'Leavened and unleavened: some theological implications of the schism of 1054'. *St Vladimir's Theological Quarterly* 14, no. 3, 1 (January), 155–76.

— (2005), 'Jaroslav Pelikan: The Living Legend in Our Midst' in Valerie Hotchkiss, Patrick Henry and Jaroslav Jan Pelikan (eds) (2005), *Orthodoxy and Western Culture: A Collection of Essays Honoring Jaroslav Pelikan on His Eightieth Birthday*. New York: St Vladimir's Seminary Press.

Famerée, Joseph (1995), 'Orthodox influence on the Roman Catholic theologian Yves Congar, OP: a sketch'. *St Vladimir's Theological Quarterly* 39, no. 4 (January), 409–16.

Florovsky, Georges (1949), 'Legacy and the task of Orthodox theology'. *Anglican Theological Review* 31, no. 2 (April), 65–71.

— (1950), 'The doctrine of the church and the ecumenical problem'. *Ecumenical Review* 2, no. 2 (December), 152–61.

— (1950), 'Eastern Orthodox Church and the ecumenical movement', *Theology Today* 7, no. 1 (April), 68–79.

— (1952), 'Christianity and civilization'. *St Vladimir's Seminary Quarterly* 1, no. 1 (September), 13–20.

— (1954), 'The Church Universal'. *St Vladimir's Seminary Quarterly* 2, no. 4 (June), 2–4.

— (1957), 'Empire and desert: antinomies of Christian history'. *Greek Orthodox Theological Review* 3, no. 2 (December), 133–59.

— (1960), 'The ethos of the Orthodox Church'. *Ecumenical Review* 12, no. 2 (January), 183–98.

— (1960), 'Saint Gregory Palamas and the tradition of the fathers', *Greek Orthodox Theological Review* 5, no. 2 (December), 119–31.

— (1964), 'Function of tradition in the ancient church'. *Greek Orthodox Theological Review* 9, no. 2 (December), 181–200.

— (1972), *Bible, Church, Tradition: An Eastern Orthodox View*, Vol. I of the *Collected Works of Georges Florovsky*. Belmont, Massachusetts: Nordland.

Gaillardetz, Richard (1997), *Teaching with Authority: A Theology of the Magisterium in the Church*. Collegeville, Minnesota: Liturgical Press.

Gallaher, Brandon (2013), 'The "sophiological" origins of Vladimir Lossky's apophaticism'. *Scottish Journal of Theology* 66, no. 3 (January), 278–98, http://dx.doi.org/10.1017/S0036930613000136.

Gavrilyuk, Paul (2005), 'The kenotic theology of Sergius Bulgakov'. *Scottish Journal of Theology* 58, no. 3 (January), 251–69.

— (2012), 'Sergii Bulgakov' in Augustine Casiday (ed.), *The Orthodox Christian World*. London: Routledge.

Geffert, Bryn (2005), 'The charges of heresy against Sergii Bulgakov: the majority and minority reports of Evlogii's commission and the final report of the bishops' conference'. *St Vladimir's Theological Quarterly* 49, no. 1–2 (January), 47–66.

Geffré, Claude (2002), 'Double Belonging and the Originality of Christianity as a Religion' in Catherine Cornille (ed.), *Many Mansions?* Maryknoll, New York: Orbis.

Gilson, Étienne (2002), *God and Philosophy*. New Haven: Yale Nota Bene.

Gros, Jeffrey, FSC, McManus, Eamon and Riggs, Ann (1998), *Introduction to Ecumenism*. New York: Paulist Press.

Gudziak, Borys (2001), 'Towards an analysis of the neo-patristic synthesis of Georges Florovsky'. *Logos* 41 (January), 197–238.

Gutiérrez, Gustavo (1973), *A Theology of Liberation*. Maryknoll, New York: Orbis.

— (1999), 'The Task and Content of Liberation Theology' in Christopher Rowland (ed.), *The Cambridge Companion to Liberation Theology*. Cambridge: Cambridge University Press.

Harnack, Adolf von (1957), *What is Christianity?*, trans. Thomas Bailey Saunders. New York: Harper & Row.

— (1959), *Outlines of the History of Dogma*. Boston: Beacon Press.

— (1961), *History of Dogma*, Vols I and II, trans. Neil Buchanan. New York: Dover.

Hayes, Stephen (1990), 'Orthodoxy and liberation theology'. *Journal of Theology for Southern Africa*, no. 73 (December), 12–23.

Heim, Maximilian Heinrich (2007), *Joseph Ratzinger: Life in the Church and Living Theology*. San Francisco: Ignatius Press.

Henry, Patrick and Hotchkiss, Valerie (2005), 'Was wir Ererbt Haben' in Valerie Hotchkiss, Patrick Henry and Jaroslav Jan Pelikan (eds) (2005), *Orthodoxy and Western Culture: A Collection of Essays Honoring Jaroslav Pelikan on His Eightieth Birthday*. New York: St Vladimir's Seminary Press.

Hussey, M. Edmund (1975), 'Nicholas Afanassiev's Eucharistic ecclesiology: a Roman Catholic viewpoint'. *Journal of Ecumenical Studies* 12, no. 2 (March), 235–52.

Iakovos, Abp of the Greek Orthodox Archdiocese of North and South America (1970), 'Ecclesiology of Yves Congar: an Orthodox evaluation'. *Greek Orthodox Theological Review* 15, no. 1 (March), 85–106.

Jacobsen, Douglas (2011), *The World's Christians: Who they are, Where they are, and How they got there*. Oxford: Wiley-Blackwell.

John of the Cross, St, *The Dark Night*, 'Stanzas of the Soul', https://www.ewtn.com/library/SOURCES/DARK-JC.TXT.

John Paul II, Pope (1995), *Orientale Lumen* (Apostolic Letter), 2 May, http://www.vatican.va/holy_father/john_paul_ii/apost_letters/documents/hf_jp-ii_apl_02051995_orientale-lumen_en.html

— (2001), 'John Paul II, Pope (2001-05-04) "A liberating process of purification of memory"', *Origins*, 31, no. 1 (n.d.).

Kalaitzidēs, Pantelēs, and Edwards, Gregory (2010), 'Orthodoxy and Hellenism in contemporary Greece'. *St Vladimir's Theological Quarterly* 54, no. 3–4, 365–420.

Kasper, Walter (1993), *The God of Jesus Christ*. London: SCM Press.

— (2001), 'From the President of the Council for Promoting Christian Unity,' *America*, 26 November.

— (2001), 'On the Church'. *America*, 23 April, 8–14, http://www.americamagazine.org/content/article.cfm?article_id=1569.

Kehl, Medard, SJ, and Löser, Werner, SJ (eds) (1982), *The von Balthasar Reader*, trans. Robert J. Daly SJ and Fred Lawrence. New York: Crossroad.

Kitamori, Kazoh (1965), *Theology of the Pain of God*. Richmond, Virginia: John Knox Press.

Ladouceur, Paul (2012), 'Treasures new and old: landmarks of Orthodox neopatristic theology'. *St Vladimir's Theological Quarterly* 56, no. 2 (January), 191–227.

Lossky, Nicolas (1999), 'Theology and spirituality in the work of Vladimir Lossky'. *Ecumenical Review* 51, no. 3 (July), 288–93.

Lossky, Vladimir (1973, first published 1944), *The Mystical Theology of the Eastern Church*. Cambridge: James Clarke & Co.

— (2001), *Orthodox Theology: An Introduction*. Crestwood, New York: St Vladimir's Seminary Press.

Louth, Andrew (2005), 'Father Sergii Bulgakov on the Mother of God'. *St Vladimir's Theological Quarterly* 49, no. 1–2 (January), 145–64.

— (2007), *Greek East and Latin West: The Church AD 681–1071*. New York: St Vladimir's Seminary Press.

Lowrie, Donald A. (ed. and trans.) (1965), *Christian Existentialism: A Berdyaev Anthology*. London: George Allen & Unwin.

Manning, Clarence Augustus (1929), 'Bulgakov and the Orthodox Church'. *Anglican Theological Review* 11, no. 4 (April), 332–41.

McDonnell, Kilian (2002), 'The Ratzinger/Kasper debate: the universal church and local churches'. *Theological Studies*, June, 227–50.

McGrath, Alister E. (2006), *Christianity: An Introduction*. Oxford: Blackwell.

McGuckin, John Anthony (2008), *The Orthodox Church: An Introduction to its History, Doctrine, and Spiritual Culture*. Oxford: Blackwell.

McManus, Eamon (2000), 'Aspects of primacy according to two Orthodox theologians'. *One In Christ* 36, no. 3 (January), 234–50.

McPartlan, Paul (1993), *The Eucharist Makes the Church: Henri de Lubac and Zizioulas in Dialogue*. Edinburgh: T & T Clark.

Meyendorff, John (1983), *Byzantine Theology: Historical Trends and Doctrinal Themes*. New York: Fordham University Press.

— (1983), *Catholicity and the Church*. Crestwood, NY: St. Vladimir's Press, 1983.

— (1996), 'St Peter in Byzantine Theology' in John Meyendorff (ed.), *Primacy of Peter*. Crestwood, New York: St Vladimir's Press.

— (ed.) (1996), *Primacy of Peter*. Crestwood, NY: St Vladimir's Press.

— (1996), *The Orthodox Church: Its Past and its Role in the World Today*. Crestwood, New York: St Vladimir's Press.

Moltmann, Jürgen (1967), *Theology of Hope*. New York: Harper & Row.

— (1972), 'The "Crucified God": a trinitarian theology of the cross'. *Interpretation* 26, no. 3 (July), 278–99.

— (1974), 'The crucified God: perspectives on a theology of the cross for today'. *Journal Of Theology for Southern Africa* no. 9 (December), 9–27.

— (1974), *The Crucified God: the Cross of Christ as the Foundation and Criticism of Christian Theology*. London: SCM Press.

— (1974), 'Crucified God'. *Theology Today* 31, no. 1 (April), 6–18.

Nassif, Bradley (ed.) (1996), *New Perspectives on Historical Theology: Essays in Memory of John Meyendorff*. Grand Rapids, Michigan: William B. Eerdmans.

Negrov, Alexander I. (2005), 'An overview of liberation theology in orthodox Russia', *Hervormde Teologiese Studies* 61, no. 1–2 (March), 327–45.

Newman, Barbara (1978), 'Sergius Bulgakov and the theology of divine wisdom'. *St Vladimir's Theological Quarterly* 22, no. 1 (January), 39–73.

Nichols, Aidan, OP (1989), *Theology in the Russian Diaspora*. Cambridge: Cambridge University Press.

— (2005), *Wisdom from Above: A Primer in the Theology of Father Sergei Bulgakov*. Herefordshire: Gracewing.

— (2010), *Rome and the Eastern Churches*. San Francisco: Ignatius Press.

Noble, Ivana and Noble, Tim (2012), 'A Latin appropriation of Christian hellenism: Florovsky's marginal note to Patristics and modern theology and its possible addressee'. *St Vladimir's Theological Quarterly* 56, no. 3 (January), 269–87.

Nucho, Fuad (1966), *Berdyaev's Philosophy: The Existential Paradox of Freedom and Necessity*. New York: Anchor Books, Doubleday & Co.

Pain, James and Nicolas Zernov, editors. *A Bulgakov Anthology*. Philadelphia: The Westminster Press, 1976.

Papademetriou, George C. (1996), 'Father Georges Florovsky: a contemporary Church Father'. *Greek Orthodox Theological Review* 41, no. 2–3 (June), 119–26.

Papanikolaou, Aristotle (2003), 'Divine energies or divine personhood: Vladimir Lossky and John Zizioulas on conceiving the transcendent and immanent God'. *Modern Theology* 19, no. 3 (July), 357–85.

Pelikan, Jaroslav (1959), *The Riddle of Roman Catholicism*. New York: Abingdon Press.

— (1961), 'Introduction to the Torchbook Edition' in Adolf von Harnack, *The Mission and Expansion of Christianity in the First Three Centuries*. New York: Harper Torchbooks.

— (1969), *Development of Christian Doctrine: Some Historical Prolegomena*. New Haven: Yale University Press.

— (1971), *The Emergence of the Catholic Tradition (100–600)* (Vol. I of *The Christian Tradition*). Chicago: University of Chicago Press.

— (1974), *The Spirit of Eastern Christendom (600–1700)* (Vol. II of *The Christian Tradition*). Chicago: University of Chicago Press.

— (1984), *The Vindication of Tradition*. New Haven: Yale University Press.

— (1989), *Christian Doctrine and Modern Culture since 1700* (Vol. V of *The Christian Tradition*). Chicago: University of Chicago Press.

— (1993), *Christianity and Classical Culture: The Metamorphosis of Natural Theology in the Christian Encounter with Hellenism*. New Haven and London: Yale University Press.

— (1996), 'In Memory of John Meyendorff' in Bradley Nassif (ed.), *New Perspectives on Historical Theology: Essays in Memory of John Meyendorff*. Grand Rapids, Michigan: William B. Eerdmans.

— (1998), Open letter to members of Bethesda Lutheran Church, New Haven, Connecticut; 'Pelikan to Orthodox church', http://www.thelutheran.org/article/article.cfm?article_id=1897.

— (2005), 'A Personal Memoir: Fragments of a Scholar Autobiography' in *Orthodoxy and Western Culture: A Collection of Essays Honoring Jaroslav Pelikan on His Eightieth Birthday*. New York: St Vladimir's Seminary Press.

Petersen, Rodney L. (1996), 'Local Ecumenism and the Neo-Patristic Synthesis of Father Georges Florovsky.' *Greek Orthodox Theological Review* 41, no. 2–3 (June), 217–42.

Ratzinger, Joseph (1965), 'The pastoral implications of episcopal collegiality'. *Concilium* 1, 20–33.

— (1987), *Principles of Catholic Theology*. San Francisco: Ignatius Press.

— (1996), *Called to Communion: Understanding the Church Today*. San Francisco: Ignatius Press.

— (2004), *Truth and Tolerance*. San Francisco: Ignatius Press.

— (2005), *Pilgrim Fellowship of Faith*. San Francisco: Ignatius Press.

— (2008), *Church, Ecumenism and Politics*. San Francisco: Ignatius Press.

Richardson, David B. (1969), *Berdyaev's Philosophy of History*. The Hague: Martinus Nijhoff.

Roberts, Hannah (2014), 'Francis "plotting a path to unity with the Orthodox Churches"'. *The Tablet* 268, no. 9060 (2 August).

Roberts, J. Deotis (1964), 'Bergson as a metaphysical, epistemological, and religious thinker'. *Journal of Religious Thought* 20, no. 2 (January), 105–14.

Ruddy, Christopher (2006), *The Local Church: Tillard and the Future of Catholic Ecclesiology*. New York: Crossroad.

Sauvé, Ross J. (2010), 'Florovsky's tradition'. *Greek Orthodox Theological Review* 55, no. 1–4 (March), 213–41.

Savich, Milan (1986), 'Catholicity of the Church: "Sobornost"', http://www.orthodoxresearchinstitute.org/articles/dogmatics/savich_catholicity.htm

Schreiter, Robert J. (1997), *The New Catholicity: Theology between the Global and the Local*. Maryknoll, New York: Orbis.

— (2008), 'Sharing memories of the past: the healing of memories and interreligious encounter'. *Currents in Theology and Mission* 35, no. 2 (April), 110–17.

Sicari, Antonio M., and Walker, Adrian (2000), '"The purification of memory": the "narrow gate" of the jubilee'. *Communio* 27, no. 4 (December), 634–42.

Slesinski, Robert (1994) 'John Meyendorff: A Churchman of Catholic Outreach'. *Diakonia* 27, no. 1 (January), 5–17.

— (2007) 'Sergius Bulgakov on the glorification of the Mother of God'. *Orientalia Christiana Periodica* 73, no. 1 (January), 97–116.

Spinka, Matthew (1949), *Nicolas Berdyaev: Captive of Freedom*. Philadelphia: Westminster Press.

Tataryn, Myroslaw (1998), 'Sergius Bulgakov (1871–1944): time for a new look'. *St Vladimir's Theological Quarterly* 42, no. 3–4 (January), 315–38.

Thomas Aquinas, *Quaestiones Disputatae de Potentia Dei*, Q. VII, Article V: 'Do These Terms Signify the Divine Essence?', http://dhspriory.org/thomas/QDdePotentia.htm.

Visser 't Hooft, Willem Adolph (1979), 'Fr Georges Florovsky's role in the formation of the WCC'. *St Vladimir's Theological Quarterly* 23, no. 3–4, 135–8.

Ware, Bp Kallistos T. (1973), 'Scholasticism and Orthodoxy: theological method as a factor in the schism'. *Eastern Churches Review* 5, no. 1 (March), 16–27.

Ware, Timothy (1972), *The Orthodox Church*. Harmondsworth: Penguin.

Whalen, Brett E. (2007), 'Rethinking the schism of 1054: authority, heresy and the Latin rite'. *Traditio* 62, (January), 1–24.

Wilken, Robert Louis (2003), *Spirit of Early Christian Thought: Seeking the Face of God*. New Haven: Yale University Press.

Williams, Rowan (ed.) (1999), *Sergii Bulgakov: Towards a Russian Political Theology*. Edinburgh: T & T Clark.

Wooden, Anastacia (2010), 'Eucharistic ecclesiology of Nicolas Afanasiev and its ecumenical significance: a new perspective'. *Journal of Ecumenical Studies* 45, no. 4, 543–60.

Zizioulas, Metr. John D. (1988), 'The mystery of the church in Orthodox tradition'. *One In Christ* 24, no. 4 (January), 294–303.

— (1993), *Being as Communion*. New York: St Vladimir's Seminary Press.

— (1993), *The One and the Many: Studies on God, Man, the Church and the World Today*. New York: St Vladimir's Seminary Press.

— (2001), *Eucharist, Bishop, Church: The Unity of the Church in the Divine Eucharist and the Bishop During the First Three Centuries*. Brookline, Massachusetts: Holy Cross.

— (2008), *Lectures in Christian Dogmatics*, ed. Douglas Knight. London: T & T Clark.

— (2011), *The Eucharistic Communion and the World*, ed. Luke Ben Tallon. London: T & T Clark.

## Church Documents

Benedict XVI, Pope (2006), 'Faith, Reason and the University', lecture at the University of Regensburg, 12 September, http://www.vatican. va/holy_father/benedict_xvi/speeches/2006/september/documents/hf_ ben-xvi_spe_20060912_university-regensburg_en.html.

'Called Together to Be Peacemakers', Report of the International Dialogue between the Catholic Church and Mennonite World Conference (1998–2003), http://www.vatican.va/roman_curia/pontifical_councils/ chrstuni/mennonite-conference-docs/rc_pc_chrstuni_doc_20110324_ mennonite_en.html.

*Common Declaration of His Holiness John Paul II and His Holiness Moran Mor Ignatius Zakka I Iwas* (1984), http://www.vatican.va/roman_curia/ pontifical_councils/chrstuni/anc-orient-ch-docs/rc_pc_christuni_ doc_19840623_jp-ii-zakka-i_en.html.

*Common Declaration of Pope Paul VI and of the Pope of Alexandria Shenouda III* (1973), http://www.vatican.va/roman_curia/pontifical_councils/chrstuni/ anc-orient-ch-docs/rc_pc_christuni_doc_19730510_copti_en.html.

Dogmatic Constitution on the Church – *Lumen Gentium* (1964), http:// www.vatican.va/archive/hist_councils/ii_vatican_council/documents/ vat-ii_const_19641121_lumen-gentium_en.html.

*Dominus Iesus* (2000), Declaration on the Unicity and Salvific Universality of Jesus Christ and the Church, http://www.vatican.va/roman_curia/ congregations/cfaith/documents/rc_con_cfaith_doc_20000806_ dominus-iesus_en.html.

International Joint Commission for Theological Dialogue (2009), *Nature, Constitution and Mission of the Church* (29 January), http://www.vatican.

va/roman_curia/pontifical_councils/chrstuni/anc-orient-ch-docs/rc_pc_
christuni_doc_20090129_mission-church_en.html.

International Theological Commission (2014), '*Sensus fidei* in the life of
the Church', http://www.vatican.va/roman_curia/congregations/cfaith/
cti_documents/rc_cti_20140610_sensus-fidei_en.html.

John Paul II, Pope (1995), *Ut Unum Sint: On Commitment to Ecumenism*,
http://www.vatican.va/holy_father/john_paul_ii/encyclicals/
documents/hf_jp-ii_enc_25051995_ut-unum-sint_en.html.

— (1998), *Fides et Ratio*, http://www.vatican.va/holy_father/john_paul_ii/
encyclicals/documents/hf_jp-ii_enc_15101998_fides-et-ratio_en.html.

Ratzinger, Joseph, Congregation for the Doctrine of the Faith (1992),
'Letter to the Bishops of the Catholic Church on some aspects of the
Church understood as Communion.' http://www.vatican.va/roman_
curia/congregations/cfaith/documents/rc_con_cfaith_doc_28051992_
communionis-notio_en.html.

— (2001), 'The Ecclesiology of Vatican II,' Conference of Cardinal
Ratzinger at the opening of the Pastoral Congress of the Diocese of
Aversa (Italy), http://www.ewtn.com/library/curia/cdfeccv2.htm.

— (2002), 'Eucharist, Communion and Solidarity', lecture at the Bishops'
Conference of the Region of Campania in Benevento (Italy), http://
www.vatican.va/roman_curia/congregations/cfaith/documents/rc_con_
cfaith_doc_20020602_ratzinger-eucharistic-congress_en.html.

'Relations with the Churches of the East: Syrian Orthodox Church' (1971),
http://www.vatican.va/roman_curia/pontifical_councils/chrstuni/anc-
orient-ch-docs/rc_pc_christuni_doc_19711025_syrian-church_en.html.

*Unitatis Redintegratio*, the Decree on Ecumenism (1964), http://www.
vatican.va/archive/hist_councils/ii_vatican_council/documents/vat-ii_
decree_19641121_unitatis-redintegratio_en.html.

# Index

*You may be interested in*

# The Mystical Theology
# of the Eastern Church

## By Vladimir Lossky

Print ISBN: 9780227679197
Epub ISBN: 9780227905081
PDF ISBN: 9780227905098
Kindle ISBN: 9780227905104

Through a combination of careful scholarship and the warmth of the deep personal devotion of the author, this book provides the authoritative English study of Eastern Orthodox theology.

Lossky's account makes clear the profound theological differences between East and West, as well as offering an important contribution to ecumenism and to the life of Christian devotion. The tradition of the Eastern Church is presented as a mystical theology with doctrine and experience mutually supporting each other.

*Available now with more excellent titles in Paperback, Hardback, PDF and Epub formats from James Clarke & Co*

www.jamesclarke.co

*You may be interested in*

# The Philokalia
# and the Inner Life
## *On Passions and Prayer*
## By Christopher C.H. Cook

Print ISBN: 9780227173428
Epub ISBN: 9780227900079
PDF ISBN: 9780227900055

The *Philokalia*, published in Venice in 1782, is an anthology of patristic writings from the Eastern Church spanning the fourth to the fifteenth centuries, and which has been the subsequent focus of a significant revival in Orthodox spirituality. It presents an understanding of psychology and mental life which is significantly different to that usually encountered in Western Christianity.

This book provides an introduction to the history of the *Philokalia* and the philosophical, anthropological and theological influences that contributed to its formation. Written with an international academic readership in mind, the book is also accessible to a more general readership and anyone interested in Christian theology, particularly in relation to mental health issues, addictions and psychotherapy.

*Available now with more excellent titles in Paperback, Hardback, PDF and Epub formats from James Clarke & Co*

www.jamesclarke.co